DATE			

A TASTE FOR PAIN

On Masochism and Female Sexuality

by

MARIA MARCUS

Translated from the Danish by Joan Tate

ST. MARTIN'S PRESS

Library of Congress Cataloging in Publication Data

Marcus, Maria.
  A taste for pain.

  Translation of: Den frygtelige sandhed.
  1. Masochism.   2. Women—Sexual behavior.
I. Title.
HQ29.M3713   306.7   81-18239
ISBN 0-312-78619-0   AACR2

Germaine Greer was in Copenhagen in 1972 and a meeting was held at which she addressed and talked with Danish women. The atmosphere in the hall was high-spirited and optimistic, when suddenly a young woman cried out with desperation in her voice:

"But how can we start a women's movement when I bet three-quarters of us sitting in this room are masochists?"

This book is dedicated to that young woman, in the hope that she can use it, and to all those who think as she does, but daren't say so out aloud.

> We regard our personal experience, and our feelings about that experience, as the basis for an analysis of our common situation. . .
> The first requirement for raising class consciousness is honesty, in private and in public, with ourselves and other women.
>
> *Sisterhood Is Powerful* (Redstockings Manifesto)

> And Sister, if you can't turn on to a man who won't club you and drag you off by the hair, that's yours (hang up). Keep your hang ups the hell out of this revolution.
>
> *Sisterhood Is Powerful* (Lilith's Manifesto)

Acknowledgements

The author is grateful to the following:

Jonathan Cape Ltd, London, and Alfred A. Knopf, Inc, New York, for permission to quote from *The Second Sex* by Simone de Beauvoir, translated and edited by H. M. Parshley; Martin Secker & Warburg Ltd, London, and Alfred A. Knopf, Inc, New York, for permission to quote from *The Trial*, Definitive Edition by Franz Kafka, translated by Willa and Edwin Muir; Kegan Paul, Trench & Trubner, London, for permission to quote from *The Fear of Freedom* by Erich Fromm; Granada Publishing Ltd, London, and Stein & Day, New York, for permission to quote from *Psychopathia Sexualis* by Dr R. von Krafft-Ebing, copyright © 1965 by Franklin S. Klaf; Neville Spearman Ltd, Sudbury, for permission to quote from *The ABZ of Love* by Inge and Sten Hegeler, translated by David Hohnen; Sphere Books Ltd, London, for permission to quote from *Venus In Furs* by L. von Sacher-Masoch; Doubleday & Co Inc, for permission to quote from *Sexual Politics* by Kate Millett, copyright © 1969, 1970 by Kate Millett; Helene Deutsch for permission to quote from *The Psychology of Women* by Helene Deutsch, published by Grune & Stratton, New York; Marion Boyars Ltd, London, for permission to quote from *Boy Girl Man Woman* by B. H. Claësson, translated by Christine Hauch; Grove Press, New York, for permission to quote from *Three Complete Novels: Justine, Philosophy in the Bedroom, Eugenie de Franval and Other Writings* by The Marquis de Sade, translated by Richard Seaver and Austryn Wainhouse; Farrar, Straus & Giroux Inc, for permission to quote from *The Function of the Orgasm* by Wilhelm Reich, translated by Vincent R. Carfagno, copyright © 1973 by Mary Boyd Higgins as Trustee of The Wilhelm Reich Infant Trust Fund; Marion Boyars Ltd, London, for permission to quote from *Erotic Minorities* by L. Ullerstam; International University Press, Inc, for permission to quote from *Female Sexuality* by Marie Bonaparte, translated by John Rodker; Robin Morgan for permission to quote from *Sisterhood is Powerful* ed. Robin Morgan; Sigmund Freud Copyrights Ltd, The Institute of Psychoanalysis and The Hogarth Press Ltd, London, and W. W. Norton & Co Inc, New York, for permission to quote from The Standard Edition of the *Complete Psychological Works of Sigmund Freud*, translated and edited by James Strachey; Basic Books Inc, New York, for permission to quote from *Three Essays on the Theory of Sexuality* by Sigmund Freud, translated and revised by James Strachey, with a new introduction by Steven Marcus, © 1962 Sigmund Freud Copyrights Ltd, Introductory Essay © 1975 by Steven Marcus; George Allen & Unwin, London, and Liveright Publishing Corporation, New York, for permission to quote from *Introductory Lectures* and *Beyond the Pleasure Principle* by Sigmund Freud; W. W. Norton & Co, New York, for permission to quote from *The Ego and the Id* by Sigmund Freud; W. W. Norton & Co, New York, for permission to quote from *Feminine Psychology* by Karen Horney, M.D., edited by Harold Kelman, M.D., copyright © 1967 by W. W. Norton & Co; Morton Hunt for permission to quote from *Sexual Behavior in the 1970's* by Morton Hunt, published by Playboy Press, New York, and Editions Pauvert for permission to quote from *The Story of O* by Pauline Réage, published in English by Corgi, London.

Contents

PART I

1 Laying Eggs

When I was between four and seven years old, I used to play a game called 'Laying Eggs'. It was a game you played alone. You threw a ball backwards against a wall in a certain way, and when you missed, you were punished.

You had to stand against the wall and draw a semicircle round you, so that the wall formed the circle's diameter, and you were standing enclosed between the wall and the semi-circle. Every time you missed the ball, you had to draw another semicircle inside the first one, so that you had a smaller and smaller space to stand in, and had to press further and further back towards the wall. Finally, you literally stood with your back to the wall and inside a semicircle that was so minute, your feet only just fitted in, and you simply couldn't move any more.

I know I was between four and seven, because I can remember the place where I played the game. I can also remember a vague tickling sensation when I played it. It was a very special sensation, associated with a very definite part of my body, but why it should happen just between my legs, naturally I never gave a thought to, except that I thought it was because of the name of the game – 'Laying Eggs'. Not until later did I realise that it was the first of a long series of games that were similar – anyhow, the first I can remember. But not the last – nor the last I played alone, or without direct intervention by a partner.

My next memory of a similar kind comes from when I was eight. That summer we were mad on some handsome masculine boys with hard knees and uniform shirts, and we spent hours and hours standing to attention, marching and shouting in unison. I think we attained quite a degree of discipline.

I can remember a scene that same summer in a park, when I tried to get an innocent nursemaid to play punishment games with us – but she was very reluctant. It could be that she sensed what it was all about.

This pattern was repeated in the following years. I discovered various games involving various kinds of tests with attached punishments, and wrote them down in a notebook. In a given time, you were not to do this or that, or you had to do something you didn't want to do, or you were given so many blows by a given object. There were very detailed rituals in the notebook, and I can remember it being exciting writing them down, but I could rarely get other children to play with me. Perhaps they also sensed that there was something forbidden about those games.

Only once did I get a girl in my class, still in junior school, to play with me. I made her order me to sit under the desk and hit me with a ruler. I found it dead boring moping under the desk without anything happening. But I can also remember that it was horribly unpleasant when she hit me. It hurt. So we soon stopped that game, and I can remember the whole thing confusing me slightly and making me feel disorientated.

My favourite game in the playground was 'Girls after Boys'. This was usually 'Boys after Girls', and I didn't think that much fun. Maybe the boys weren't all that keen on catching me, or else I hadn't dared do enough to provoke them. But on special occasions, anyhow, it was 'Girls after Boys'.

It was played all over the playground at once – I think we had to catch the boys and corral them in one place. Anyhow, I can remember that I always threw myself at the biggest, strongest and most unapproachable boy and fought to the death with him, now that I seemed to have permission. I enjoyed being stronger than he thought I was – but most of all I enjoyed not being as strong as he was, and naturally it always ended up with him subduing me, which was what I had intended all along. Unfortunately, we didn't play that game very often.

There were also a couple of girls who subdued me physically. That was when I was at the top of middle school, and it was not a game. Two of them scrubbed me with snow. They were on top. I couldn't do anything and thought the situation completely hopeless and desperate, for two reasons – first, because they had no reason to be scrubbing me and were doing it because they hated me, which really shocked me; and second, because they had transformed their hatred into something physical I couldn't get away from. To me it seemed that against my own will, the game had become reality. Now I really did have my back to the wall and I couldn't get away.

I didn't really think it extraordinary that they hated me. I was small and fat, I had developed young, I was a new girl, and to cap it all, I was clever at school. I would have given a lot to be as stupid as the others, to be ten centimetres taller, have sharper knees and a different name, and to be good at gymnastics. In fact, many other children in a great many schools felt the same, but I didn't know that then.

That I was bad at gymnastics had something to do with the fact that my gym teacher made me a scapegoat in that special way that has affected thousands of people for life. It's such a well known pattern that there is no reason to go into it. The only thing there is good reason to mention is that I worshipped her, because she was unpredictable and not always my tormentor, exposing me to the laughter of the class. We also had her for Danish, and in Danish lessons she had other victims, whom we dutifully scorned and mocked at the slightest sign from her. I joined in with a nasty taste in my mouth. Perhaps the others did, too, I don't know. I worshipped her.

I loved all the hooligans in the class, all the cheeky toughs, the ones with the hardest knees and the boldest eyes. But I was more concerned with the teachers. School was the place, outside home, where you first met men.

My favourite teachers were those who kept the best discipline. When I think back, most of them were probably dreadful dry sticks, with no sense of humour, rather empty-headed, enclosed in their narrow little world of formalities. I'm not even sure that any outside world did in fact exist for them; anyhow they never mentioned one.

But in school, they were in their element. They strode about the classroom interrogating us in military manner on what we knew. Their pointers were combined sceptres, music batons and instruments of law and order. Law and order – they certainly had that. *Their* law and order. We were just ciphers. I liked their lessons. They were cold, unfeeling and unapproachable, and dealt out precise marks according to a higher, no doubt divinely inspired, scale of values, which they administered strictly and fairly. Rewards were just as precise – a nod before the next on the list. Our names were read out in

alphabetical order, and for exams according to marks. We had
duties, but no rights, and no one dreamt of wasting emotions
or indulgent chat on us. Everything was just as it should be.

Everything was just as it should be, because there wasn't
much room for error. You knew your place. You knew who
you were, and where you belonged.

Not until I got into high school did I have a teacher who
radiated warmth and I begin to realise that teacher-pupil relationships could also exist in other ways than through orders,
interrogation, punishment and small, carefully measured
rewards.

It was when I moved into puberty that it became serious, if I
can put it that way. One of my teachers became the centre of all
my fantasies. I loved him because he had a beautiful voice and
sorrowful eyes that I thought saw straight through me, making
me turn away, melt, and at the same time nailing me to my
seat. I loved him and worshipped him for years in that pre-
adolescent way. Now and again he slapped us quite hard,
though it was according to our common yardstick always well
deserved punishment – but never me. I was a polite girl, who
always sat still and did what I was told. I felt a sweet shudder at
the thought of a beating from him, but that somehow seemed to
be beyond the bounds of possibilities.

But before I fell asleep every night, I thought about what else
he could do to me. I constructed a whole fantasy world with
myself and him at the centre – or to be more precise, with him
doing something to me, and me being the person having
something done to by him. In time these fantasies became
more and more elaborate and drastic, and also more ritualistic
– they always followed a definite pattern. I was hung up in a
tree – by him. There was some question of being beaten, but
I'm not certain whether the threat was ever carried out in
reality. I had discovered that it wasn't nice when something
hurt. But I wanted to be hung up by the arms. I imagined
myself stretched out, unable to move or get away, the sense of
having to wait for what I wanted the person I loved to do to me
– with no possible chance of preventing it.

Oddly enough, I found out many years later that two of the
teachers in my old school became Nazis. He was one of them
and my idolised gym-teacher the other.

I abandoned myself systematically and passionately to my fantasies, but I had no idea what it was really all about. At that time, I knew nothing whatsoever about sex.

Well, I knew that men had genitals and what those looked like, but I didn't know they were used for anything except peeing. In fact I didn't really know that I myself had genitals, although I was menstruating and knew how children came out. I couldn't *see* those genitals, and I certainly didn't know that they were put to any use. I had never masturbated, either, although I can well remember a special feeling when I slid back and forth on the edge of a chair.

But I had no idea what to do about all this. I never dreamt of talking to anyone about it, and I was sure it was something I ought to keep to myself. On the other hand, I couldn't get away from my fantasy games. There was nothing to do but experiment on my own.

Once or twice, when I knew I was going to be alone at home for a while, I carried out some ingenious projects – which I had spent much time and thought planning. I managed to tie myself into unpleasant positions, once to the door handle, another time to my bed. I had also decided beforehand just how long it was to last, down to the last second.

I cannot remember if I watched the time. There was nothing to stop me getting free, and it was both boring and unpleasant – and also, there was no one controlling me, no one to see me, no one who had decided that this should happen to me. Once or twice I tried hitting myself, too, but not very much. The whole thing was very complicated. But it was titillating – especially when I planned it. And it was perfectly clear that the tickling feeling was *something definite* over which I simply didn't have any control.

What were the sources of material for all these fantasies I constructed so purposefully?

I may have invented it all myself, but not necessarily. When I think back, it is amazing how much nourishment my imagination received from literature – from children's books, that is, the good old ordinary, approved children's books that you borrowed from the school library or from the real library in the town.

There was material everywhere, and I can still remember a

great deal of it.

There were the books about boarding school, in which small boys slaved for the bigger boys and were punished by them if they didn't do exactly what they were told. There were books about the initiation rites of exotic people. There was *Uncle Tom's Cabin*, and other books about black slaves in America. There were books about armies with iron discipline and military justice and punitive expeditions. There were books about Chinese and Japanese and Indian systems of torture.

Then there were of course the Greek myths about all those people condemned to eternal punishment: the Danaides, who had to fill a bottomless vessel; Sisyphus, who had to roll a heavy boulder up a mountain only to watch it rolling down again and have to start all over again; then Tantalus. Imagine being Tantalus, condemned to stand in water all his life and still be thirsty, have the most delicious fruit within reach and still be hungry, because the water and fruit retreated each time he stretched out his hand for them...

There were also historical novels – stories from the Catholic Middle Ages with their refined and imaginative interrogation techniques, stories from the days of the Nordic Vikings, when bondsmen were subdued by cruder, but nevertheless extremely effective, methods, and then all those stories from antiquity. Antiquity was best, especially ancient Rome, in which slavery gave rise to all kinds of systems of punishment that were graphically described.

History books were otherwise heavy and often boring tomes. But I obviously found a semi-conscious use for them. I could almost smell which books would contain ''good material'', and tortures thus became part of my own imagination. I got a lot more out of historical novels than out of comic strips and weekly magazines, probably because there was more description in them.

Nevertheless, history textbooks – the ones we used in history lessons – were the best of all, because there were no fantasies in them. They were *reality* and you could really rely on them in quite a different way.

Very often it was the small print of history that became most important to me, because that was where there were descriptions of prisoners being tortured or rebellious peasants being punished. There were often pictures, too, of pillories and whips and stocks and Spanish hooded cloaks. I could use it all. I swallowed it all whole.

For years I was actually unhappy about the civilised times I lived in, full of envy for people who had lived in the Middle Ages, in the days of witch-hunts and the Inquisition. Why couldn't I have been born a slave or a villein in a different and more colourful epoch of history! My unhappy yearning love for the golden days of torture was exceeded only by my terror when I heard the first reports from reality, the real reality – accounts of the same things going on in my own times. It was as if there were two kinds of reality – one in books and one that affected myself, or someone I knew, or just someone I could see and hear, or just someone alive today. I had not meant it to be *that* real. I simply couldn't use it that way!

But now I couldn't stop it. I sometimes wondered whether it was all a refined game, a revenge by fate, a punishment for my fantasy-desires. But it wasn't. It was only reality.

All the intensity I had put into my fantasies was now transferred to the level of reality. I became hypersensitive, if it can be put that way, to everything to do with authority, to the relationship between executioner and victim, to violence, compulsion and torture. I was obsessed with terror at the thought of torture, and reality was full of fantasy material. For years my waking nightmares were about what was done to people – in concentration camps, in war, under interrogation. I put myself in their place, myself and my nearest and dearest, in other words, my family. I thought about it all the time. It never stopped.

I thought a lot about what would have happened if I had been a little older and had had to decide whether I should join the resistance movement or not – whether I would have dared, and what would have happened. Even now, I do not forget that at any time, and almost without notice, you can find yourself faced with the choice of whether or not to get seriously involved in your own times. How would I react? How would I be broken down if I let reality in too close – if I myself were subjected to torture, or if I were forced to witness torture, or if my children or someone I loved, or just someone I could hear, were subjected to torture?

That kind of idea was and still is constantly in my mind and will probably never leave it. I try as much as possible not to think these things through to the bitter end, but if the right situation is there – a high temperature, a dream, the influence of a mind-expanding drug – I know that I cannot escape. That is one of the reasons why I would never dare take LSD or any equivalent.

Awareness is always there, in everyday circumstances as well. It is there every time I sit in a dentist's chair, with all its refined instruments of torture. And when I lie on the couch with my legs in the air at a gynaecological examination. It is there at any sort of *treatment*, whether meted out by a doctor, a beautician, a masseuse or a chiropractor.

It is also there in the sense that the slightest external reason makes my thoughts go off at a tangent with merciless dream-logic. What if you now had to stay on this bus for days and days, en route to an unknown destination? What if the eggs you're cooking were put boiling hot under your armpits, as was done to Hans Egede? What if they locked the door of the sauna so that you couldn't get out? What if someone took your cigarette and stubbed it out on your skin? And so on and so on. It is inexhaustible, not a single day passing without it appearing.

Neither could it be said that there is any lack of nourishment around us for waking nightmares. You can hardly go to the cinema, switch on a television thriller or open a morning paper without coming across refined forms of torture or kinds of violence that you would have to be very thick-skinned to be able to withstand. Many people clearly are able to do so, but I long ago reached the point where I recognised that I would never acquire a thick skin. I have to switch off the television and go away and close my ears and eyes.

But that is only entertainment. There are always political realities: rebellions crushed, juntas demonstrating their power and authority.

It is not even that simple and unequivocal. There is always something else. There is always something titillating in it. When I come across descriptions of maltreatment, the following usually occurs. I cautiously let my eyes glide over the story – to find out if I dare even start reading it. If it is too close, smelling too much of reality, I hurriedly turn the page to avoid

it becoming etched into my mind so that I can't get rid of it
again, however much I want to. But if it lies just below a certain threshold, I cannot help using it as fantasy material. It is
no longer a question of whether it is actually fantasy or reality
that is involved. Because I know there's no difference.

Germaine Greer said in a *Playboy* interview that we must make
sure we find out why we become sexually excited at the sight of
a Nazi uniform. I am not excited by a Nazi uniform, but I can
understand that she is. For her, it is the past, history, fantasy,
for her it is on the same level as the wooden horse and pillories
in the history books are for me. A Nazi uniform for me is, and
will continue to be, reality, because I myself experienced the
time when it *was* a real threat, which might affect myself and all
the people I knew.

I dimly remember a novel in which some people in a concentration camp stimulated each other sexually by talking about
the prisoners. It is one of the most obscene situations I have
ever read. But the obscenity did not lie in the use of reality as
pornography, because one often does that provided it is at a
safe distance. It lay in the fact that it was reality to them *at the
same time*, leaving the victims out in the cold, waiting...That
would be the equivalent, for me, of using Santiago's football
stadium or a contemporary prison in my sexual fantasies. My
hold on reality is not that weak...

But everything is relative. I cannot use reality until it is sufficiently distant from me no longer to appear as reality, and I
can persuade myself that it is fantasy. Then I can prostitute it
instead, buy it like goods to be used as sexual stimulants. Then
I can devote myself to its pornographic worth.

These are only some examples of the conflicts that exist for
me to this day, but which I experienced as conflicts many years
earlier. I did not know what I should do with this sordid
mishmash I felt was going on in my head – or wherever it was.
What was it all about?

I had to find out, so I started seeking at random, in the kind
of books you would expect to contain something relevant. For
naturally I didn't dare speak to anyone about it.

2 Something Called Masochism

Early informative books: Fabricius-Møller, Krafft-Ebing, etc.

An unmarried man in his forties, in a good position, rational and attractive, was every now and again overtaken by a frenzy. He went to a certain woman and paid her to be allowed to polish her tiled stove. By doing this naked, while she watched, ordering him to make the tiled stove really clean, he had an erection, an orgasm and ejaculation of sperm.

Thus he was at peace for a while, but would again ask to clean the stove, humiliating himself to an extreme.

This description has etched itself on my memory. It was the first description of its kind I had read in a serious book, one I happened to find on a shelf in our municipal library. The book was *Sexual Life* by J. Fabricius-Møller, and the extract was introduced in the following way:

In this same category of Masochism, the following account must also be included, the most remarkable I have experienced.

Masochism. So there was a name for it.

So I was a masochist and belonged in books about *sex*, though not under descriptions of genitals or sexuality in the early years, but after abortions, venereal diseases and abnormalities. I was not included in normal sexual life, but came under *abnormal* sex, right at the end of the book. There I was, together with a whole series of other abnormal phenomena:

Narcissism (love of self), fetishism (arousal caused by a certain object), pygmalionism (arousal caused by statues and pictures), exhibitionism (urge to expose sexual organs), senile indecency, algolagnia (there I am – the masochist – together with the sadists), urolagnia (drinking urine), coprolagnia (eating faeces), paederasty (when the anus is used in intercourse), cleptolagnia (arousal from stealing), pyrolagnia (arousal from seeing fire), voyeurism (peeping toms), paedophilia (indecency with minors), zoophilia (indecency with animals), necrophilia (indecency with corpses), homosexuality and bi-sexuality. Altogether, we filled fourteen pages of this 256-page-long book.

I think I was pleased to have a name, as if I were no longer floating about in the air. But I was also somewhat frightened when I realised the furtive nature of the group to which that name consigned me. But I reckoned Fabricius-Møller was sure to be a respected author, and this was later confirmed for me. For many years, his book was the most widely read information book on sex in Danish.

I was also pleased that he was not in the least condemnatory either; on the contrary, he was very tolerant:

It can safely be said that there is not *one single thing* devised by the human mind that is not used in the field of sex, sometimes of an ugliness so great, one must turn away from it in disgust. But however repulsive it may be to one's feelings, we must never forget to have compassion for these people and show them understanding. They are often wretched souls with more or less unhealthy minds, who are as much deserving of our help as any other unhealthy people.

And at the end of the book, he wrote:

Should you have been depressed by anything that I have told you, especially today when we look at the more revolting aspects of sexual life, then tuck it away in a distant corner of your mind. But not so far away that you cannot retrieve it, should you again come across it on your way through life, so you can then with understanding rise above that which revolts you.

And if you have hidden away the ugly things, then I would ask of you in exchange to remember that there is nothing more beautiful in life than faithful love between two people who love each other. Love makes people beautiful and good.

That was truly beautifully said, so beautifully that I almost forgot the words were also referring to me, though unfortunately in a particular way: I was one of the revolting ones, not one of the faithful lovers. I tried to forget it, but that was not easy. It is hard to forget something that is beautifully written.

Fabricius-Møller's book was published in 1944, and reactions to it were very varied, especially to his tolerance. Most reviewers were full of praise for his style – but there were also some who were angry. They accused the author of being 'shockingly open-minded', clearly indicating that I simply should not have been included in such a book. Reviews said that "the section of the book dealing with sexual deviations could have been excluded without harm", that his realism "at times contains almost a touch of cynicism", and that what was very much lacking was "not just moral, but also aesthetic evaluation". There were also critics who thought that if one is involved "in ensuring that young people should be sound and healthy, with strong personalities, a command over sex and the most profound respect for love between men and women, then there is not much help to be found in Dr. Fabricius-Møller's book".

One individual reviewer said:

On purely humane grounds, it is a book one would not put into the hands of young people indiscriminately. It might come as a shock to many honourable young people, not least innocent young women, a brutal intrusion into a world that it would be healthier for them not to know about, or perhaps should be revealed to them only slowly. The publisher writes on the back of the book that every parent could without fear give this book to a young son or daughter, and at this I definitely protest.

Fortunately, I read all these reviews some years later, or I would probably have been slightly shocked that young people were not even supposed to know I existed. But they did know, nevertheless, because Fabricius-Møller's book went into a great many homes. So one can assume that he has contributed to a great many people's understanding of what is normal and what is not normal. He distinguishes between the two in this way:

> By normal sex life, we mean the forms of sex that commonly occur in healthy natural people, and we group in abnormal sex all forms of sex that occur only rarely, and in their form deviate from ordinary forms in essential points. The borderline between normal and abnormal is, however, by no means sharp, and there are all kinds of intermediate stages.

I was slightly confused to find that there were all kinds of intermediate stages between me and the others, but nevertheless there was an unmistakable borderline, and it was clearly a kind of numerical, statistical borderline – the others were normal because there were so many of them and I was not normal because there were not so many of me. How many, I wondered?

Fabricius-Møller also knew other terms for my group, but he did not bother much with those. He mentioned them, however, for the sake of order: *perversions, unnatural sex and sexual deviations.* And on page 237, the page about me, there is a picture of various instruments of torture, among them handcuffs, whips and studded belts. The pictures interested me greatly, and naturally I also revelled in the section on Algolagnia. I still felt slightly honoured that a whole page and an even more peculiar name were devoted to me.

I would like to quote the whole section here:

> *Algolagnia.* We comprehend this form of sex as sexual pleasure roused, or exclusively finding satisfaction in, tortures of one kind or another. We speak of an *active* form, *sadism*, after the Marquis de Sade, who wrote books on the subject, and a *passive* form, *masochism*, after Sacher-Masoch, who described this form.

> *Sadism.* In this form, sexual pleasure rises to orgasm by the violent tormenting of the other partner. This violence is usually carried out purely physically, but we also speak of psychic sadism. An incredible variety of violent instruments are brought into use for this purpose. The illustrations show

you a collection of such things that have been used for
sadistic and masochistic purposes.

The sadist may be utterly demonic in his actions, so may
use considerable violence, even to the extent that his victim's
death may result; this is called *sexual murder*.

Masochism. This is the opposite of sadism. The masochist enjoys sexual satisfaction through suffering, in
this case also in both physical and psychic form.

An example from my practice demonstrates what this
entails better than words. There was a middle-aged man
who sometimes allowed himself to be whipped by his wife.
He pulled his underpants tightly across his buttocks and bent
over an armchair, and she then struck him as hard as she
could with a dog-whip until both his underpants and skin
were covered in blood. At this he had an erection and
reached the highest sexual pleasure with orgasm and ejaculation.

This is a typical case of masochism. If his wife had had
sexual satisfaction from hitting her husband, which was not
the case, then she would have been a sadist.

In this same category of Masochism, the following account
must also be included. (The story of the man polishing the
tiled stove comes here.)

I have mentioned these cases to show you how extraordinary apparently healthy people can be in their sex life.

That leanings towards the sexual urges mentioned, particularly sadism, can involve great unhappiness needs no
explanation. But should a sadist and a masochist find each
other, naturally they can live happily together.

After that follows the section on urolagnia, sexual arousal
from drinking urine.

This was the general introduction young women and men
from reasonably informed backgrounds in Denmark – myself
included – received to something called "abnormal sex". For
safety's sake, I supplemented this by looking it up in Salomon's
Danish Dictionary for which I had always nourished a venera-
tion. Yes, I was in there, too:

Masochism, an abnormality in the field of sex, its name deriving from the Austrian author Sacher-Masoch.

Masochism is manifested in the individual whose sexual urge is in such a direction as to find sexual satisfaction during intercourse (or outside intercourse) only from pain being administered, usually in the form of blows or bites; on some occasions this desire veers towards added suffering in the psychic field, produced by scolding or mocking. Masochism is the opposite of sadism, the desire to cause the other person pain. Slighter elements of masochism are found in many people in whom sexual urges on the whole are normal. Those comparatively rare cases when the sexual urge can only be satisfied by masochistic actions are considered truly unhealthy.

K.H.K.

I had learnt not a little, all in all. There was normal and abnormal sex, and I was one of the abnormal, although there were all kinds of intermediate stages and many normal people felt slightly the same way as I did.

I represented the most revolting sides of sex, but all the same tolerance as well as compassion should be shown towards me and people of my kind.

I was one half of a couple. Sadism formed the other half of the couple (and clearly the grandest, as it is always mentioned first). So I was actually the opposite of a sadist.

I was harmless...in contrast to the sadist.

If one day I could find my sadist, I should have a chance of being happy.

I had been very slightly aware of the latter, but where does a young girl find a sadist? In general, I had a great deal to think about, for there were many inner contradictions in what I had read. But the most important thing I had gained was the simple matter of having acquired a name. So I was *something definite*. I was included in a definite category. I had my own place. The drawer I belonged in didn't smell quite so nice as the others, but it was a regular drawer with a label on it. In some way or other, this seemed comforting, a kind of acknowledgement.

Being given a name seemed to be the first act of consciousness-raising, as if a whole disorganised mess of granules had gathered themselves together into a solid picture, not only something definite, but also something *special*, something not really as it should be. Not quite like a crime, but something close to it.

I consulted many more books, wanting to know much more. At first I wanted more detailed and realistic descriptions of what you did when you were a masochist. Explanations could wait.

I wanted the most extensive and comprehensive description of myself possible, because I had no wish to go round feeling like an indescribable scrap-heap. I also wanted to know how much of what I felt was shared by others. Perhaps I would be able to plan a strategy that way – that is, put my life right according to my abnormal condition.

Finally, I think quite early on, I admitted that I found it exciting to read about sadists, and especially about masochists, on this "authoritative" level. The details were guaranteed, as it were, because, other things apart, the clinical cases were often years old.

When I came across particularly detailed descriptions in these books, there were often references to a particular book called *Psychopathia Sexualis*, by Dr. R. von Krafft-Ebing. One day I took my courage in my hands and acquired the book itself. It was a huge work of four hundred and fifty pages, of which over a hundred were about my sadist and me, truly a goldmine. I soon found out why Krafft-Ebing is still regarded as a classic, although his book was published as long ago as the end of the last century.

But you have to know Latin to be able to get the best out of the book. It is *not* written for people who like being excited by reading about sexual deviations in detail: on the contrary. The really intimate parts are written in Latin, for safety's sake. If it refers to buggery, it says *coitus a tergo*. In those days that kind of book was not written for ordinary people or patients, but for academics, scientists and the medical world. No one ever meant *me* to see it.

Dr. R. von Krafft-Ebing's discretion makes his book just as beautiful reading as Fabricius-Møller's, despite the fact that he certainly doesn't pull any punches. But his starting-point is in itself beautiful and is also concerned with *love*.

He writes in the introduction that in his opinion love is a natural urge, but none the less the field in which human beings rise above animals:

> Man puts himself at once on a level with the beast if he seeks to gratify lust alone, but he elevates his superior position when by curbing the animal desire, he combines with the sexual functions ideas of morality, of the sublime, and the beautiful.

So there are grounds for optimism: love is beautiful and will probably tame our lowly nature. But it is also necessary to look soberly upon love, anyhow in some of its forms. As a doctor, you see a great deal that is nasty, and it is all this nastiness that Krafft-Ebing undertook to write about because he saw himself facing:

> dark sides of his existence, the shadow of which contorts the sublime image of the deity into horrid caricatures, and leads astray aestheticism and morality.

The people we meet in this fat volume offend us, because they are neither good nor beautiful. But they themselves cannot help that: they are sick. I am sick. What does Dr. von Krafft-Ebing say about me?

Well, to start with, naturally, it isn't actually me he is talking about, but my grander opposite, the sadist. He writes sexual murder, necrophilia, maltreatment of women and defiling women, about "ideal" sadism, boy-beaters and animal-tormentors. But then he comes to me:

> Masochism is the opposite of sadism. While the latter is the desire to cause pain and use force, the former is the wish to suffer pain and be subjected to force.
>
> By masochism I understand a peculiar perversion of the psychical sexual life in which the individual affected, in sexual feeling and thought, is controlled by the idea of being completely and unconditionally subject to the will of a person of the opposite sex; of being treated by this person as by

a master, humiliated and abused. This idea is coloured by lustful feeling; the masochist lives in fantasies, in which he creates situations of this kind and often attempts to realise them. By this perversion his sexual instinct is often made more or less insensible to the normal charms of the opposite sex – incapable of a normal sexual life – psychically impotent.

But this psychical impotence does not in any way depend upon a horror of the opposite sex, but upon the fact that the perverse instinct finds an adequate satisfaction differing from the normal – in woman, to be sure, but not in coitus.

Whether masochism is absolute or supplemented by normal sexual life, whether it is purely psychic or must be acted out, whether the capability for normal intercourse survives or not – all these things are dependent on how strong the perversion is and how strong the individual's ethical and aesthetic inhibitions against them are, as well as on how robust the sick person is. But common to all masochists, whether severely or less severely afflicted, is this concept in which submission and maltreatment dominate.

Then comes a whole series of case histories, written down in detail and with care. They are divided up in the following clinical manner:

(a) The Desire for Abuse and Humiliation as a Means of Sexual Satisfaction
(b) Latent Masochism – Foot- and Shoe-Fetishists
(c) Disgusting Acts for the Purpose of Self-Humiliation and Sexual Gratification – Latent Masochism – Coprolagnia
(d) Masochism in Woman

Then follows an attempt to describe the origins of masochism, and a summary in the last section on masochism and sadism. There are also attempts to find *reasons* in each individual category: Krafft-Ebing describes his patients' genitals, shape of head, body-build, deviations in the family, concussion, diseases of the nose, hereditary predispositions to diseases of the central nervous system; and he examines their masturbatory history, any unusual family antecedents, whether the patient has lived too hard, as well as many other things.

There is a mass of material in Krafft-Ebing's case sheets for the person who has run out of fantasies – and all of them are real people doing a great variety of special things.

There is the man who leaned over a chair and let a woman ride on him for three-quarters of an hour at a time, enjoying the feel of the bridle, the pressure of her thighs and the woman's cheerful voice as she gave him orders.

There is the man who had a girl stand on him in high-heeled shoes with one heel on one of his eyeballs, the other on his throat.

There is the man who hired a servant to come rushing in while he was courting a lady, and then throw him out.

There is the man who had a prostitute beat him as a punishment because he wouldn't go to school. Then she had to give him a little basket with bread and fruit in it, and tell him to go off to school.

There is the man who could have an orgasm simply by hearing a dominating woman (a cashier, for instance) scolding a man (a servant for instance).

There is the man who dreamt only about being trained like a dog or a horse, and who asked his lady in writing to do the same to him, as slave-owners used to do with their slaves.

There is the man who dreamt about a slave existence in which he was given nothing to eat but potato-peelings and gnawed bones, and in which he had to sleep on bare earth.

There is the man who every fourth week sent a letter to a girl in a brothel in which he said: 'Dear Peggy, I shall be with you tomorrow evening between eight and nine o'clock. Whip and knout! Kindest regards...'

And there are all the others who paid girls in brothels to imprison them, beat them, whip them and treat them in one humiliating way or another.

Some of these people pursued their preferences in practice, others were content to do so in their fantasies. A number tried to turn their fantasies into reality, and were deeply disappointed. Others suffered most from a fearful revulsion that overcame them at the actual moment of orgasm.

Krafft-Ebing sketches some of the case histories with a swift but sure hand; other cases are described more fully and create a fascinating picture of how hard people have tried to make a pattern of the details of their lives, and to find out what was fundamentally going on inside themselves. Here is one of those fuller examples which I wish to quote at length, written by the patient himself:

CASE 57: I am thirty-five years old, mentally and physically normal. Among all my relatives in the direct as well as in the lateral line, I know of no case of mental disorder. My father, who at my birth was thirty years old, as far as I know, had a preference for voluptuous, large women.

Even in my early childhood I loved to revel in ideas about the absolute mastery of one man over others. The thought of slavery had something exciting in it for me, alike whether from the standpoint of master or servant. That one man could possess, sell or whip another, caused me intense excitement; and in reading *Uncle Tom's Cabin* (which I read at about the beginning of puberty) I had erections. Particularly exciting for me was the thought of a man being hitched to a wagon in which another man sat with a whip, driving and whipping him. Until my twentieth year these ideas were purely objective and sexless – that is, the one in subjugation in my fancy was another (not myself), and the master was not necessarily a woman. These ideas were, therefore, without effect on my sexual desires – that is, on the way in which they took practical shape. Although these ideas caused erections, yet I have never masturbated in my life, and from my nineteenth year I had coitus without the help of these ideas and without any relation to them. I always had a great preference for elderly, voluptuous, large women, although I did not scorn younger ones.

After my twenty-first year my ideas became objective, and it became an essential thing that the 'mistress' should be a woman over forty years old, tall and powerful. From this time I was always in my fancies the subject; the 'mistress' was a rough woman, who made use of me in every way, also sexually; who harnessed me to a carriage and made me take her for a drive, whom I must follow like a dog, at whose feet I must lie naked and be punished, that is, whipped, by her. This was the constant element in my ideas, around which all others were grouped. In these fancies I always found endless pleasurable comfort which caused erection, but never ejaculation. As a result of the induced sexual excitement, I would immediately seek a woman, preferably one corresponding exteriorly with my ideal, and have coitus with her without any actual aid of my fancies, and sometimes also without any thought of them during the act. I had, however, also inclination towards women of a different kind, and had coitus with them without being impelled to it by my fancy.

Notwithstanding all this, my life was not exceedingly abnormal sexually; yet these ideas were certain to occur periodically, and they have remained essentially unchanged. With growing sexual desire, the intervals constantly grew shorter. At the present time the attacks come every two or three weeks. If I previously were to have coitus, the occurrence of the fancies would, perhaps, be postponed. I have never attempted to realise my very definite and characteristic ideas – that is, to connect them with the world without me – but I have contented myself with revelling in the thoughts, because I was convinced that my ideal would not allow even an approach to realisation. The thought of a comedy with paid prostitutes always seemed so silly and purposeless, for a person hired by me could never take the place of my imagination of a 'cruel mistress'. I doubt whether there are sadistically constituted women like

Sacher-Masoch's heroines. But, if there were such women, and I had the fortune to find one, still, in a world of reality, intercourse with her would ever seem only a farce to me.

Indeed, I can only say that, were I to become the slave of a nymphomaniac, I believe that owing to the other necessary renunciations, my desired manner of life would soon pall on me, and in my lucid intervals I should make every effort to obtain my freedom at all hazards.

Yet I have found a way in which to induce, in a certain sense, a realisation. After my sexual desire has been intensely excited by revelling in my fancy, I go to a prostitute and there call up before my mind's eye with great intensity some scene of the kind mentioned, in which I play the principal role. After thinking of such a situation for about half an hour, with a constantly resulting erection, I perform coitus with increased lustful pleasure and strong ejaculation. After the latter, the vision fades away. Ashamed, I depart as quickly as possible, and try not to think of the affair. Then for about two weeks I have no more such ideas! Indeed, after a particularly satisfactory coitus, it may happen that until the next attack I have not even any sympathy whatever with masochistic ideas. But the next attack is sure to come sooner or later. I must, however, state that I also have coitus without being prepared by such ideas, especially, too, with women that are acquainted with me and my position, and in whose presence I abhor such fantasies. Under the latter circumstances, however, I am not always potent, while, with masochistic ideas, my virility is perfect. It does not seem superfluous to add that otherwise in my thought and feeling I am very aesthetic, and despise anything like maltreatment of a human being. Finally, I will not leave unmentioned the fact that the form of address is of importance. In my fancies it is essential that the 'mistress' address me in the second person (*Du*), while I must address her in the third (*Sie*). This cir-cumstance of being thus familiarly addressed (*Du*) by a person so inclined, as the expression of absolute mastery, has from my youth given me lustful pleasure, and does today.

I had the fortune to find a wife who is in everything, but especially sexually, attractive to me; though, as I scarcely need say, she in no way resembles my masochistic ideals. She is gentle, but voluptuous, for without the latter characteristic I cannot conceive such a thing as sexual charm. The first few months of married life were normal sexually; the masochistic attacks did not occur, and I had almost lost all thought of masochism. Then came the first confinement and the necessary abstinence. Punctually, then, with the occurrence of libido came the masochistic fancies again, which, in spite of my great love for my wife, necessitated coitus with another, with the accompaniment of masochistic ideas. It is here worthy of note that marital coitus, which was later resumed, did not prove sufficient to banish the masochistic ideas, as masochistic coitus always does. As for the essential element in masochism, I am of the opinion that the ideas, that is, the mental element, are the end and aim...

Finally, I should mention that, according to my experience, the number of masochists, especially in big cities, seems to be quite large. The only sources of such information are – since men do not reveal these things – statements by prostitutes, and since they agree on the essential points, certain facts may be assumed as proved.

Thus there is the fact that every experienced prostitute keeps some suitable instrument (usually a whip) for flagellation, but it must be remembered that there are men who have themselves whipped simply to increase their sexual pleasure. These, in contrast with masochists, regard flagellation as a means to an end.

On the other hand, almost all prostitutes agree that there are many men who like to play ''slave'' – that is, like to be so called, and have themselves scolded and trod upon and beaten. As has been said, the number of masochists is larger than has yet been dreamed...

I must also confess that, in spite of its marked pathological character, masochism is not only incapable of destroying my pleasure in life, but it does not in the least affect my outward life. When not in a masochistic state, as far as feeling and action are concerned, I am a perfectly normal man. During the activity of the masochistic tendencies there is, of course, a great revolution in my feeling, but my outward manner of life suffers no change; I have a calling that makes it necessary for me to move much in public, and I pursue it in the masochistic condition as well as ever.

I have mixed reactions when I read accounts such as this one, by a man who is perhaps a senior official, perhaps a lawyer, perhaps a newspaper editor, perhaps a theatre director. First I feel powerful sexual excitement reading his detailed clinical facts and varied fantasies. Second, I feel as if I have had a handshake from a fellow-sufferer over almost a century. There is something comforting and almost friendly that there are so many of us, that we are so varied and yet so united.

I find it interesting to read Krafft-Ebing's descriptions of different people's experiences. But on the other hand his own analyses are not particularly convincing – his attempts to explain why some people become masochists and others don't. Among his attempts to find an explanation, there are also some that directly contradict each other: in one place he says that masochism is due to sexual response being pathologically high, so that everything, even pain, becomes a sexual stimulant; and in another place he says the opposite, that masochism is found in people who have lived too intensely and thus have blunted their senses to an extent that something extra in the way of titillation is needed for potency.

Potency...I suddenly realised that practically all the cases

Krafft-Ebing described were men. But weren't there any women masochists at all – except me?

On further investigation, it proved that in Krafft-Ebing's section on masochism, there were thirty-four male cases compared with three female. This has a natural explanation in his theories on what men and women are – two human types that are (and should be) so different that they seem to come from different planets:

> Man has beyond doubt the stronger sexual appetite of the two. From the period of pubescence he is instinctively drawn towards woman. His love is sensual, and his choice is strongly prejudiced in favour of physical attractions. A mighty impulse of nature makes him aggressive and impetuous in his courtship. Yet the law of nature does not wholly fill his psychic being. Having won the prize, his love is temporarily eclipsed by other vital and social interests.

> Woman, however, if physically and mentally normal, and properly educated, has but little sensual desire. If it were otherwise, marriage and family life would be empty words. As yet the man who avoids women, and the woman who seeks men are sheer anomalies.

For woman, love is not sensual, but spiritual, and when she becomes a mother, sexual life for her is largely a proof of her spouse's love and affection:

> Woman loves with her whole soul. To woman love is life, to man it is the joy of life. Misfortune in love bruises the heart of man; but it ruins the life of woman and wrecks her happiness. It is really a psychological question worthy of consideration whether woman can truly love twice in her life. Woman's mind certainly inclines more to monogamy than that of man.

As far as actual sexual life is concerned, the roles are divided in an unambiguous manner:

> In the intercourse of the sexes, the active or aggressive role belongs to man; woman remains passive, defensive. It affords man great pleasure to win a woman, to conquer her; and in the art of love making, the modesty of woman, who

keeps herself on the defensive until the moment of surrender, is an element of great psychological significance and importance. Under normal conditions man meets obstacles which it is his part to overcome, and for which nature has given him an aggressive character.

This sexual division of the roles involves a corresponding division of roles in the field of perversions:

In the first place, sadism, in which the need of subjugation of the opposite sex forms a constituent element, in accordance with its nature represents a pathological intensification of the *male* sexual character; in the second place, the obstacles which oppose the expression of this monstrous impulse are, of course, much greater for woman than for man.

So we don't often become sadists. But why then do we seldom become masochists? There are two reasons:

First, woman has so strong a feeling of shame and virtue that out of physical necessity she reacts to every attack of perverse sexual desire with an almost insurmountable resistance. Briefly it is almost impossible for us to be perverse, because we are both too unsensual and – purely morally – too elevated. But when it finally comes to masochism in women, the situation is different.

In woman voluntary subjection to the opposite sex is a physiological phenomenon. Owing to her passive role in procreation and long-existent social conditions, ideas of subjection are, in woman, normally connected with the idea of sexual relations. They form, so to speak, the harmonics which determine the tone-quality of feminine feeling. . .

Thus it is easy to regard masochism in general as a pathological growth of specific feminine mental elements – as an abnormal intensification of *certain features of the psycho-sexual character of woman – and to seek its primary origin in the sex.*

So women are in a way born masochists, while it is men who become sadists. But men can also be masochists, and when such cases are investigated, it is important to find out whether the subjects show other female characteristics. (Krafft-Ebing mentions anxiety, irritability, weakness of will and so on.)

There can be no doubt that the masochist feels he is in a passive, female role towards his dominator, and his sexual satisfaction is governed by the success his illusion experiences in the complete subjection to the will of the consort. The pleasurable feeling, call it lust, resulting from this act differs per se in no wise from the feeling which woman derives from the sexual act.

But in the case of masochistic men, it is sad that it is so difficult for them to find woman dominators in the world of reality. They have to imagine them and then masturbate to their fantasies, which again can bring on psychic impotence...

So a masochistic man takes on a kind of female role, and the other way round; the few women who can really be called masochists, imagine they are men.

I found it difficult to understand the latter statement until I realised how astonishingly logical Krafft-Ebing's reasoning really was. If a woman has to imagine that she is thoroughly humiliated, then it is no use her imagining herself a woman, that is, a creature already humiliated. In fact only men can be dragged down into the mud, because women are already there...

Besides, most women simply aren't masochists. They are simply women. This applies not least to certain alien cultures. Krafft-Ebing has a particularly nice example he found in a book from 1698, and which has been quoted in one book after another since. It is the story about Russian peasant wives:

There are some nations, *viz*, the Persians and Russians, where the women regard blows as a peculiar sign of love and favour. Strangely enough, the Russian women are never more pleased and delighted than when they receive hard blows from their husbands, as John Barclarus relates in a remarkable narrative. A German, named Jordan, went to Russia, and pleased with the country, settled there and took a Russian wife, whom he loved dearly, and to whom he was always kind in everything. But she always wore an expression of dissatisfaction, and went with sighs and downcast eyes. The husband asked the reason why, for he could not understand what was wrong. 'Aye,' she said. 'Though you love me, you do not show any sign of it.' He embraced

her, and begged to be told what he had carelessly and unconsciously done to hurt her feelings, and to be forgiven, for
he would never do it again. "I want nothing," was the
answer, "but what is customary in our country – the whip,
the real sign of love." When Jordan adopted the custom his
wife began to love her husband dearly. Similar stories are
told by Peter Petreus of Erlesund, who adds that husbands,
immediately after the wedding, among other indispensable
household articles, provide themselves with a whip.

It is impossible to avoid noticing Krafft-Ebing's enthusiasm
for the women in this primitive Russian society. They are
really people who are close to the soil. But he thinks it probable
that even women on a higher cultural level see their role during
the sex act as pleasing simply because it is passive. And he
thinks the more elevated the society is, the greater the difference between men and women in that society. It will always
be so that "the man's bold conduct exercises a sexual attraction
on the women".

Thus he seems to have explained both why there are so few
real female masochists – and why, despite all the grim case-
histories, there is nevertheless no reason to despair in a world
where men are men and women are women.

On the other hand, he says nothing about how men become
men and women become women, apart from just "that's how
it is". And I knew that already, because it was in the air –
then. That needed no investigation. Everyone knew what was
manly and what was womanly, and it was nature herself speaking.

It was also in the air that nature spoke with emphasis and
some menace, so it would be no good speculating too much on
that. Not doctors, nor women nor authors ignored nature's
voice. Whatever was unnatural the doctors would have to cure.
Judgement as to what was natural was made by taking a deep
breath, closing your eyes and concentrating on nature's voice,
which also aligned itself with the voice of common sense. It was
easy then, and the reason why I have made relatively much of
Dr. R. von Krafft-Ebing here is that I think he is such an
excellent example of what everyone agreed on, and what
hardly anyone dared discuss out of anxiety about being called

unnatural.

Krafft-Ebing also had proof: that is, that so many men and so few women consulted him. Naturally, at the time, it would never have occurred to a doctor that there might be other reasons why more women did not consult him. Perhaps they simply couldn't afford to? Then, only very few women had money of their own, and how many wished to present their husbands with a bill from the author of a book about abnormal sex life?

Presumably there was an added reluctance when it came to discussing perverse urges. That is still so today, as long as we still feel slightly guilty that we have strong sexual urges at all.

And why should they have consulted him if they sensed that he would perhaps pat them on the shoulder and say it was only natural? They would certainly have found it difficult to articulate what they were afraid was really wrong with them. And they certainly would have been frightened of being put on the list of revolting diseases. They probably felt under pressure of a kind similar to that felt by the young woman at the Germaine Greer meeting, who expressed the desperate suspicion that three-quarters of us are probably masochists anyway!

3 Columbine

Not so very long after I lost my virginity, as it is called (or was called), I sat down in my room one day with a strong sense that I simply had to *write* something.

I had never tried to write before, and I had no idea of what to write about or how to set about it. But there was a poster on my wall, the famous Harlequin poster advertising the Tivoli Gardens in Copenhagen, so I wrote about that.

I am not including this piece because I think it is a literary masterpiece, but because I have always had a special relationship with it. I think it was logical that my very first attempt to put words together should reflect the essential conflict that is mine, and, I think, many other women's.

I was overwhelmed with bewilderment and bitterness that love was not enough for the person I loved to be able to read me like an open book, that he could not unveil the secret I felt I was brooding over, that he could not help me find out what kind of secret it was. Was it the secret of actual womanhood? And who could help me solve the puzzle − could no one else but myself?

Harlequin and Columbine
Something must happen today.

They are right in among the flowers, in the centre of the bouquet, a garden of roses and bluebells, pink and yellow stars and hanging scented vines. The sun is shining down on them through the leaves and she hears the last violins. She has been dancing with Harlequin and she is still on the tips of her toes, in the centre of her white rose. She looks up at him as he stands there, his hand still on his heart, his eyes turned to her.

But now the music has gone, his hand sinks and he is breathing deeply. She seeks his eyes − and as always, they turn away, vanish, looking beyond her, fading away like the notes. There is no one else now, only her − why is he so far away? Harlequin, come closer. If you love me, we must plumb the depths of each other's eyes. If you love me, you must answer all my questions before I ask them. And it must happen today. Today she must catch Harlequin's eyes. Now he really is looking at her, and is speaking, but his voice is hard.

"Columbine," he says. "What's the matter with you today? You simply weren't with me. You weren't keeping time. You must pull yourself together a bit."

They start to go, he a few steps ahead of her. That doesn't matter, because she is crying slightly, and that would annoy him.

But then he turns round and she feels his hand on her shoulder. She kneels down in the grass and buries her face in the tall daisies. She cannot keep her tears back and it is a pleasure to give in – the roses are scented, the sun mild and the air still. It is June – she hears the cuckoo not far away. Now he is wholly with her. Never has she loved him as at this moment. It will always be June for them. They will walk among the flowers.

"Little Columbine," he whispers. "Columbine, can you forgive me? It's my fault. My white rose, you mustn't cry. Come, let us go now." She rises, the grass soft and winding itself round her ankles. He presses her to him. "Yes," he repeats. "You're my white rose." She begins to feel cold.

They move on to the path, the sun now behind a cloud, and she sees with surprise that the flowers are dead. They have come into a forest, and the moss on the roadside is damp. He stops, pulls her to him and stands with his hands on her waist, looking down into her face. His eyes are blurred, his voice tender: "Your eyes are so clear, your forehead so fine – I love you, Columbine, my dove, my white flower. I will look after you. You will always be with me, where no one can do you harm."

She looks up at him. There's something on his nose, a piece of fluff from a dandelion. She brushes if off. "And your lovely fair hair!" he says. "It shines like the sun, bright and transparent, like a still lake, a halo around you. Your lovely fair hair!" His eyes are radiant, and at last she can see right down into them, right down to the bottom of Harlequin's eyes. She lets her hand glide through her hair, quite slowly, taking a strand and winding it round her fingers; she doesn't have to look at it.

He bends down to kiss her, but she pulls herself out of his arms and runs away, the rain weeping a tear for her. But the wind comes and dries it for her, stroking softly and firmly through her hair – her pride, her lovely black hair.

4   Deviants in a Sexually Privileged Society

Kinsey, Auken and Hunt, and other more recent informative books: Claesson, Inge and Sten Hegeler, and Ullerstam.

Is it not possible to find out whether it is really true that seventy-five per cent of all women are masochists? Whether three quarters of us feel that deep down inside us we are as dark as night or sin, because we really long only for a man who will treat us badly, crush us, beat us and pull us around by the hair? Are we slaves, three out of every four of us?

It would be good to have some facts to hand, but that, at least in the days when I was trying to come to grips with the problem, was not as easy as it sounds.

I tried, for instance, looking up the Kinsey reports. But the first one is concerned with the sexual behaviour of American *men*, and only four of the book's eight hundred pages have even a few words on masochism. There is no investigation into how many men are masochists in practice.

The Kinsey report on men appeared in 1948. Kirsten Auken's report on the sexual behaviour of Danish women came out in 1953, and that was largely set up like Kinsey, so includes no investigation into masochism in women. If she had waited a few years, she could perhaps have used the second Kinsey report (on American women) as a model. Then perhaps we would have known a *little* more about this side of Danish women's sexual behaviour. But the Kinsey report on women came out in 1953, at the same time as her own.

The second Kinsey report, which (in contrast to the first) included women, also included another area, the psychic stimuli. It maintained that women are far less likely than men to be sexually stimulated psychically. The conclusion drawn from these observations was that women are to a greater degree sexually stimulated *physically*, and men were advised to take this into consideration when they initiated intercourse.

For instance, it was found that American women are less aroused than American men from listening to sado-masochistic stories. On the other hand, women are just as aroused as men by seeing films, reading romantic literature – and by being bitten. Furthermore, there are rather more women who are aroused by being bitten than there are men. But the Kinsey report does not discuss whether or not this is because women are more masochistically inclined than men (or because men perhaps bite more...).

Since the publication of the Kinsey report, several researchers have questioned the finding that women do not react sexually to psychic stimulants. The couple Phyllis and Eberhard Kronhausen interviewed women who reacted very strongly to various forms of pornography, and other researchers also persuaded women to tell them about their fantasies during intercourse.

All these investigations were interesting to read, but none of them could be used for statistical purposes, partly because so few women were consulted.*

But on the twenty-fifth anniversary of the first Kinsey report, the Playboy Foundation published a broadly based report on the sexual behaviour of American men and women in the 1970s, edited by Morton Hunt. It was based on questionnaires spread over a representative sample of the same kind as Kinsey's, and involved two thousand people.

It follows up the Kinsey report, but in some respects goes a step further. For the first time, there are concrete figures for sadism and masochism. According to Hunt, sado-masochism has increased during the past twenty-five years – but the figures are still astonishingly small; anyhow, nowhere near seventy-five per cent. On the other hand, the division of sadism and masochism between men and women is what would traditionally be expected; most female masochists and most male sadists.

* Even the *Hite Report*, which was published in the 1970s, rather late in the stage in my life I am describing in this chapter, contained little or no material on sexual fantasy; and Nancy Friday's *My Secret Garden*, which did – I was deeply impressed by the wealth of rape and sado-masochistic fantasy material – did not appear until 1975, nor did it provide any statistical analysis of these fantasies.

Here are the figures:

Ever Obtained Sexual Pleasure from Inflicting or Receiving
Pain: by Sex. Total National Sample. Per cents.

	Males	Females
Inflicting Pain	4.8	2.1
Receiving Pain	2.5	4.6

It also turned out that sado-masochistic activities hardly ever
take place within marriage, but only with partners to whom the
person is not married. Hunt thinks this is because unmarried
people and people practising sado-masochism have certain
problems in common: each may have emotional problems of
some considerable severity.

A third point worth noticing is that there are many more
young people than older who practise sado-masochism. On the
other hand, sado-masochism is not practised just for the sake of
experiment; by far the majority of those who attempt it, continue to practise it. Further, the figures for *active* sadists and
masochists are very low. They have also never really been
recognised as a sexual minority: there are no, or only very few,
bars where they can meet, and, in contrast to modern attitudes
to homosexuals, there is no public openness or emerging social
acceptance applied to them.

But what about the psychic form? Here Kinsey notes that
only ten per cent of men and three per cent of women became
sexually aroused by reading pornographic stories. And only
four per cent of the women in the Kinsey report had used sado-
masochistic fantasies while masturbating. The *Playboy* report is
more to the point, but the questions the researchers asked had
been rather narrowly formulated. They asked whether during
masturbation, any fantasies about forcing someone, or being
forced, into intercourse ever surfaced – which of course far
from covers the whole of the sado-masochistic field. But here
are the figures (including all the people who have at some time
masturbated):

Ever Had Thoughts, While Masturbating, of
Being Forced to Have Sex. Per cents.

Male		Female	
Under 35	35 & Over	Under 35	35 & Over
14	5	24	12

Yes, it seems that the numbers are rising, if you count the masochism that develops in the imagination. But it is still impossible to say what would have emerged if more questions had been asked – and if they had been phrased in a different way. For instance: What do you think about while you masturbate? Do you feel anything when you hear the word "slave", when you become erotically aroused and are kept there, when your partner is heavy-handed during intercourse, when he disregards your request to be less violent? There are a thousand things that could be asked, but one also has to think carefully before phrasing the questions to avoid making most women, for conscious or unconscious reasons, say no.

We will have to be content with the figures we have. But there must be many more people aroused by sado-masochistic pictures, films, books, etc. than the *Playboy* statistics indicate. This can be seen by the turn the international wave of pornography has taken in recent years in the direction of sado-masochism. The number of sado-masochistic magazines has increased enormously, and today it is hardly possible to open an "ordinary" pornographic magazine without coming across whips, chains and various forms of rape and torture. There must be money in it, so there must be people who want it. Why then do they not carry it out in practice? Because it is difficult to find a partner (when so few people dare speak of their "distinctive" leanings)? Because it is dangerous (as it is difficult to defend yourself from what might happen if, for instance, you are tied up)? Or just quite simply because most people do not even dare admit to *themselves* that they have these kinds of leanings?

When *Playboy* made some of the results of its report public for the first time, it followed them up with a conference. The delegates were psychologists, authors and various others well known in the public debate on the subject. Here are some of the questions discussed in connection with sadism and masochism:

Is the incidence of sado-masochism more widespread than before (perhaps because of greater openness brought about by the Kinsey report) – or is it simply that we dare talk a little more about it and buy a few more magazines? Have we become slightly more tolerant?

According to the record of the *Playboy* conference, Eberhard Kronhausen thinks that sadism and masochism are built into our whole system of upbringing. He mentions English-type boarding schools especially, with their canings and schoolboy hierarchies, in which small boys have habitually been the slaves of the bigger boys. He also reckons that today's sado-masochism can be traced back to the great wars we have been through. He describes wartime pilots' accounts of having orgasms when bombing an enemy town, and how they maintained that it was better than going to bed with a woman. Kronhausen also believes that everyone should be allowed to develop his or her private sexual desires, provided no one is forced into anything – and provided that children are not involved, even if they should provoke it themselves. However, as a psychologist, he is not happy about the rise in sado-masochism, because in his opinion this is connected with an inability to give oneself over to sexuality and enjoy it, and to develop a healthy sensuality that he sees as potentially almost without limits.

Another delegate – also a psychologist – estimated that ten to fifteen per cent of women's fantasies are masochistic; the rest in his opinion are fairly ordinary intercourse fantasies with the woman underneath and the man on top. He also felt women should fantasise much more, because this would help them develop their creativity.

Who is actually in charge of a sado-masochistic encounter, was another question discussed – is it the sadist, which one would think likely, or is it really the masochist, who proclaims when the boundaries are about to be overstepped? In this connection, W. B. Pomeroy, one of Kinsey's collaborators, described a scene they once filmed for their archives. A sadist had tied up a masochist and was dropping hot wax from a lighted candle on to the partner's genitals. But at the same time, he was very carefully watching the expression on the other's face, and when he could see that it was becoming too much, he raised the candle a little and waited until the candle-grease had cooled off. "It suddenly occurred to me that the masochist was almost literally controlling the sadist's hand," said Pomeroy.

Another delegate was of the opinion that a genuine sadist is generally not interested in a masochistic partner who enjoys it – but only in people who hate it.

Do the sadist and masochist regularly exchange roles? As for instance in *Who's Afraid of Virginia Woolf*, or when the man stimulates his wife's clitoris with a dry finger so that it hurts, and she does not dare to say anything – but perhaps the next day "happens" to throw away some papers that were lying on his desk?

It is true, as one delegate maintained, that the majority of the female sadist's customers are among the most successful, influential and important pillars of society? And in this case, what is the explanation – does their position make them guilt-ridden, so that they feel a need to be maltreated? Does this mean there is guilt-feeling behind masochism?

On the other hand, I am reminded of Linda Lovelace, star of the film *Deep Throat*. She confesses to a great number of masochistic fantasies. She loves to imagine being tied up and having a variety of things done to her, while she is totally unable to move, until in the end she feels she is about to ex-plode. But she protests violently against the theory that masochistic fantasies arise from feelings of guilt. She states quite definitely that she feels no guilt.*

How is it that we still find it so difficult to realise our masochistic fantasies, even in these days of tolerance?

It is very often clear that views on sexual deviations have become more liberal. Fabricius-Moller was certainly not con-demnatory, and no one was to be imprisoned for, or weaned off, masochism. But he was tolerant in the way people are about those who order white wine with meat, or have forgotten to zipp up their trousers: tactful, but absolutely cold.

* In her memoir *Ordeal*, published in 1980, Ms Lovelace repudiated many of her earlier statements and claimed that she had been forced into playing these roles.

In a more recent sex information book for young people, there really has been a change of tone, now almost free of paternalism. The book is called *Boy Girl Man Woman* by Bent H. Claesson, and was first published in Danish in 1968.

In the original Danish version of the book, the author says that it is normal to have fantasies while you masturbate:

> If the fantasies have a strong sprinking of masochism (page 118) or sadism (page 118), naturally this indicates something about what lies hidden deep down inside you, but that does not by any means mean that you are abnormal. So you have to try to accept that that is what you are like – and generally be on your guard in case these tendencies suddenly show themselves in relation to other people...

So I mustn't worry. But why then should I be on my guard? Because my sexual leanings may infect other conditions of life? Or because people are so uniform that the same pattern will necessarily be imprinted on them in all fields?

Or perhaps I am not the one who should be on my guard, but only the sadists?

And what do I find on page 118? And where is page 118? It is no longer *after* venereal diseases, but is huddled together with them. I am there again with the homosexuals, exhibitionists, people who sleep with animals, take part in group sex and commit incest. But it says:

> Quite often a person can be a sadist and a masochist at the same time. Many people show streaks of sadism or masochism in their love play, and so long as this is acceptable to both partners it can hardly be called anti-social.
>
> For some people, however, such behaviour becomes a necessary precondition for sexual stimulation or satisfaction, and in this case it is but a small step from rough love play to a real desire to hurt the other person.

So it's not so bad after all. But undoubtedly it is not that good, either. Anyhow, I don't think the naked young girl on the front cover of the Danish edition running happily together with a naked young man can be me. Neither do I think I am the person in the pictures of intercourse, nor presumably of the girl masturbating. There must be limits when it comes to young people. So there are no pictures of a lovely young girl being tied up or hit by a handsome young man.

But there is something else that is interesting; we can exchange roles, my sadist and I. I was not prepared for that, and to be honest, I found it somewhat confusing.

And another thing – how do you decide at what point elements of sadism and masochism are a *condition* for sexual stimulation and satisfaction?

And what if they are a condition? If they are a condition for me? Then I am not normal, anyhow...

It would be a great relief to be quite certain about what was normal...and fortunately we can be. All we have to do is to ask the newspaper columnists Inge and Sten Hegeler, authors of the widely translated *ABZ of Love*. Their answer is short and terse.

They confirm that happiness is to know what is normal. And they insist that what is normal has very wide boundaries.

They do not say so straight out like that, but they do convey quite clearly that *everything* is in fact normal, as long as you don't do to other people anything they don't like. Everything is...well, perhaps not normal, but anyhow quite in order and not to be speculated about too much. If you look up Masochism in their book *ABZ of Love,* the article begins with the words: "is a speciality in the sphere of sex life".

There are a great many things you can look up in *ABZ of Love* – apart from Masochism and Sadism, there are references to words like Governess, Dippoldism, Upbringing, Minority, Perversity, Nature, Personality, Sex Life, Flagellant, etc. Under Masochism itself is the following:

Masochism, masochist: A speciality in the sphere of sex life. A person who becomes particularly sexually stimulated by being tortured or humiliated is called a masochist. But let us not forget that we are all slightly familiar with the sensation – with masochism as well as sadism and all the other isms we call perversities. All these things exist in normal sexual relationships as a form of adult play – just as when children play at war, torture, prisons and the like. It is when any one of them is pursued to the exclusion of all others that it becomes dangerous, for it then indicates a state of being "stuck".

Masochism – the term – comes from the name of a German author, Leopold von Sacher-Masoch, who lived during the nineteenth century and described in his books the pleasures he obtained from being mishandled by hi⸱ ⸱ife. Religious history furthermore provides us with c⸱ ⸱ess examples of people who have tortured themselves because in so doing they satisfied sexual urges they were otherwise forbidden to permit a more natural release. We have instances of it amongst nuns obliged to live in celibacy but who derived intense pleasure from the cruellest tortures and forms of humiliation of their own selection, from hunger and whipping to drinking the blood of persons infected with the pox and licking the wounds of the leprous. Some of them were made into saints. Nation-wide movements of religious flagellants have also existed – but their supporters never realised that sexual urges were behind it all.

As will be seen from a small-scale investigation referred to elsewhere in this book (see Governess) many fairly pronounced practitioners of masochism exist in England today. In the case of a great many of them it is obvious that the seed which has resulted in these special wishes was sown long ago during childhood. Occasionally childhood experiences bound up with humiliating, sadistic forms of punishment have been the cause: or they may be a legacy of infantile guilt-feelings of other kinds.

We have many other proofs of the way upbringing can form personality, but few give such food for thought as this.

Both men and women can become masochists; the fact that adults who seek a "governess" are often men who long to be "brought up" by a dominating type of woman is probably bound up with the fact that it is easier for women to find a dominating type of man in our patriarchal society, without a special parade.

It may be added that for a woman who possibly finds it a little difficult to have sexual feelings (see Frigidity), even her husband's "misuse" of her, i.e. using her to obtain his own sexual satisfaction, can sometimes give her a passive form of pleasure reminiscent of masochistic feelings. A lot of normal couples occasionally enjoy tussling, pretending to rape each other or be each other's slaves – this is play not perversion. The time to worry, and ask for advice, is when one partner is "stuck" with some ritual which upsets intercourse and drains off his or her capacity to enjoy sex. (See also Bondage, Deformity, Fetishism and Transvestism.)

All the work the Hegelers have done is intended to comfort those of us who are worried and harassed because we feel out in the cold as a minority of perverse people. But, they insist, we are not that. We simply do some things that others dare not do – or we do a little more of what everyone else does a little. "Most of these things hover quite mildly in the minds of most people", it says under Perversity. And under Fantasies it says:

> There is nothing whatsoever perverse about it – this sort of thing is merely one of the many safety valves of a normal healthy mind.

You always feel very healthy and normal when you have read what Inge and Sten Hegeler have to say.

Yet the Hegelers have no actual *explanation* for sado-masochism. They have seen it as their mission to comfort their readers – to abolish anxiety about their being abnormal by abolishing the division between normal and abnormal. They reassure us that the normal has a wide framework, that most of us have our little oddities in the sexual field, which may perhaps be shared by a "few hundred thousand other people on this earth".

The sad thing is that even if we are all almost normal, there are indeed some people who are rather more normal than others. If you once again open *ABZ of Love* and look under *Perversion, perversity, perverse,* it suddenly says something that makes me uneasy:

> Real perversity is a deformity of the mind, a fanatical one-sided choice amongst the many possibilities existing within the range of natural comprehensive sexual relationships.

So we're none the wiser.

So it doesn't help much that Sten Hegeler says in his advice column in the press (for instance, when a masochist dies through the practice of the "speciality") that we all possess a little of this potential for violence (for instance, when we bite each other's shoulders), and that it is perhaps most widespread in social strata in which the opportunity to pay for a suitable partner exists, but that otherwise it is enormously widespread, and that people who die from it must have a very high orgasm threshold, because it seems that they need so much physical pain until satisfaction is achieved. It is no help to anyone to know that it "is a matter of knowing yourself and understanding each other".

Yes, it does help to know. It helps to know that you are not alone. It does in fact help to be reminded that the business of being *normal* is not that important. What is much more important is how you cope with it. Perhaps you should really enjoy what you have, instead of longing for something else?

That is what the Swedish psychiatrist, Lars Ullerstam, says in his book *The Erotic Minorities*, first published in 1964.

At first glance, I thought I simply wasn't in the book. But that was because my sadist and I were put together in one chapter headed Algolagnia. For a moment I felt homeless, but then I saw I was surrounded by my usual friends, and not only that, there were a few more added to them – incest, exhibitionism, paedophilia, saliromania, homosexuality, and scoptophilia – and then followed not only transvestism, necrophilia, fetishism, zoophilia, gerontophilia and pyromania, but also new blood, namely onania, autoerotism (onania), troilism and sexual collectivism. The last I was both pleased and amazed to find in such a place.

But it was intentional that we should meet there. Ullerstam intended to show that sexual life takes may forms and that it is absurd to call anything perverse. He recognises only the expression "minority", a smaller number. And he recognises that from one point of view only: that the minorities do not have the same rights as the majority.

Ullerstam says this comes from our having a dual attitude to sexuality. On the one hand, we have introduced a kind of welfare morality into the sexual field by admitting that sexual intercourse should be used as a means of enjoyment. But on the other hand, we have not extended this welfare morality to include the so-called sexual perversions. Instead, a sexually privileged society has been created:

> Thus erotic enjoyment has become, in our society, the privilege of people with a specific pattern of heterosexual needs. The debate on morals that is kindled at regular intervals in Sweden, with its participants firmly convinced of their progressiveness, concerns itself almost exclusively with the possibilities of increasing the advantages enjoyed by this already well-favoured caste.

If you are not one of the majority, the case is quite different:

> Thus it seems that we do not find originality praiseworthy when it comes to sexual matters. In fact, we don't use the word "originality" in that context at all; we apply the term "abnormality" instead (together with "perversion"), and that is no compliment.
>
> In sexual affairs, the statistical and the ideal norms obviously coincide. It is accepted that the majority is right, in this case, and that we should all conform to their sex habits. The only approved variations are purely technical, that is, variations of coital postures to achieve as effective an excitation of the sexual organs as possible. On these questions handbooks and sex instructors are very willing to give advice, as long as it concerns a heterosexual act between two persons. But if someone wanted to know how to vary techniques in acts, for example, of troilism (three persons taking part in the sexual act) or sodomy, I wouldn't advise him to visit the R.S.F.U. [that is, the official clinics. Ed.]. For the adult, the sexual objective is an unthinking conformism.

The result is a conflict between different norms:

> On the other hand, it is accepted that every person should be allowed to be blessed in his own way, and there is nothing wrong with helping the *handicapped towards happiness*. But

on the other hand, it is not right for the "perverse" to be allowed freely to experience sexual happiness, and no one wishes to help them achieve that happiness.

Christian morality must take some of the blame for this attitude, and now we also have a new form of puritanism. Not that Ullerstam thinks there shouldn't also be a place for puritans! He only means they should not be permitted to force their attitudes on others. And puritans still do that.

True, they do not hide behind religion so much today, but they often hide behind scientific medical terminology. If you want to forbid something today, the best thing to say is that it is *unnatural*. Actually, there is only one thing that is more important than being natural, and that is to be "sane". We live in an era of a kind of Reign of Terror by the sane. This sanity, which has nothing whatsoever to do with mental hygiene seems to be an American import and consists of a peculiar melange of sun-tanned rude health, brutality, and prudishness.

Ullerstam goes on:

Away with the society of sexual privilege! I would like to raise the cry: erotic minorities of all categories, unite! It is only too easy to realise why this exhortation stands less of a chance of success than the Marxist battle cry. The sexual deviates are too embarrassed and too guilt-ridden to dare to challenge public opinion. The initiative must come from another direction.

Ullerstam has a number of suggestions for what could be done to help erotic minorities to get together, especially sadists and masochists. Actually he uses the other name, algolagnia, which he then divides up into active algolagnia (sadism) and passive algolagnia (masochism).

He does this because he thinks people entertain the most grotesque delusions about sadism. As soon as a child is maltreated or a policeman is too heavy-handed, the newspapers start talking about sadism. The word is partly a term of abuse, partly an indication of sexual peculiarity, and should preferably be avoided in factual discussions because of its strong emotional overtones.

But what do we know about this "algolagnia"?

We don't really know anything at all, Ullerstam writes straight out. Quite a lot is written about it, but we don't actually know very much partly because, according to him, sexual-scientific authors are not interested in qualified knowledge in this field:

> The only certain knowledge we have of algolagnia is that it has a great potential for happiness.

Ullerstam mentions several of the more special forms this happiness can take:

> Quite a few masochists have testified to considerably sophisticated experiences during torture: experiences of a religious, visionary, and aesthetic nature, sometimes intensified to the point of revelation.

As an example of this kind, Ullerstam mentions the French writer Jean Genet, and especially his book *The Miracle of the Rose.* He also mentions a British Colonel Sparkers, who published a book called *Experimental Lecture* in 1873:

> According to this educator, sensual pleasure is achieved by arousing the strongest possible feelings in a person. Now pain is the strongest of all feelings, he continues, and its effect is certain and unmistakable. Thus, the man who is able to make the strongest impression on a woman, who can drive the female organism to the absolute peak of excitation, can be assured of reaching the highest degree of sexual enjoyment himself.

So men with masochistic wives have not much to grumble about. But men who on the other hand are themselves masochists have:

> There is a type of man who marries only in order to experience the delicious humiliation of waiting on his wife and her lover, who engage in intercourse in his presence.

Unfortunately, for the men, their wives' sadism often isn't all that genuine, but in many cases they know how to take artful and unscrupulous advantage of their husband's inability to resist their whims, using this as a means to gain various nonsexual profits.

Finally, Ullerstam has a simple explanation for what surprised some of the delegates at the *Playboy* conference – why it was so often men with success, money and position who went to be humiliated in English brothels, which were often equipped as torture chambers:

After all, they were the only ones who could afford to pay for it. Nevertheless a number of authors have been tempted to profound meditations on the rulers' need to expiate their guilt in front of the people held in thraldom.

But what practical suggestions does Ullerstam make? He says the masochist should be helped to sexual satisfaction by a specialist in a brothel:

However, certain individuals require the "executioner" to be sexually excited also: such cases one would wish to introduce to suitable sadists, as this could result in an excellent symbiotic relationship.

And he goes on to propose a number of steps to improve public education on sexual matters, as well as what he calls "pornographic services". Ullerstam sees his book as his own contribution; and he ends modestly with the hope that it will meet a wide range of sexual needs, and help nourish respect for all sources of sexual pleasure, even if some of these have their origins in some degree of emotional damage.

But there is far to go before such high aims are achieved. Even if all we wish for is a rather more relaxed attitude to the whole subject, there is still a very long way to go.

As far as I am concerned, I kept my mouth shut, but I read a whole lot of books. Not all at once, even if that is what it looks like here; my reading stretched over many years. But what the books had to say clearly settled into a definite slot inside my head, where they stayed and argued with each other.

For each book, I became a little wiser, but also more confused and eager to find out more. I alternated between feeling more perverse and more original. I alternated especially between feeling more like a man and less like a woman. There was only one thing I read that I could not accept, and that was the theory that I was at the same time something of a sadist.

Should I go on reading or should I take the plunge and experiment on my own?

Well, in time I did a bit of both.

5 Some Day My Prince Will Come

At one point, as I mentioned before, I lost my virginity, but I didn't seem to have lost it properly. The books confirmed that I still had some dark undiscovered places deep down inside myself. I had "become a woman", as they say. But I still felt I was different from the others. I felt guilty of some obscure crime, yet at the same time suspected that it was not a crime, but the innermost nature of sexuality itself.

I was certain that when I first met the man who would see straight through my sunny innocence, right down into the depths of my being, I would also have my first orgasm. I hadn't actually had one yet, and the years went by. But I was certain that masochism and orgasm belonged together – for me, anyhow, and perhaps for all women.

When a man attracted me sexually, it was never because of his looks; anyhow, not in the same way as a man feels attracted to women because of their looks. I thought men with good bodies, handsome faces and beautiful hair were nice, but not especially attractive sexually. They also frightened me. I reckoned they could not possibly fall in love with me. They were too perfect, so I wrote them off beforehand.

If one of them fell in love with me all the same, I never really believed it. I was always sure I had a whole lot of rivals who would win in the long run; the girls he had known before me. I studied old photographs of him, and he always seemed to have had an expression that he did not have when he was with me, an expression which attracted me, but which was brought out by someone else – someone better, someone who had what I hadn't got, someone who was more of a woman, presumably, but what was that? Someone who dared live with her masochism perhaps – someone who dared be more provoking?

Naturally looks counted for something, but in another way, more as an expression of something internal. What was decisive for me, for instance, could be a sad expression that I interpreted as uneasiness, dissatisfaction with the world as it was – as rebellion, as evidence that he wanted to live his own life and would decide the conditions and if necessary reform the world. So it was not so much his body or hair that said anything to me, but his lips and eyes. His eyes when he was absorbed in his work, when he was talking to an equal opponent, when he was chairing a meeting, when he headed straight for something without paying me any attention. When he finally looked at me with those eyes, I felt I was melting away, disappearing, becoming blissful nothing.

If his lips were narrow and hard, then I imagined that he was commanding me, giving me orders, and how I thirsted for him to give me orders! Or for him to keep silent with those grudging and demanding lips.

I also fell in love with his way of walking, because that told me something about how purposeful he was, and how able to attain his goal, take matters into his own hands and manage things. I hardly dared look at his hands, as they affected me physically and I daren't think the thought out. Hands were the most arousing thing in a man.

Or was it his voice? Because a voice was something so impalpable that it seemed to contain everything. All the fantasies and yearnings in the world could be invested in it. I listened hopefully to every note of confidence, superiority, omniscience, conviction, of indulgence and paternal protection, or of scepticism, cynicism and remoteness. I found many voices that sounded like that. They really all sounded rather like that...perhaps that was one of the reasons why I always remained full of hope.

The most important thing to me, however, was that a man be perfect in some way or other. What it was he was perfect at was not so important, but preferably something to do with his work. Whether that was playing a double-bass, building a road, running a business, or skating, didn't matter, as long as he did it well, efficiently, brilliantly, as long as he was successful at it, as long as he was the winning type. I was always prepared to fall on the neck of the victor – regardless of what the battle was.

The loser also interested me, but in another way. If the loser was a woman, I had a peculiar feeling that I was witnessing something shameless, slightly pornographic, almost like a voyeur.

Naturally, that is only half the truth. I was really always on the side of the weaker in any form of struggle. But I am not talking about sympathy or compassion now, but about sexual feelings, and in that field the opposite mattered.

The whole thing was mixed up in an extraordinary way, and it was almost impossible to say what was sexual and what was not.

In any case, there was a thread running right through the whole thing, and that was something to do with subject and object. I felt that the man I was going to love had to be the subject, i.e. *someone who was something in himself,* who dealt with things himself and was active of his own free will. I felt that before I could love a man, he had to make me into an object, i.e. *someone who wasn't anything in herself,* who did not deal with things, but who was dealt with, and who was passive because there was no free will for me.

For a relationship to function, he had to be as much a subject as possible, and I had to be as much an object as possible. Naturally I did not think all that out at the time, but later on I realised that was what was behind it all.

I think there was another reason why I wanted to be the object. I felt that would be the safest. Then I would perhaps keep a rather better hold on myself, because I often felt as if I did not know where I was. I tried looking in the mirror, but was that really me? If a man looked at me, I seemed to exist more clearly. If I simply walked the streets alone, I felt as if I were not there, and when anyone greeted me, I was astonished that they recognised me. I also wanted to get somewhere in life, as they say. In bed it was rather the other way round. There I was most sure of myself, when I was as small as possible and counted as minimally as possible and preferably hauled off by the hair. As an object, I would be able to be sure I really existed – but that demanded the right subject, the right man.

That was why I was constantly on the look-out for a man who was taller, older, stronger, cleverer and more self-confident than I was. Otherwise I felt forced to drop him. Once I had a lover whom I thought to be my own age; and then saw on his driving licence that he was in fact two years younger. I got a flat taste in my mouth and hurriedly ended the affair. To me, such a relationship seemed at variance with the whole idea of sexuality – being with a man not superior to oneself was like turning nature's order upside-down, slightly perverted, and anyhow wholly against my own nature, as I saw it. I had been born small and sweet and had loved the teacher's firm hand, the doctor's authoritative voice and the butcher's perfect professionalism. I was good at exams, at waiting politely until spoken to, and at playing down my own abilities, without ever admitting what an enormous advantage I also got out of the game. For who does not take pleasure in helping the person who is small and humble, and who plays up to the grown-ups? Who cannot afford to be gentle and good towards the person who stakes all on her weakness so that in exchange his own strength can be heavily underlined?

I did not consciously play up to strict people, but I probably sensed that it was a question of calculation and that certain privileges would accompany the role of the weak – the female role. In many ways it was a comfortable position, a good one for the indolent, so to speak.

I did not think about the price I would have to pay as I went round looking for the lover of my life – the man who would be like a solid rock, a rock I could lean my head against, a solid unshakeable point in the centre of the great precarious confusion of living. On the whole, I did not think at all; I went round feeling, feeling that I must find a man with a strong firm male will, and then I could be a little girl nestled up to father, leaving everything difficult to him. Or was it to mother? For although he was to be the unshakeable rock, strict and just in all vicissitudes, he was also to be loving. Stern and just, undisputed and demanding, hard, imperious and full of contempt – at the same time gentle and understanding and loving. It really was a very strange sexual partner to be looking for, and the conditions were very difficult for the men I met to live up to! So it was not surprising that I had to wait so long...

Fortunately I also met many men of quite a different mould, for things were not quite so one-sided as I describe them here, where I am trying to isolate a part of myself that one does not usually show publicly and hardly even to oneself. It is precisely because certain things are not talked about, that they come to play such an unnaturally large part in one's life. As long as it was a dark secret I was dragging around, and as long as I could not do anything about realising my fantasies, as long as I went round searching and searching for a highly peculiar ideal – the whole think continued to be irresolvable: was this mysterious thing, this masochism, just a part of myself, or was it really my innermost nature?

Meanwhile, I was constantly falling in love, and I also came quite seriously to love some of the men I met. I married and had children and my life was secure and comfortable. But at a certain time I had to continue with the search because I still had not met *him,* the man who was to annihilate my own will and make me melt, crumple and not be there – or perhaps swell up like a balloon and grow larger and larger, and then collapse the moment the whole thing cracked and burst, when the orgasm came. The orgasm which never came. Because *he* never came, I thought.

I was quite sure that he would make himself known, so I had no doubts. His hard eyes and calm voice would announce him. Then everything he would do to me would make the whole thing clear, which role we would each separately adopt, and what the nature of our relationship would be.

I did not know whether he would hit me or beat me, whether he would tie me up and abandon me, or treat me scornfully and force me to do things that would make me explode with pain and shame and desire. Or whether he would simply use me as his slave, so that I could wait on him, serve him obediently and humbly, run errands for him and carry out his slightest order, under threat of punishment for anything not done correctly in the tiniest detail. I was not quite clear about the details of what it would be like, but I was quite certain there would be no doubts in my mind when he came.

The reason the search lasted so long I thought was perhaps that I myself had also to make a move, and express my wishes more clearly – although I could not really see why that was necessary. So I tried provocation, despite the fact that this seemed unnatural to me and it meant that *I* seemed to be the one who had to do violence to myself, not him.

For instance, it was not easy to provoke someone into rape, when you yourself nearly always felt like it; then it wasn't as it should be; then it wasn't rape.

It was even more difficult to provoke a lover into hitting me; I tried to wrap it up in a thousand ways, and I clearly wrapped it up so well that no one understood. Now and again, I was successful enough for the occasional well meaning but reluctant man to try out a few slaps. But not of the right kind.

I also tried provoking people into being rough with me, by resisting, for instance; but that simply became a fight (or attempts at persuasion, and endless arguments). I tried telling them to stop – in the hope that they would catch the undertones, enforce their overbearing will, and not stop. But they always stopped when I asked them to...

Gradually, as time went by, I began to doubt I would ever meet him. I hoped again every single time I met a man who attracted me. I took the chance every time I saw a hard glint in an eye or heard a faint note of command in a voice. I fell in love for several years with the faintest reflection of my ideal: in a man who defied my protests and told me I could stand *much* more; in someone who looked at me with distant cold eyes during intercourse; in someone who told me how he had terrorised another girl he had been with; in someone who enjoyed half-killing flies; in someone who forced me down on a hard floor; in someone who said that if I ever went to bed with anyone else, then...; in someone who taught me something new, so that once again I became a little ignoramus anxious to learn...

But when it came to the crunch, even the oldest, biggest, cleverest, wisest, hardest and most unapproachable man was too soft. The moment I was about to have a climax of a kind, his own climax would be just round the corner – and that meant an anti-climax for me: the strong man was transformed into a weak man, groaning and gasping and loving, or just lying there like a passive lump and falling asleep. Although I became clever at interpreting all kinds of things into all kinds of other things, so that I could blame his falling asleep on hardness and indifference (which it also was), for instance – that was still not enough. So I lay there with all my accumulated longings and my pent-up desire, unable to go further. That time, too.

Thus I screwed and balled and fucked for years, and it was always wonderful and also often awful. But what I was expecting never happened.

Sometimes I faked it – I pretended to have orgasms, but that was rare. Usually it was unnecessary, because men usually were not sufficiently interested in that side of the story to discover that I didn't come. But I also often told them I hadn't come. Some were grumpy, but not many; most were concerned in an irritating way, or their own self-esteem was damaged, so *I* had to console *them* and build them up again. But usually they were sure they could soon clear up that little problem – they were usually able to, they said. That encouraged my sense that I was different from other girls. Naturally I did not know that other girls were faking too – and at the time I never gave the possibility a thought. I was quite certain all other girls just *came.*

I also had a feeling that my orgasm was going to come like manna from heaven – all by itself. I couldn't really take my men coming over all considerate and careful. Some of them became technical, but that was unquestionably a minority, and I could in any case not have helped them with the technical details at the time. Today I would presumably say they were not technical *enough,* or perhaps simply not erotic enough. I would also have felt it wrong if *I* had to teach *them* something. Should the child teach the father? I wanted them to be ruthless, like the men in the books. He threw her ruthlessly down on the bed, ignoring her resistance, it always said.

I loved it when someone threw me roughly down on to the bed and tore my clothes off, sending buttons and straps flying. The rougher the better. But it always turned out ordinary, normal roughness when it came down to it – and the effect wore off quickly. It wasn't long before it simply became irritating, his rhythm quite out of tune with what I wanted, I being kneaded in the most amazing places while my own erogenous zones lay unused, my own will generally not getting a look-in at all – then my lovely ruthless lover just became a crude unfeeling youth with no sense at all of what sex really was, although he thought himself the greatest lover in the world.

I thought it all rather extraordinary. I kept wishing for a ruthless lover, and then suddenly the whole thing was just boring and frustrating and desperate.

Why could I not achieve release? Theoretically, it might have been my lover's fault, if for instance he came too quickly. But I did not take that theory seriously at the time – because it was just the same in lengthy intercourse. I loved the foreplay. I loved noticing my desire becoming stronger and stronger, but it always peaked at the wrong place, before I had really reached the top, yes, before I could even see it. The top always seemed to be hidden in the clouds, so that I couldn't even see the beginning of the path I knew would take me up there. I could only find the way down again.

Just abandon yourself, they always said. But it was all right for them to lie there saying that – what was I to abandon myself to? What did that entail? It must mean that I should stop *thinking* about that orgasm. But that was like being told you must not think about a white elephant – it becomes the only thing in the world you can think about. So I always lay there thinking that I must not think about the orgasm I could not achieve.

With hindsight, I can now see only too well how comical it was, but at the time I was desperate. For years I went round thinking about literally nothing else but that orgasm I could not achieve. It took up an incredible amount of my thoughts and energy and became the symbol of my lack of a decisive attribute, for orgasm was to me the decisive sign that a woman was a hundred-per-cent woman. So I was not a hundred-per-cent woman, and nothing could have made me more desperate.

I can now hardly remember why I simply had to be a hundred per cent woman. I mean I have gradually come to realise how powerful the forces are that drive us to adhere to the female image. Yet it was an ideal so full of contradictions that it was impossible to live up to – with orgasm its mysterious crown. I kept meeting that orgasm everywhere, implied or directly described. And everywhere it seemed to mock me.

My masochistic fantasies slid into the background compared with my speculations on orgasm, which now took up a greater and greater part of my waking hours. But I still had a dim feeling that the two things had something to do with each other. The reason why I wasn't a hundred-per-cent woman must be because I was a masochist: a masochist who had not found her sadist. If I found him, he would be able to carry me into the forbidden room, into the promised land of orgasm. Into woman country.

I felt like Sleeping Beauty waiting for her Prince, but not a glittering Prince on a white horse. The Prince I was waiting for was the Black Prince.

6 Pornology, Pornography and other P-ratings

Sacher-Masoch and de Sade, pornography, Shakespeare, Kafka, etc.

Masochism derives its name from the author Leopold von Sacher-Masoch. He was born in Galicia in 1835. His novel *Venus in Furs* was published in 1869 as the first in a cycle of novels, though it is the only one to have become famous: so famous that the names of his two main characters have today become symbols for the mistress-slave relationship and are often used in advertisements by people seeking partners of this kind.

Wanda and Severin are two people from a background in which money and time are of no importance, and there are plenty of opportunities for anyone to satisfy any special desires. These desires first present themselves, however, when Severin finds it impossible to form a more normal relationship with Wanda. Wanda is an independent-minded modern woman who believes that love cannot last longer than two months – and she does not intend to stay with a lover for whom she no longer feels passion.

She is also a beautiful woman, and she often wears furs. Presumably this is supposed to indicate that she is cold and impossible to conquer – and at the same time too hot-blooded for our latitudes, so people burn themselves on her. Presumably also Severin's preference for an ordinary romantic relationship with Wanda is only a cautious formality, and he becomes a "masochist" the moment she denies him this.

Severin loves Wanda and wants to be with her for the rest of his life. To persuade her, he suggests he become her slave.

Wanda protests violently at first, but he begs and pleads for so long that she finally gives in. She accepts him as her slave and starts ordering him about and using a whip – at first to his great and undiluted delight.

Gradually the relationship develops and is consolidated with a contract. Wanda and Severin travel as a couple – the mistress and her livery-clad servant. Wanda bosses Severin about, allowing herself to be waited on by him and punishing him if he does not obey immediately. At the same time, there is still a love-relationship between them that is mutual. Severin can still break out. Wanda warns him. She feels he has called out emotions in her that are dangerous.

Now Severin's duties begin to take on a more serious character. He is to help Wanda make contact with other men. He is forced to see their yearning eyes as they look on Wanda, and to watch her conferring her favours upon them. At one time, he almost despairs and tries to break the relationship – but he cannot, he has become too dependent on it. And then everything goes wrong. The climax is reached when Wanda starts an affair with a handsome Greek, making him whip Severin while she herself looks on, then she goes away with the Greek.

Now Severin is at last cured. He is cured so thoroughly that he changes completely. As he expresses it himself: in future he will no longer be the anvil, but the hammer. So in future he will treat women just as Wanda has treated him.

Venus in Furs is a very strange book – a romantic love story in picturesque surroundings, running the whole romantic gamut of emotions, and complete with numerous details of such precision and solidity that the romantic apparatus seems to function only as background for the essential core – the masochistic scenes. Perhaps it would have been unthinkable to publish such a book without all this background, even for a distinguished author such as Sacher-Masoch – or perhaps just because he was such a distinguished author.

There is considerable style about the purely physical sufferings Wanda inflicts on her slave. Occasionally the whole seems operatic, and at other times more like an operetta. Apart from whipping him (with a whip they have been out together to buy), she also ties him up – not only to the bedpost, but also to a plough he has to haul along with a yoke over his shoulders. She gets some black girls to stab him with golden hairpins. She orders him to carry her cases and run up and down stairs for her. But there is very little about all this hurting Severin – and nothing whatsoever about him being sexually aroused, still less achieving sexual release from his slave experiences. We are on a much higher plane than that.

Neither are Severin's sufferings only physical. They are

equally psychological. The author seems to have at least one foot on the ground when it comes to describing mental tortures. Wanda summons him in the middle of his meals. He has to travel third class, while she herself goes first. He has to exchange his ordinary clothes for livery and his own name for the slave name of Gregor. She uses the familiar "*Du*" to him, while he has to address her formally. Added to the physical pain of whipping is yet another degradation, in that she does not always whip him herself, but allows her lover to do it – or four *black* women (clearly the most degrading thing of all in those days), and he is always being made to wait for his orders and for his punishment.

The relationship is confirmed in a written form of contract – or rather, in two contracts that he has to sign. The contracts are drawn up as follows:

AGREEMENT BETWEEN MME. VON DUNAJEW AND SEVERIN VON KUSIEMSKI

Severin von Kusiemski ceases with the present day being the affianced of Mme. Wanda von Dunajew, and renounces all the rights appertaining thereunto; he on the contrary binds himself on his word of honour as a man and nobleman, that hereafter he will be her *slave* until such time that she herself sets him at liberty again.

As the slave of Mme. von Dunajew he is to bear the name Gregor, and he is unconditionally to comply with every one of her wishes, and to obey every one of her commands; he is always to be submissive to his mistress, and is to consider her every sign of favour as an extraordinary mercy.

Mme. von Dunajew is entitled not only to punish her slave as she deems best, even for the slightest inadvertence or fault, but also is herewith given the right to torture him as the mood may seize her or merely for the sake of whiling away the time. Should she so desire, she may kill him whenever she wishes; in short, he is her unrestricted property.

Should Mme. von Dunajew ever set her slave at liberty, Severin Kusiemski agrees to forget everything that he has experienced or suffered as her slave, and promises never under any circumstances and in no wise to think of vengeance or retaliation.

Mme. von Dunajew on her behalf agrees as his mistress to appear as often as possible in her furs, especially when she purposes some cruelty toward her slave.

That was contract number two. Contract number one is short. He has to write it in his own handwriting and sign it before her. It runs as follows:

Having since many years become weary of existence and its illusions, I have of my own free will put an end to my worthless life.

At that, Severin's degradation is complete. He has no rights even to his own life any longer. At the same time, he has renounced all external indications of being a self-sufficient individual: his name, his clothes – and his money. As it becomes clear that he has no means of doing anything in life without money, he is really totally paralysed and declared incapable – his situation begins to overwhelm him, and for a brief while he considers breaking the contract. Wanda scornfully offers him money. But it is too late. Deep down inside him, he has no wish to be free, and so he stays with her. The relationship does not break up until Wanda herself leaves her slave.

In those days women did own their own clothes, but they did not have their own names and certainly no money of their own. So Severin is placed in a role that is closely analogous to that of women of the time. But he is a man, a man who has given a name to a characteristic as heavily female-weighted as masochism.

This has evidently been a problem for the author. Anyhow, he has gone to a great deal of trouble to bring a balance into the sex roles. He has also made a point of apologising for his wishful dreams on the division of roles: in which women are hard mistresses and not, as nature demands, soft and passive, and in which men are not brave and active, but have renounced their male privileges so that Wanda can say: "How handsome you are – you have a martyr's eyes."

Perhaps Severin was not really "manly" from the start. But

on the other hand Wanda is fundamentally a "real woman". She has to be persuaded at great length, and very forcefully, to adopt her role of mistress, and she is persuaded not once and for all, but repeatedly along the way. Severin actually has to place her in the part – to teach her, so that in one way she becomes his pupil – a "natural" sex role. But once she has learnt the part properly, the catastrophe happens. She abandons her slave, thus inflicting on him the ultimate punishment and humiliation – but at the same time putting an end to the development of their relationship.

Why does she leave him? She does so because she has at last met a real man, a man of quite different calibre from Severin. She can only truly love Severin in situations and at times when he – in his own way – lives up to his male role, in which he is self-sufficient, headstrong, takes the initiative and uses imagination. She loves him just before the end, when he withdraws and is prepared to break the contract.

But when it comes to the point his rebellion is without backbone. He *must* feel the whip again. He even begs for it. He longs to be humiliated and his slave soul will not leave him in peace. That is what Wanda cannot bear. Her love collapses and becomes the opposite. She hands Severin over to her lover and watches the handsome Greek whipping her slave, as we suspect he will later on whip Wanda. The reason she has chosen to go away with him is that he can subdue her in the same way as she has earlier subdued Severin. Fundamentally, then, Wanda is a "real woman", who would never be able to love a masochistic man, who is not really a man.

So it is good that Severin really *is* cured, and becomes the hammer instead of the anvil. Then everything is as it should be again, and the natural balance restored. Yet it is difficult for the reader to forget that Severin *has* been a full-blooded masochist all through the book, and that masochism has taken its name from a book about a masochistic man...

Pornographic literature is full of masochists, by far the majority of them women. This is possibly because those women in reality simply aren't real masochists, but only passive victims, as it is known that nearly all pornographic literature is written for men. And when men read pornography, they probably often do so in order to be able to treat a woman in their imagination in the way "women like", thus confirming the idea that women are masochists by nature anyhow.

Are the women in the books written by the father of sadism also masochists (for sadism really has a father, as is fit and proper, just as most of the books in the past had a father and no mother, except the one looking after the children while father wrote)?

The books by the Marquis de Sade are full of women being raped, whipped and maltreated in every possible and impossible way. Under all circumstances, they are victims. A few of them enjoy it, possibly, namely those who have been whipped into being soft and graceful in the course of their erotic upbringing. The others apparently do not enjoy it, either before, during or after. But as they are only characters in books, they rise again after each assault like tumblers, prepared to allow themselves to be tumbled again by the first, best, most lecherous person whose path they happen to cross.

That is so for *Justine*, anyhow, the main character in de Sade's first and most famous book. It was written in the Bastille in a fortnight in 1787, and the sub-title is *The Misfortunes of Virtue*.

Misfortunes certainly follow the virtuous Justine. They hail down upon her so copiously that it is impossible to relay the plot of the book at all. This is true even of the first edition, in which the misfortunes that afflict her from twelve different directions, are limited to beating, unsuccessful or successful rape, and diverse abominable but not especially imaginative assaults.

Why do things go so badly for poor Justine? They do so simply because virtue does not pay. The book is really a minor, seditious, anti-religious, moral story in the style of Voltaire's slightly earlier *Candide*. Like the naive main male character in *Candide*, Justine is a starry-eyed and stupidly innocent child, who believes the fairy tales she has heard about virtue and goodness always winning through. There are actually no sadists in de Sade's first book, only a number of men spouting morals and beautiful emotions while taking what they desire. And Justine – is she a masochist? No, she is not. She's just stupid.

She's stupid because she relies on virtue. The violent times in which de Sade lived were hardly likely to encourage a belief in the goodness of people: torture and the uninhibited use of force were part of everyday life, so it was reasonable enough to scorn anyone who expected goodness to triumph, and virtue to be its own reward. But in de Sade, the logic becomes as sharp as a knife, and virtue is punished instead.

Elsewhere, de Sade makes himself spokesman for the only sensible attitude to take up in his world: to indulge all your desires without restraint. The only regrets when you die should be for those desires you have *not* given in to. Once you accept that as a starting point, says de Sade, it follows quite logically that there is no point in considering whether your desires may cause pain and unhappiness to the person on whom you are satisfying them.

Naturally, this especially concerns men's attitudes to women:

> If then it becomes incontestable that we have received from Nature the right indiscriminately to express our wishes to all women, it likewise becomes incontestable that we have the right to compel their submission, not exclusively, for I should then be contradicting myself, but temporarily. It cannot be denied that we have the right to decree laws that compel woman to yield to the flames of him who would have her; violence itself being one of that right's effects, we can employ it lawfully. Indeed! has Nature not proven that we have that right, by bestowing upon us the strength needed to bend women to our will? . . .
>
> The law which will oblige them to prostitute themselves, as often and in any manner we wish, in the houses of debauchery we referred to a moment ago, and which will coerce them if they balk, punish them if they shirk or dawdle, is thus one of the most equitable of laws, against which there can be no sane or rightful complaint.
>
> A man who would like to enjoy whatever woman or girl will henceforth be able, if the laws you promulgate are just, to have her summoned at once to duty at one of the houses; and there, under the supervision of the matrons of that temple of Venus, she will be surrendered to him, to satisfy,

humbly and with submission, all the fancies in which he will
be pleased to indulge with her, however strange or irregular
they may be, since there is no extravagance which is not in
Nature, none which she does not acknowledge as her own.

It would be wrong to think, however, that de Sade sees women
as masochists born to suffer, or just as inferior creatures with
whom you can do as you please. That's all right but:

But we will redress the balance. Yes, we will redress it;
doubtless we ought to. These women we have just so cruelly
enslaved – there is no denying we must recompense
them...
     I say then that women, having been endowed with con-
siderably more violent penchants for carnal pleasure than
we, will be able to give themselves over to it wholeheartedly,
absolutely free of all encumbering hymeneal ties, of all false
notions of modesty, absolutely restored to a state of Nature;
I want laws permitting them to give themselves to as many
men as they see fit; I would have them accorded the enjoyment of all sexes and, as in the case of men, the enjoyment of
all parts of the body; and under the special clause prescribing
their surrender to all who desire them, there must be sub-
joined another guaranteeing them a similar freedom to enjoy
all they deem worthy to satisfy them.

In the same way, a man may certainly beat a woman in order
to achieve the greatest possible erotic enjoyment; but the
woman may also beat him, yes, indeed, and she is welcome to
it. The girl here addressed is exhorted to enjoy being beaten,
but she has also been asked to do the same thing for the man
later on:

'Twill embellish our buttocks by lending colour to them...
Courage, my angel, courage; bear in mind that it is always
by way of pain one arrives at pleasure.

So it is also logical that a young girl should learn to look on
the conditions of life with open eyes:

May atrocities, horrors, may the most odious crimes
astonish you no more, my Eugenie; what is of the filthiest,
the most infamous, the most forbidden, best rouses the
intellect...'tis that which always causes us most deliciously
to discharge.

The most wonderful satisfaction...yes, there it is. In relation to the social conditions of the day, the Marquis de Sade
was in fact a progressive man. He was an opponent of im-
prisonment and not least of capital punishment (because, he
said, if you execute a criminal, you simply have two dead men
instead of one). And in the world of sexuality he believed that
everything should be allowed:

The imagination is the spur of delights; in those of this order,
all depends upon it, it is the mainspring of everything; its
greatest triumph, its most eminent delights come of ex-
ceeding all limits imposed upon it.

Most of what de Sade wrote is a weighty mixture of
philosophical argument and erotic orgies. In the later editions
of *Justine* and its sequel, *Juliette*, his fantasies do indeed overstep
all boundaries. Everything is allowed, and there is a wealth of
description of the most barbaric and ingenious tortures – including intra-vaginal torture – that one would call absurd if
one didn't know what goes on in the world today. Presumably
de Sade has been a rich source of inspiration for the professional sadists of more recent times.

How sadistic the Marquis himself was, we don't really
know. But we do know a little. For instance in 1768, in Paris,
when he was twenty-eight, he spoke to the thirty-six-year-old
Rose Keller in the street and got her to go with him to his house
in Arceuil. When they got there, he forced her to undress, tied
her up and beat her.

We also know that Leopold Sacher-Masoch found a woman
who took the name of his heroine Wanda, and who exchanged
contracts with him for a regular mistress-slave relationship.

If you compare what happens in Sacher-Masoch's and de
Sade's books, this contract is one of the first points of contrast.
For the masochist, it is important to have this lasting link; he

makes provision for it voluntarily, signs it himself – for it binds the mistress as much as the slave. The mistress has in reality her own part of the burden to carry, just as the slave also has first to train her for her job. He is her teacher. He has to train her for her mistress-role until it is in her very bones; not until then can he be sure of having his desires properly governed – or more than that.

With de Sade, on the other hand, there is no contract whatsoever. But there is an inflexible philosophy, a whole system following his inflexible laws. The victims can complain and wail as much as they like, but there are no sensitive ears to hear. Generally speaking, there are no feelings at all, no warmth, and no trace whatsoever of the great romantic feeling that underlies the story of Wanda and Severin. There is only cold logic and over-excited sensuality.

Neither is there any of the dreamy semi-darkness that encloses the Sacher-Masoch couple. In de Sade there is a garish harsh light everywhere, that allows no detail or organ or obscenity to be overlooked.

But the two authors have one thing in common. Although both have given a name to a perversion – or whatever it can be called at this stage – the extent of excitement in reading them is limited. If a kind of consumer service for the general public was to be produced assessing pornographic values (a kind of P-rating scale, for instance), then Sacher-Masoch would not come very high, as his book is too romantic for that; and de Sade too would come fairly low down, because a fearful mass of argument has to be ploughed through to get to the goodies.

On the other hand, if you want to read a book that really rushes to the top of the P-ratings, then you must read *The Story of O* – but I want to keep that until later on.

Not that anyone has ever suggested that de Sade's and Sacher-Masoch's books had particularly high P-values. They can, for instance, be borrowed from many public libraries, and libraries don't stock pornography; so their books can't be pornographic.

In many countries in recent times, serious criteria have been set up to distinguish what is "art" from what is "pornography". In the post-war period there was a whole series of court cases in Denmark, in which publishers were accused of having overstepped the obscenity laws and were threatened with the confiscation of their books.

In England, the most famous case was the prosecution by the Crown of Penguin Books for publishing *Lady Chatterley's Lover* by D. H. Lawrence. These were all extremely peculiar court cases. Testimony was sought from experts – not porn-experts, but experts in literature. The publishers' hope of success lay in finding experts to testify that the suspected book was of literary value. If this were found to be true, then suddenly it was not porn any longer, but literature, and the publishers were free to publish.

Then Danish pornography laws were abolished and a wave of pornography followed. Today, pornography is sold freely over the counter, no longer even wrapped up discreetly to look like a tax return.

Neither *is* it a tax return. Make no mistake about the magazines brought home from kiosks, they are neither art nor literature, but regular porn, produced for a definite market to satisfy a definite need. If this had to be labelled art, then it would be "functional art".

There are presumably two groups of people who form the majority of the pornography industry's customers: those who use normal pornography, and those who use specialised porn – in this case, sado-masochistic porn.

Normal pornography is presumably used by people who are temporarily or permanently cut off from sex (because they are in prison, for instance), and by people who want to, have time to, and can afford to purchase a little extra excitement, to give them an outlet in moments of leisure. Seen from society's point of view, this occupation can be compared with watching sports on television, in that it distracts the mind from more constructive matters. From that point of view, pornography should be grouped with other instruments for maintaining "the system" – it is part of a cycle of alienation, in which the system in turn increases and satisfies the need for porn by alienating us from each other, so that our sexual life comes in the end to resemble an exchange of goods: I'll give you a couple of beers, but you must screw with me in return; or, You should be pleased that I can go on for two hours and seventeen minutes; or, If I give you an orgasm, you must give me an orgasm, and then we're quits...

Nor is pornography free of society's attitudes to women. Most of the pictures in porn magazines are of women, naturally, as it is mainly men who buy them: women performing together with one or more men, or alone; women taking their clothes off for two pages or a whole magazine. The men can simply take their choice of dish. The women are presented as nothing, freely available for use. If they have any will of their own at all, it is only to get into bed with the men (if they are not raped – but then that only means in the end that they like it). If sexuality is nothing but goods, women naturally become goods, too. Women – or just their various orifices – become consumer goods.

The majority of these normal-porn magazines (in text and/or pictures) deal with normal authorised heterosexual intercourse with variations in the numbers of people involved, skin colour, social status and age, intercourse positions, and the number of orgasms following on each other.

But there are also numerous leaflets and magazines dealing with less authorised forms of sex, including sado-masochism, with or without final intercourse. There are some papers that specialise in the two main forms for sado-masochists: spanking (hitting of one kind or another), or bondage (erotic compulsion, usually in connection with being tied up), and there are also some very sophisticated kinds that draw their inspiration from the torture chambers of the Nazis and other tyrants. It is obvious that the supply is decided by the varying fantasy worlds of customers.

Customers who buy these magazines do so (one has to presume) because they are sexually dependent on stimulants that are regarded as perverse, viler than others, or anyhow extremely furtive.

For a sexual relationship in the established style, it is usually fairly easy to find partners, provided you are not particularly unfortunate and living conditions allow it. But things are quite different in the field of "specialities". Most people with such needs know that they are labelled as abnormal, and are deeply ashamed of them. Many of them drag out a miserable existence in what is a frustrating secret search for a partner – if they do not make do with those they can pay for at specialist massage clinics.

The purpose of the magazines is to supply their customers with fantasy material – details, situations, pictures, chains of thought, methods, formulations, etc. – that can be *used*. They can be used directly for masturbation, or indirectly – stored away and used during the next "normal" intercourse, to make orgasm possible with a partner who perhaps must not know anything about such leanings. There is also the possibility that sado-masochistic pornography gives people ideas they can use to carry out their fantasies in reality. But in that case, according to the Hunt report, they will be disappointed because only a minority of those who carry out sado-masochistic activities in practice achieve orgasm during their actual activities. This is not what you read in the pornographic magazines, and neither does everyone react in this way, though clearly a considerable number do.

On the other hand it has never been proved, although some people have tried, that there is any connection between criminal violence and sado-masochistic pornography. There is nothing to indicate that unstable souls use this form of porn as inspiration for violence.

Unfortunately, we have no idea whether sado-masochistic pornography is addictive, either. As things are, there can be no doubt that it influences the user's sexual life more than normal pornography influences *its* customers. Neither can there be any doubt that a lot of money is made out of our sexual deviations. But as long as we have no evidence that it also colours the sexual life of people who did not have sado-masochistic tendencies to start with, then I think we have to accept it as an emergency solution. Forbidding it would amount to removing the *symptoms* of a disease, instead of its causes.

Men appear in masochistic roles in sado-masochistic magazines as well as in ordinary porn magazines, but there are far more women in them. There is also a great difference between the men and the women in the pictures. The men really do crawl about like dogs, and are usually weakly and unaesthetic, sorry figures in every way. But even during the crudest maltreatment, the girls are still delectable and pretty. Why is that?

This is because the girls are usually simply not masochists. They are really consumer goods to a much greater extent than ordinary strippers. They are packaged and labelled masochists like tins of beans. But they actually function only as victims for sadists – or for men who are aroused by the thought of girls "getting what's good for them". So they have to keep on being good-looking – because there are not many submission-hungry women who are supposed to identify with them, in the way that male masochists must be able to identify themselves with the slobbering dogs in the pictures. In that way yet again it is hammered home that it is natural for pretty young girls to be masochists...

Most women hesitate at the thought of going to buy simply an ordinary old-fashioned sex magazine, not only because it is traditionally the men who have the most money, but because it is traditionally the men who are interested in pornography...it is very unfeminine to be so. So a woman has to pluck up a hundred times more courage to go in and buy a real sado-masochistic publication. We still don't talk openly about our perfectly normal sex life, so we are prepared to crawl into a mouse-hole if we feel suspected of perversion.

There is yet another reason why there are so few women pornography buyers: women (according to investigations) are more stimulated by words than by pictures. This is presumably something to do with the fact that women also do not habitually use their eyes to assess a man's body, in the way that art, advertising and many other things have trained men's eyes to look at women's bodies.

So most porn papers contain far more pictures than text, and if papers that have both are looked at together by a man and a woman, he will linger over the pictures while she lingers over the text. Not so much the short stories, which are usually rather humdrum, but the correspondence columns, the advertisements and readers' own contributions. They often contain a wealth of detail of such astonishing precision that they have a harsh smell of reality – if not of actual reality, then at least of daydreams dreamt by real people...

In sado-masochistic press advertisements too, the division of the sexes is not an even one. There are many more men looking for ruler-mistresses than there are women looking for dominant men. Is this because there are more male than female masochists? That would probably be drawing too hasty a conclusion, as there are so many other possibilities: that there are so many dominant men, there is no need to advertise for them; or that women don't dare put in advertisements because of their reputation; or that they are afraid of a real sadist...But there are still a great many advertisements from men looking for slave girls.

Sado-masochistic advertisements can be seen not only in porn magazines, but also, in some countries, in the personal columns of ordinary papers. But there is a difference in language. In the ordinary papers the language is a code, using expressions such as "old-fashioned upbringing", "firm hand" and "interest in discipline". In the porn magazines, there is more free play and many real pearls can be found in them. I will quote just one I came across:

> Where is my masochistic woman – uninhibited, perverse – who will let herself unconditionally be trained and humiliated, *and who loves chocolate*? Write to me...(My italics, M.M.).

The P-rating of such an advertisement is very high, because it offers the imagination a puzzle that can be solved in several ways, according to individual needs. Will she be given chocolate afterwards as consolation? Does he sit eating chocolate in front of her? Does he tie her up and put a box of chocolates beside her? There are a great many possibilities.

Recently some daily papers in Denmark have launched sex correspondence columns, in which people with special interests can communicate with each other. These have dual aims, first to remove taboos and make life easier for people oppressed by the dictatorship of the sexual majority, and second to increase circulation, since a great many people find titillation for their own fantasies in the wording of the advertisements.

This kind of material can also be found on the news pages of the daily papers, which are full of sex murders, child-battering, corporal punishment cases, accounts of torture, reports from prisons, interviews with prostitutes with diverse specialities, interviews with doctors on sexual minorities. And it is not only the popular dailies – the "quality" press is also involved, although there is rather more camouflage there.

Even television is not free of it, if programmes are investigated according to the P-ratings. I do not mean war reports, but all those serials in which the hero, watched by children and adults, is either threatened with or becomes a victim of torture if he doesn't confess or cooperate. Electrical apparatus is applied carefully to sensitive parts of the body, chemicals are prepared and ropes are made ready, all to release the terrible things that can provide material for nightmares in children and sex dreams in adults. The fact that they usually remain threats, or happen outside the picture, is of secondary importance – we have *already* seen or heard in detail what the point is.

In these productions, victims are usually *men*, because heroes are men. But they are only victims, not masochists. The sadists who prepare the tortures are also usually men. Women have access to this world only if they have the right statistics – or as victims to be rescued by the heroes.

So it is not necessary to take to pornography to be stimulated in sado-masochistic directions. For the unclean, all things are unclean. There are plenty of sources of inspiration, and it is impossible to investigate what motives lie behind them all; whether the motive is making money out of our anxiety to acknowledge our various leanings – or whether it is a reflection of our culture, which is full of victims and tormentors wherever we look.

So there is no need to go to pornographic films if you lack the courage. Just go to an ordinary cinema and see Catherine Deneuve being tied to a tree and whipped, or Maria Schneider being ordered to go out and buy butter before Marlon Brando screws her per anus as he forces her to say all the things that most humiliate her. You can go and see films by people like Bergman, Warhol, Cayatte, Pinter, Godard, Fassbinder, Dreyer, Bunuel and many more experts at demonstrating how people torture and oppress each other and play cat and mouse with each other.

Neither need you go and buy pornographic photographs, if you don't want to. There are plenty of P-values in beautiful art books full of pictures of the sufferings of Christ, scenes of the martyrdoms of saints, and surrealist visions of hell – as well as symbolic or realistic pictures of political realities, persecuted and tormented people.

If you do not care to go and buy pornographic magazines, and don't wish to read violent horror magazines, you can always go to the library and borrow a sex manual. You can buy guides to the art of love from the *Kama Sutra* to those by the most "liberated" American experts, all of which include their share of sado-masochism. You can buy one of the "erotic" books that have become fashionable in some circles to have lying around on the coffee table alongside the most recent good food guide. All literary pornography with any self-respect includes a sado-masochistic story, and in all the books describing innocent young women going from the hands of one man to those of another, at least one of those hands is what is called in the advertisements "firm".

Naturally it would be much better if there were some "real" autobiographies of sadists and masochists, but they are hard to find. One Danish example is *Jeg – en Kvinde* (Me – a woman), by Siv Holm, which is halfway between a novel and an autobiography, clearly not written to be titillating. She writes openly about her fantasies:

> And what are the fantasies of a woman who prefers masturbating to being screwed by a man whose hands she does not like?
>
> She dreams of other hands, strong hands: take me, kiss me, tie me, hit me. Let me go, kiss me, screw me. Yes, now – that's it, I'm nothing, see, I creep right under you, sink right down into the ground until I'm nothing. Put me in a pocket – with buttons! The button must be on the outside, as I don't want to decide when the pocket shall be opened or closed. I don't want to decide anything – a-n-y-thing – nothing.

At last a dyed-in-the-wool female masochistic fantasy – which you can use! At last a woman daring to admit to being a masochist! At last someone daring to say outright that she doesn't want to decide anything herself...

But if Siv Holm is a masochist, then she is not a wholly tradi-

tional one. Only in sexual situations does she not want to
decide, and in all other situations she refuses to allow anyone to
decide for her. She says so in an interview:

> As a woman, I want to be ruled, as a person I want to be
> respected.

It is slightly confusing – or is it? Perhaps it only seems confusing because the great majority of women masochists in
books are described by men. The number of men who have
described masochistic women is endless, and it is almost easier
to name those who haven't, so I will not produce a list. Here
are just a few examples of the way even a most gilt-edged
classic approved by the Danish Teacher's Federation can contain definite sado-masochistic material: such as J. P.
Jacobsen's novel, *Marie Grubbe*.

The novel is set in the eighteenth century, when wheels and
stakes, wooden horses and women whipped out of town were
still part of the order of the day – very handy for a writer who
wants to tune his reader's mind to violence and sensual
pleasure in one fell swoop.

The first time we meet the young Marie Grubbe, distant
chords are at once struck. She is daydreaming and although
her daydream is of a literary figure of centuries ago, there is no
mistaking it. This is how it starts, amid the suffocating scent of
roses and honeysuckle:

> In the room, with its purple rugs and gilded alcove, Griseldis
> lies at the feet of the Margrave, but he thrusts her away; he
> has just snatched her from the warm couch and now he
> opens the small arched door, the cold air streaming in on the
> wretched Griseldis, lying there weeping on the floor, nothing
> between the cold night breeze and her warm white body but
> a thin shift. But he pushes her out and closes the door behind
> her. Sobbing, she leans her naked shoulders against the
> smooth cold door, listening to him walking softly over the
> rugs inside...

Griseldis is the sorely tried, repeatedly bruised innocent that
so many renaissance writers produced in their works: and she is

the person who sets the tone for the way in which Marie
Grubbe's life will be shaped. Of noble birth, married into the
court, Marie is attracted only to the black princes, the men who
treat her in a masterly manner, and she rejects all those who
proclaim weakness. Ulrik Christian attracts her because he is a
hero and grasps her firmly by the wrist. Yet she cannot stand
Ulrik in the long run because he is too easy-going. She first falls
in love with Stig Hog when she finds out that his faint melancholy also contains fierce and violent scorn – and she tires of
him when she realises that he also has doubts and is not so
proud as she had thought.

Marie Grubbe ends her days with a man who is consistently
inferior to her – Søren the farm worker, with his peasant
speech, his manual labours, his workworn body and coarse
gluttony. But she loves him, and follows him through thick and
thin. She becomes his obedient wife and countenances being
beaten when she behaves too self-confidently. From the beginning she has known that:

> ...she would bow to it all, love it all, accept good and evil
> from this black hand...there was a rare pleasure in this self-
> abasement that was partly related to base sensuality, but also
> to what is said to be the noblest and best in a woman's
> nature...

Marie Grubbe has character, strength and sufficient will to
defy prejudice and the conventions of society and – to go her
own way as a woman, that is the way of self-abasement. As a
genuine woman, she finds her true strength in extreme
weakness, dependency, humility, self-effacement. She even
takes total responsibility for her own life. All through the book,
it is she herself who chooses between the various possibilities –
and wherever possible, she chooses weakness before strength
(in herself) and strength before weakness (in men).

Marie Grubbe is only one of innumerable masochistic
women who populate literature and have been partly responsible for creating the impression in the reader that women are
born slaves of their innermost natures. And those who are not
will no doubt become slaves: just like the heroine in
Shakespeare's *The Taming of the Shrew*. This is a classic story of

how, with the minimum of physical superiority, a free woman may be transformed into a masochist *against her will,* so that in the end she becomes a caricature of a woman in a male society.

The Shrew, whose real name is Katherine, is perhaps not accidentally called Kate, which especially in Danish sounds like "cat". When her animal tamer, Petruchio, whom she has never seen, breezily tells her that he is going to marry her, she is naturally furious at this insolence. But as she has previously been portrayed as a loud-mouthed virago, we are supposed to laugh and to gloat at the sportive struggle that is to come. For Kate is not only psychically strong, but she is also physically a worthy opponent.

But Petruchio is just a little stronger than she is. In addition, he has all the means of mental humiliation to hand. He lets her wait at the wedding, to be derided by the "public", he tantalises her with food when she is most hungry, clothes when she is exhausted from cold, sex on her wedding night.

It is a swift but efficient brainwashing. Kate is transformed from a wildcat into a tame domestic cat. She has become punctual, obedient, unpretentious, sweet and smiling. She has learnt to agree when he talks rubbish. She complies with his slightest order and admonishes her fellow-sisters when they do not do the same with their husbands.

In her final speech of tribute to natural female slavery, it may, with an ounce of goodwill, be *just possible* to detect a milligram of irony. But it is really much more convincingly interpreted as a trailer for more exciting struggles, lovely sporting fights in which she will have her make-up smudged with sperm and find it hard to breathe, desperately trying to transform her hopeless struggle against superior forces into masochism – to get *something* out of it.

There is a great deal of material of this kind in this classic comedy, material for the imagination of masochistic women, as well as for all those men who wish to have their belief confirmed that women love exactly the way they love themselves.

The dream (I suppose it can be called that) of the masochistic woman is so common in pornography, literature, art and advertising, that we have learnt to believe that it is so – that women are like that. So it is often difficult to see the wood for the trees – to be clear in one's mind about just how much this image of women actually fires our most intimate fantasies, as well as our concept of ourselves.

There is also another category of books which does this in a wholly different way, and which is usually not about women at all, but comprises accounts of society as a machine directed by cold unfeeling laws, over which we have no influence; as in de Sade's system, a society that turns us all into marionettes and helpless victims. Accounts of that kind are on the increase, but the most telling example is still that of Franz Kafka.

In Kafka, we have an example of a whole body of work showing such marked masochistic undertones that it can be read as pornography (if you so wish), although most of it has nothing whatsoever to do with sex or gender. The most obvious example of masochistic feeling detached from sexuality, traditionally speaking, is his novel *The Trial*.

The main character is called Josef K. He is a confidential clerk in a bank. One fine day... yes, that is how the book starts:

Someone must have been telling lies about Joseph K, for without having done anything wrong he was arrested one fine morning. His landlady's cook, who always brought him his breakfast at eight o'clock, failed to appear on this occasion. That had never happened before. K waited for a little while longer, watching from his pillow the old lady opposite, who seemed to be peering at him with a curiosity unusual even for her, but then, feeling both put out and hungry, he rang the bell. At once there was a knock at the door and a man entered whom he had never seen before in the house. He was slim and yet well knit, he wore a closely fitting black suit, which was furnished with all sorts of pleats, pockets, buckles and buttons, as well as a belt, like a tourist's outfit, and in consequence looked eminently practical, though one could not quite tell what actual purpose it served.

"Who are you?" asked K, half raising himself in bed. But the man ignored the question, as though his appearance needed no explanation, and merely said: "Did you ring?" "Anna is to bring me my breakfast," said K, and then with silent intensity studied the fellow, trying to make out who he could be. The man did not submit to this scrutiny for very long, but turned to the door and opened it slightly so as to report to someone who was evidently standing just behind it: "He says Anna is to bring him his breakfast." A short guffaw from the next room came in answer; one could not tell from the sound whether it was produced by several individuals or merely by one. Although the strange man could not have learned anything from it that he did not know already, he now said to K, as if passing on a statement: "It can't be done."

It can't be done; and after that there is nothing that can be done for the man, whose name has been reduced to a letter. He is told to move to a shabbier room, his guard eats his breakfast, and he receives no answers when he asks what he is accused of. He has to obey orders, comply with summonses, adapt to the system, act and think and feel in agreement with its laws. For a while K walks around quite freely, but he is watched, an eye is kept on him from somewhere...where he does not know. He seeks out authorities who might be presumed to take on his case, and is thus drawn straight into the mysterious court-houses. But he never becomes quite clear about whether they *are* court-houses or whether it is *his* case that is in question, or even what kind of laws he is to be judged by, what his crime is supposed to be, and what his sentence in that case would entail. Neither has he the right to defence counsel in his trial, which in reality is no trial at all, but only a protraction of his execution. One day he is taken away by two men, his clothes removed, then he is placed on the ground with his head against a stone in a "forced and impossible position", and after a few polite formalities...

But the hands of one of the partners were already at K.'s throat, while the other thrust the knife into his heart and turned it there twice. With failing eyes K could still see the two of them, cheek leaning against cheek, immediately before his face, watching the final act. "Like a dog!" he said. It was as if he meant the shame of it to outlive him.

K dies like a dog, shamefully – but the story had started

with a statement that he had never done anything wrong. What has happened?

What has happened is that he has accepted the accusation. He feels it is just – and he feels this more and more, gradually, as time goes by and the mysterious machinery works. He also feels that in fact he should take the knife from the two gentlemen and stab himself with it, and he thinks:

> He could not completely rise to the occasion, he could not relieve the officials of all their tasks; the responsibility for this last failure of his lay with him who had not left him the remnant of strength necessary for the deed.

So he ends regarding himself as a guilty person who deserves his punishment. He has squirmed and wriggled a little – like a marionette, like the mouse the cat is playing with. But not for long. There was nothing he could do about it. The circle round him grew smaller and smaller: with no name, no clothes of his own and no rights, caught in the dim corridors of jurisprudence and bureaucracy, he is left alone, alienated from the world and other people. The brainwashing has worked, and he has assumed the values of the superpower. And with that he has given up his freedom of action, his will, his identity.

The system that is directing him is quite impersonal. It is arbitrary, or just, or both at the same time, with its absurd logic, utilising the labyrinths of internally contradictory laws and an impenetrable language, the only certain signs being that it is the language of authority.

This language alone – the language of authority and Kafka's judicial-bureaucratic-pedantic language – can make a man doubt his worth and make him ask: do I exist at all? Just like the whole system the book describes: its function is to paralyse, obliterate, crush. K stops existing as a man and dies a non-person, like a dog. But there is nothing about him being unhappy.

Is K a masochist? Perhaps – perhaps he is a masochist, perhaps he is a Christian. *The Trial* perhaps is a book about man's impotence in the face of the mercy of God or the absurdity of society. Common to all these various possibilities is the sense that there's nothing to be done about it. Other people decide.

But whichever way *The Trial* is interpreted, and whether or not Kafka himself can be called a masochist (he has been, just as J. P. Jacobsen has been called an algolagnian), fundamentally the main character is not K, but the system he is caught in. The central theme of the book is the way the system makes people impotent. The system is the unfeeling ruler, the kind Severin and Marie Grubbe and Siv Holm long for, and the kind de Sade creates for his heroines.

Masochistic wishful dreams, a sadistic construction, or whatever you prefer to call it, *The Trial* is for me a book with a high P-rating, because of its cold language and the way in which the language and the system humiliate the main character. That is why I have included it here. For although it is not a pornographic book in the ordinary way, I would like to take Ullerstam's words as my own and say quite clearly that I think it is good if someone acquires a pornographic return out of it. I myself have done that with so many things, and I am pleased not to have missed them. As long as you are dependent on a fairly definite form of fuel to be able to function sexually, you have to take what you can get and allow others to do the same. Anything else would be hypocrisy – both for women and for men.

Anyhow, Josef K is a man, and Severin is a man, and Leopold von Sacher-Masoch and Kafka and J. P. Jacobsen are men. It is men who have described masochism. If you say that they are really just writing about people who are alienated in relation to their own sexuality, that is simplifying the matter too much.

But let us – as de Sade says – restore the balance and turn back to women by handing the word over to a man who sounds as if he knows what he is talking about: Nietzsche.

Nietzsche is just as sure about the correct division of roles as are Krafft-Ebing, the poets, the porn-buyers and the girl at the meeting with Germaine Greer. He expresses himself briefly and clearly in a famous sentence that must have left a mark on the souls of at least three-quarters of those who heard it:

If you go to a woman, don't forget your whip!

Thus spoke Nietzsche in the book on Zarathustra, and that sentence can stand as a motto for the next chapter, which is about Freud. Freud was the first to try to investigate masochism seriously. It was Freud I plunged into in the next round, because after all these ambiguous judgements, I longed for something tangible to hang on to.

But I should warn anyone reading this book for stimulation for their sexual fantasies that the following chapter is almost entirely devoid of P-values. It is involved and dry and demands a certain concentration, and I cannot even guarantee it is worth the effort. But nevertheless I think it was worth writing.

PART II

7   The Little Penis-less Creation

Sigmund Freud

If you go to a woman, don't forget your whip!

God knows what Freud thought about that sentence. Perhaps he secretly rubbed his hands at such an excellent way of putting something that lay behind his theories too – the assumption that there is a link between femininity and masochism.

The mystery of masochism was something that preoccupied Freud all through his life. He produced three painstakingly worked out theories on the subject. And yet he did not himself ever find a solution to the problem, which is of course also why he went on trying. There are many internal contradictions in these theories, possibly because new perspectives appeared every time he peeled another layer off the problem.

The mystery of women was also something that preoccupied Freud all through his life – and to which he did not find any solution, either. But in this very formulation lies a startling thought. Why are women and femininity a problem and men and masculinity not? Could there be any explanation other than the proposition that Freud regards men as normal and women as some kind of deviation from the norm? A nice deviation, indeed, a mystery – but nevertheless a deviation from the species called man.

While Freud works with meticulous care to discover what masochism is, he happily accepts existing folk-myths about what woman is – she is passive, uncreative, morally weak and generally inferior to man. He uses these folk-myths as essential to the fundamental basis of his work – and it is on that he builds his own theories.

Freud's dependence on the old concepts of women is expressed in a great many places in his writings, though he often hides behind formal provisos such as "it is generally said", or "women are usually reproached with" and similar phrases. But he offers nothing to invalidate what women are reproached with or what is generally said of women. On the contrary, he does not even investigate what part social conditions have played in what he calls the nature of women. There is one particular point which betrays quite clearly how basic to his work is – shall we say – a *one-sided* understanding of women. It is in a special terminology that runs through his work, simply proffered to his reader without comment, in such phrases as *passive-feminine* and *feminine masochism* (the latter is used by Freud to characterise a quality of masochism in men).

This could be said to be a linguistic problem. But language is a most effective instrument for indoctrination as long as it is not analysed. It is important from the start to make it quite clear exactly what such composite phrases mean.

First, they suggest that there is no particular reason to split the pairs of words up. The only reason to do so would be that they were tautologies, that is, words that already mean the same thing, so one would perfectly well serve the same purpose. Passive *or* feminine, feminine *or* masochistic might so be used, because they do seem to represent one and the same thing. But there is a practical reason for using such phrases as passive-feminine (or active-masculine). In that way, the model for the world of the two sexes is constantly reinforced. How wisely nature has made arrangements for men and women! How reassuring that there is a system, and that we all have our proper place in it.

Because Freud makes this assumption about a sharp division between the sexes (which is naturally connected with the place, time and system in which he lived), it is impossible for us to tackle his work without some preliminary scepticism. So we are quits – he doubts us, and we doubt him.

But even if we detect a logical failure in the basis of his work, it could still be that his argument holds good. So despite our scepticism, we must set about it and find out what Freud has to tell us about masochism and about femininity. For he is the first thinker to have formed theories that take the subject truly seriously. He is not content to describe, as Krafft-Ebing does – he hardly describes at all. He does not ask *how,* but *why.*

However, if Freud's argument is to be investigated, it is not enough simply to go through the door labelled *masochism.* We have to take the route via the fundamental concepts in his thinking, if we wish to understand his more special theories.

The way in which human beings behave, think and feel is decided by a great many differing motives. Some of these motives we know – those that are quite obvious and rational. But apart from these, there is a mass of obscure motives we cannot perceive – either in ourselves or in others. This is due, Freud says, to the fact that they are *unconscious*. We have a whole series of basic attitudes, but we often have no idea they exist. These basic attitudes decide what we do, for they are the remains of fundamental experiences we have had in very early childhood – so early that we do not remember them, because our early childhood lies enveloped in darkness (despite the fact that it is in childhood we have our most powerful experiences). Many of these experiences are of a sexual nature, as we possess sexuality from the very start of life.

There is yet another reason why many of our decisive experiences are enveloped in darkness – because they have been of a negative kind, involving shock, anxiety, disappointment. Some of these experiences have been so violent that we would not have been able to live with them, if we had had to look at them for the rest of our lives. So we have tucked them away. We have forgotten them, and we have forgotten that we have forgotten them, as R. D. Laing expresses it. But they are still there, and they are still extremely active.

They are there in people who are mentally sick. These are the people Freud studied, with the aim of finding a way to the repressions that caused them to suffer from anxiety, depressions and obsessions – neuroses. Freud thought that if he could get people consciously to recognise their own repressions and look their old violent experiences in the eye instead of tucking them away, then they would be rid of their neuroses. He also came to the conclusion that it was not only the sick who went around with repressions, but all of us. The method he founded to bring the unconscious out into the light of day was called *psychoanalysis*.

In practice, the psychoanalyst tries to eliminate the patient's controlled reasoning and intellect, concentrating instead on everything that makes its own way out, so to speak, past the controls that are intended to keep dangerous things at bay.

This happens, for instance, when you dream, or when you "happen to" say or do something unintentionally, or when you allow yourself to follow your stream of thought and ideas without steering them consciously. Further, the psychoanalyst carefully investigates the attitude the patient takes to him, because from this relationship between patient and doctor – called the *transference* situation – he will retrieve patterns that go back to the patient's early past and remain decisive for his or her emotional and general behaviour.

With the help of the psychoanalytic method, Freud found a number of traits common to all his patients. On these traits he built his understanding of how our common childhood is formed, how our very earliest sexuality develops into adult sexuality, how boys become men and girls women. And how it happens that some people become masochists.

Anatomy is destiny, says Freud. By this he means that certain psychic qualities and predispositions follow of necessity from a female or a male anatomy. This particularly concerns two decisive factors. First is the child's relation to its parents, that develops quite differently in a girl and boy. Second is the two children's relationship to the penis, which in Freud's world takes on roughly the same role as the Holy Grail and the Book of Wisdom and the fairy on the Christmas tree. For a girl, therefore, a penis is something she is ashamed at not having; for a boy, it is something he is afraid will be cut off. Together, the two children's attitudes form what Freud calls the castration complex.

Against this background, "the small penis-bearer" and "the little penis-less creation" are given quite different roles in relation to their father and mother. This relationship Freud calls the Oedipus complex, after the Greek King Oedipus, who killed his father and slept with his mother.

That is what Freud thinks boys do – or rather what they would do if they could.

At first, both the boy and girl love their mother; she is the one who gives them love from the start, while the father does not really exist for them. At most, he may be a rival, stealing some of the mother's time and love from them. But one day this competitive relationship becomes so intolerable for the boy, he starts hating his father. He has discovered that his father's penis is much bigger than his own, and he can never hope to defeat his rival and realise his love for his mother by going to bed with her. He also presumes his father – his enemy – wants to cut his penis off if he can get away with it. And he can see from his mother and sisters what will happen – then he will have a wound instead of a penis.

As far as the girl is concerned, development takes another turn. She falls in love with her father, which is quite natural as he is a man, and so comes to regard her mother as a rival. Then she has the great shock that she never gets over, when she sees the wound she has where the penis should be, so her hatred is transferred to her mother, as it must be her mother who has castrated her. The only way in which she can hope for any kind of reparation is to have a child by her father.

In contrast to the boy, who can safely go on devoting his love to his mother until he is adult and finds a new mother and marries her, the girl has to go through a series of stages in relation to her parents. If she never gets any further than loving her mother, she is risking becoming homosexual later on. If she never gets any further than loving her father, this might bring with it father-fixation. On the other hand, a certain father-fixation is necessary if the little girl is to become a *natural woman*.

But this analysis also raises yet another matter connected with the penis. For the little girl has got a penis, although it is very small. This is her clitoris, physiologically the equivalent of the boy's penis, although unfortunately so much smaller. But it *is* there, and Freud regards this as evidence that the little girl has something bisexual in her – or rather, something masculine. This is very unfortunate, because she risks never becoming a real woman – if, for instance, she uses her clitoris to masturbate with and never gets further than clitoris-orgasms. At some time, she has to transfer her sexual sensitivity from the clitoris into the vagina, and at the same time stop masturbating. It is the man's penis inside the vagina that is to give her orgasms. Not until then is nature's concept of her complete.

What will have happened is also that from being active (a male quality) she has become passive (a female quality). And so all obstacles have been swept away, and she can become a genuine little woman.

This is where masochism comes in – for is there any more passive and thus feminine attitude than the masochistic? Freud thinks not, because he characterises his male masochistic patients by saying they adopt feminine attitudes. He does note in passing that there is also something childish – something infantile – in masochism: being made helpless and condemned to obedience. But the closest and most natural characterisation, however, is to say that masochistic attitudes are markedly feminine. When a man shows masochistic leanings, he becomes a kind of woman – and therefore needs treatment.

But we must go further back into childhood if we wish to follow Freud on his route to an explanation of masochism.

One of Freud's great discoveries was that at the very earliest stages, the infant has a sexual life, though hardly of the kind we later call normal:

But it is in fact self-evident: if a child has a sexual life at all it is bound to be of a perverse kind; for, except for a few obscure hints, children are without what makes sexuality into the reproductive function.

Freud describes how the child's sexuality develops. He calls the first phase in an infant's sexual development the *oral* phase. During this period, all feelings of pleasure are centred on the mouth, as when the child suckles its mother, or sucks on a bottle.

The second phase Freud calls the *anal* period. During this time, the child's feelings of pleasure are centred on excrement and the anus. There are two (opposing) urges at this time, an active urge that later may become masculine, and which concerns the bowel muscles mastering the contents of the bowel and not yielding; and the passive urge that concerns the physical pleasure, the sensual sensitivity connected with the anus.

However, Freud is not content to call this period simply anal. He uses the expression *anal-sadistic*. By this, he means that the anal period is characterised by a great urge for aggression. He thinks that children at this phase are markedly cruel to animals and playmates, and are ready to inflict on them all kinds of violence and pain with pleasure (or at least without pity). He also says that the rage often observed in infants when they are given an enema stems from the irritation of the rectum releasing rage as a kind of substitution for aggression. Hence the term anal-sadistic.

So sadism is nothing much to be surprised about. It is natural in the development of every child. It is *primary* and needs no further explanation. Whereas masochism does not necessarily appear in the development of every child. It is only there if natural sadism is distorted, or rather, if sadism is turned inwards towards the child itself. So masochism is *secondary* (Freud later changed his opinion on this).

The early stages in the child's development are unconscious. We know something about them only because psychoanalysis can bring out the unconscious – and this information later can be supplemented with observations of infant behaviour. After the oral and anal stages comes a stage in which sexuality does not manifest itself so strongly, but is latent. This stage ends when the child acquires adult sexuality in a form that should correspond with its sex.

If, however, an adult person develops a perverse sexuality, Freud says this is due to a *regression*, that is a turning back to a stage that should long ago have been put behind. The sadist turns, for instance, back to his anal phase, and can be helped only if the psychoanalyst can get him to untie the knots of the past that are clearly tying him to that stage. But this is not necessarily successful. The period is repressed and an unconscious *guardian* is found in the patient's subconscious, hindering the repression from being raised and made conscious: some experience has been so fierce that the child has had to stow it away (Freud thinks that the experience of seeing the parents' intercourse has usually played this part), and the unconscious offers *resistance* to being brought out into the light.

There is striking evidence from psychoanalysis carried out with the aid of consciousness-expanding drugs such as LSD that this concerns quite "tangible" resistance. Resistance and guardians appear in the form of unmistakable enemies – animals, dragons, warriors, horrible people – that in her imagination the patient has to fight bodily if she wishes to get as far as the memory they are there to guard and defend. But if you are fortunate enough to defeat them and look the past in the eye, then you have a chance of clearing out your repressions and being rid of some of your anxieties.

Thanks to his reconstructions of the early phases in the child's development, Freud came to a point where he could maintain:

> . . . that all these inclinations to perversion had their roots in childhood, that children have a predisposition to all of them and carry them out to an extent corresponding to their immaturity – in short, that perverse sexuality is nothing else than a magnified infantile sexuality split up into its separate impulses.

With regard to the perversions of sadism and masochism, Freud soon understood that he was dealing with important phenomena:

> A denial in the form of an evasive suggestion that after all these are only rarities and curiosities would be easy to refute. On the contrary, we are dealing with quite common and widespread phenomena. If, however, it is argued that we need not allow our views of sexual life to be misled by them because they are one and all aberrations and deviations of the sexual instinct, a serious answer is called for. Unless we can understand these pathological forms of sexuality and can co-ordinate them with normal sexual life, we cannot understand normal sexuality either.

Freud says that sadism and masochism have a special position among the perversions, as this fundamental contrast between activity and passivity is part of the ordinary features of sexual life. The whole cultural history of humanity shows us that cruelty and sexual urges are very close together. But how? Is it a question of the remnants of cannibalistic desires? Or is it just that every pain in itself contains the possibility of feeling pleasure? And is it a question of one or several psychological tendencies?

> But the most remarkable feature of this perversion is that its active and passive forms are habitually found to occur together in the same individual.

A person who feels pleasure in producing pain in someone else in a sexual relationship is also capable of enjoying as pleasure any pain which he may himself derive from sexual relations.

A sadist is always at the same time a masochist, although the active or the passive aspect of the perversion may be the more strongly developed in him and may represent his predominant sexual activity.

We find then, that certain among the impulses to perversion occur regularly as *pairs of opposites*.

This circumstance makes it tempting to set these contrasts in relation to bisexuality with its "opposing masculinity and femininity":

...a contrast which often has to be replaced in psychoanalysis by that between activity and passivity.

So perversions have their roots deep in normal sexual life. But how then does it come about that normal drives are transformed into masochism?

Freud concentrates on this in three theses. He comes to three different conclusions:

1. Masochism is sadism turned in on the person concerned;
2. In general we think we are governed by a principle of desire. But another equally important principle exists that is the basis of masochism: the death wish;
3. In reality, masochism has its source in an unconscious sense of guilt.

Freud puts forward the first theory in a thesis called *A Child Is Being Beaten*, with the subtitle *A contribution to the understanding of how sexual perversions arise.*

The starting point for the thesis is a fantasy-idea that Freud has repeatedly established in people who came to him for analysis. These fantasies are quite simply about a child being beaten, fantasies combined with feelings of pleasure.

On the other hand, the patients are not happy about mentioning these fantasies. They seem to be ashamed of them and feel guilty about them.

Freud was able to establish that the first fantasies of this kind appear very early on in childhood, before school age, probably between four and five years old. At the time when the fantasies stop, when the child grows older, they are nearly always replaced by reading – pornographic books, *Uncle Tom's Cabin* and similar stories.

Freud says that it might be thought that children who have these pleasurable fantasies (that often led to masturbation and release) would also remember having felt pleasure from actually seeing children at school being beaten. But this was not in fact the case. It was also always expressly a prerequisite in the fantasies that no serious harm should come to the children – they were only to be beaten.

One might also imagine that the patients themselves had been beaten as children, but that was not the case either. Freud adds that naturally at some time or other they must have had experience of their parents' (or guardians') physical superiority, and that there are fights in all nurseries. But every time his patients were asked what kind of child it was who was beaten, whether it was always the same child, who it was who beat the child, whether the patient herself did the beating, or whether the patient was the one who had been beaten, there was never any real answer, only a dispirited comment – I can't remember. I only know it's a child being beaten. It was not even possible to find out what sex this child was – whether it was the same sex as the person having the fantasies, or the opposite sex. For the same reason, Freud says, it was impossible to say whether the fantasy in question was a sadistic or a masochistic one.

He concludes from this that masochism is a matter of primary perversion. One of the ingredients that together form sexuality must have developed before the others. But what is remarkable is that the incident that caused the whole thing was really rather banal and had not upset other individuals, which Freud again took as evidence that the problem was something special to the make-up of the patient in question.

Freud develops a theory on the basis of a very small number of people – only six, and from them selects four women, keeping two men for later use.

What is remarkable in these women is that there is

something constantly indefinite about the way they present their problem – almost as if it were a matter of indifference.

The child being beaten is never the girl having fantasies. On the other hand, it is often a younger brother or sister, if there is one. And the person doing the beating always turns out to be an adult, who is easily recognised later as the girl's father.

Freud distinguishes between the three phases that this "beating fantasy" runs through: they can be expressed verbally in the following manner:

1. *Father beats the child* – and it is a child I hate.
2. *Father beats me.* This phase Freud regards as the most important. What is special about it is that it has never been conscious. It is exclusively a reconstruction deduced from what comes out from analysis.
3. *A child is beaten* – by father, by a teacher...but it isn't me. This phase of the beating fantasy is enlarged on with details of a great many different humiliations, and is clearly erotic and can be used for masturbation. How can this be – when it is a matter of an unknown child, or in reality about several – moreover often boys?

Let us look at these three phases in turn:

First phase (Father beats child) in reality stems from early childhood. This is the Oedipus-time, that is, the period when the girl is tied to her father and a hatred of her mother is conceived – and also a hatred of her small brothers and sisters, who steal the adult's love. So the fantasy could have been expressed in other words: Father beats the other child, so he doesn't love the other child – Father loves only me.

Although the beating fantasy appears consciously first at the age of four to five, its origins go much further back; the source lies as early as some time between two and four to five years old. So it is relevant to regard the beating fantasy as an end result, something that has a prehistory, and not as a beginning. It is evidently produced by the child's jealousy and is dependent on its love life, but it is also strongly supported by the child's egoistic interests. And it occurs independently of whether the girl has seen her father beat the other child or not.

In that, Freud says, lies the creation of material for the development of sexual *sadism* later on.

In the period when the girl is strongly tied to the father, sooner or later she will want to have a child by him. She probably doesn't yet know how that happens, but in some way or other connects it with her genitals – if nothing else, with the urinary function. But then the Oedipus complex (the strong tie to the father) is met by her "destiny", love for her father and hatred for her mother must necessarily be repressed.

Why? Because their time has passed and a new phase is starting in the child's life. And because every child, according to Freud, must in its individual development go through the same stages mankind has gone through in *its* development. The child has to repress the feelings connected with incest – in the same way as humankind has displaced or suppressed its tendencies towards incest, sexual love between children and their parents.

Simultaneously with this repression process, guilt arises in the child, probably also of unknown origin, but no doubt connected with the forbidden wish for a sexual relationship with the father. This guilt gives rise to the image of the sternest possible punishment for a little girl: No, father does not love me, because he beats me. In this way, the *second phase* of the beating fantasy (Father beats me) becomes a direct expression of the guilt that now accompanies her love for her father.

The beating fantasy has thus become *masochistic;* as far as I know, says Freud, this sense of guilt is always the reason why sadism turns to masochism. But apart from the sense of guilt, love also plays its part: beating is not only punishment for the forbidden sexual relationship, but also its regressive replacement: that is, the child turns back to an earlier point in its development to be able to recreate the love relationship to the father which is now forbidden. And that again means that the fantasy is erotic and therefore can be used for masturbation – and that now for the first time it is truly masochistic.

The second phase remains unconscious, presumably because it has been repressed so intensely, and has to be reconstructed in analysis. But Freud regards this as the decisive stage.

The *third phase* (A child is being beaten) is apparently again sadistic. It is as if the balance has been shifted in the sentence that runs "Father does not love this other child, he loves only me". Now the emphasis is on the first part of the sentence, since the second part has been repressed. But even if it is another child that has been beaten, the satisfaction is nevertheless of a masochistic kind, for it has taken on the sexual charge that tied it to the sentence's second part – and thus the guilt as well. The many unspecified children who have been beaten by the father or by a teacher appear as replacement for the child who is fantasising.

So Freud regards masochistic fantasy (or perversion) as inextricably tied to the Oedipus-complex, the girl's sexual love for her father. The beating fantasy probably does not become conscious until four to five years of age, when the Oedipal stage is over. But Freud reckons that what is remembered in such a mysterious way is something that has replaced the remains of the Oedipal period.

But if perversions in general can be traced back to the Oedipus complex, they then again become a confirmation of its great importance. Freud says quite clearly that the Oedipus complex constitutes the essential core of neuroses, and is the essential prerequisite for what later become perversions – because the Oedipal stage constitutes the peak of the child's sexuality. So perversions are a kind of "scar" left by this period.

In fact, the phases of the beating fantasy develop slightly differently in boys and girls (to judge from the two men in Freud's material). This is because the boys put themselves into female roles in their fantasies. So "their masochistic attitudes coincide with a *feminine* one", though the remarkable thing is that, for the men, the person who is doing the beating is a woman!

But never mind the boys. For the moment, what interests me most is what Freud has to say about me.

So:

Freud says there is nothing remarkable or unusual that I had masochistic feelings as young as five or six years of age. He says that comes from my having once fallen in love with my father, while hating my mother and younger brother. He says that the fantasies were a kind of wish fulfilment – it would have pleased me if my father had beaten my little brother, because he would thus have shown me that I was the only person in the whole world he loved (he should really also have beaten my mother). Later on I found that I had to forget all that about being in love with my father, and I had a guilty conscience about feeling something sexual about someone so closely related to me. Therefore – to make up for it – I imagined that my father beat *me*. That was what I deserved, as I had such wicked thoughts. But in one way it pleased me, because it was still *father* beating me! But then I more and more forgot that I loved him. Instead I started imagining that my father and later on my teacher were beating some other children; I dared not admit to myself that actually it was I being beaten (yes, to be honest, I did dare to; so perhaps I was especially bad).

That's what Freud says. I felt quite flattered that he had researched so deeply on my behalf. Nevertheless, I did not feel much wiser. But that was perhaps just because I had not gone into analysis, so I could not know whether what he said was right – I would have to be content with believing what he said. Should I believe him? Should I believe him, just because he said so much about me?

Freud's second thesis on masochism is called *Beyond the Pleasure Principle*. In this Freud finds it necessary to produce an "economic principle". That is, he has to ask how the sum can be solved? If we start out from the assumption that we are governed by a pleasure-principle, so that we always, consciously or unconsciously, choose what satisfies our desires best, what about masochism, which denies pleasure and makes non-pleasure its aim? To explain this contradiction, Freud has only two alternatives: either he has to say that masochism is not opposed to the pleasure-principle – or that the pleasure-principle does not govern everything. He chooses the latter possibility.

Freud already has some reservations with reference to non-pleasure: it only *seems* to be striven for by the masochist and is not real – anyhow not to the sadist, nor at any rate to the child at the sadistic stage. He says that when the child is cruel to animals or playmates, it is not to hurt – the pain is only a necessary secondary circumstance. But when sadism is later transformed into masochism, the pain acquires a function – for there is reason to suppose that pain, like other feelings of aversion, may overlap sexual excitement and create a state of pleasure, for the sake of which pain can also be accepted. It can be said of both the masochist and the sadist that:

> In both cases, of course, it is not the pain itself which is enjoyed, but the accompanying sexual excitation – so that this can be done especially conveniently from the sadistic position.

But nevertheless...how can pain and non-pleasure generally become something to strive for? Freud takes his starting point in an analysis situation to explain what he means.

The patient does not remember; perhaps she does not remember precisely what is most important. But her actions and her reactions nevertheless follow the same pattern all the time. This can be clearly established in the patient's relations to the analyst (in the transference situation). It seems to be a question of compulsive repetition of the same pattern over and over again. Even the situations from which it is impossible to extract pleasure – even they are repeated. So it is a question of *repetition-compulsion*. For were it not a question of compulsion, why should the patient repeat what is so painful to her in that way – why should she put herself in a situation in which she is again like the child disappointed with her parents, who is jealous of her small brothers and sisters, who wishes in vain to have a child by her father, who feels that her parents' tenderness is decreasing and her upbringing is making greater demands on her? And why should she more or less provoke a punishment that clearly reminds her of an experience that once long ago showed her that she had been rejected and despised? Is it fate that persecutes her in this demonic way? Or why do we have to accept that a repetition-compulsion displaces the pleasure-principle?

"What follows now is speculation," says Freud, and then he goes on to maintain that other urges also are subjected to the repetition-principle. Perhaps an urge exists in the organism to revert to an earlier condition.

But – an organism develops, doesn't it, growing and reproducing? Freud's paradoxical answer is that organic

development is due to "external, confusing and diverting influences". He says straight out:

> Everything living dies for *internal* reasons – becomes in-
> organic once again.

and he continues:

> ...then we shall be compelled to say that "the aim of all life
> is death" and, looking backwards, that "inanimate things
> existed before living ones".

So everything is on a detour to death, and any hypothetical
instinct for self-preservation has only one object, to ensure that
the organism does not die too soon or through a short-circuit,
but has "its own death-route" – dies in its own way. At which
Freud himself exclaims:

> "But that just isn't possible!"

But he says it is possible, although there is a kind of delaying
rhythm inbuilt in the life of organisms. The one group of drives
(death-wishes) storms ahead as fast as possible to reach the
final goal of life; the other group of drives (sexual or libido
drives) strives to extend the route.

Freud also says that in reality it is impossible to establish a
general evolutionary drive, for what is evolution? It is a question of what we mean by higher or lower stages. And even for
humankind, the real essential route goes *back*...

Originally, Freud differentiated between libido drives,
directed to an object, and the opposite, ego drives, such as the
instinct for self-preservation. Now he brings in another contradiction between the ego-drive-death-drive and sexual-drive-
life-drive, that is, an even stronger dualism than before. And
then Freud asks: is sadism not originally a death-wish that has
simply been given another direction?

The same with masochism; masochism would in this case
not be a secondary urge as Freud had presumed, but a primary
one.

Thus the ruling tendency in the mind is a striving to keep

inner tension constant, reducing it and abolishing it, Freud says, and calls this *The Nirvana principle* "to borrow a term from Barbara Low".

So there are both death-drives and life-drives in humankind. And in addition there survives an old myth about a drive that originates in a previous condition of man. This is Plato's myth from his *Symposium*, in which he posits man as a once androgynous and now divided being whose two halves (the male and the female) strive to be reunited... "But," says Freud finally, "I think this is the moment to stop."

So:

Freud says that as I am a masochist, this means I strive to return to an earlier condition: something like "from dust ye come". Can I recognise anything of myself in this theory? Yes, perhaps, in so far as in intercourse I probably seek for a moment when I disappear, forgetting myself, disappearing from myself. But as far as I know, the object of intercourse for *everyone* is a form of self-obliteration. I cannot immediately see that as anything special for me, the masochist.

And when Freud looks meaningful and says: "The Nirvana principle, to borrow a term from Barbara Low," I am not quite sure he knows what he is talking about. As far as I know, the word *nirvana* defines a condition in which the ego is abolished – not a condition of death, but the opposite, of life at its greatest intensity.

Nevertheless, there is something in the actual words *death-wish* that says something to me...

Freud apparently did not find his thesis on the death-wish wholly satisfactory – except perhaps as a vision. He continued anyhow, and wrote his thesis *The Economic Problem of Masochism*, because he was still troubled about masochism. He says that it involves "great danger". In this third thesis, he still uses the contradiction between the death-drives and the erotic life-drives. But now he is less eloquent and more systematic about it. He says it is necessary to study how the pleasure-principle stands in relation to the two forms of urges, if one is to go any further.

He differentiates among three different forms of masochism:

1. *Erotogenic masochism* (which he says is the basis of the other two);
2. *Feminine masochism* (which actually, for "material" reasons, as he says himself, he studies in men); and
3. *Moral masochism.*

About *erotogenic masochism* (that is, erotic masochism) Freud says briefly that it must have a biological and constitutional origin, that is, have its roots in the relevant person's constitution – but that it is and continues to be incomprehensible. On the other hand, what he calls feminine masochism is relatively accessible for observation.

The most obvious interpretation of *feminine masochism* might be that the masochist wishes to be treated like a small and helpless, dependent child – but more precisely, a *rude* child! However, it has been discovered that fantasies place the individual in a:

> characteristically female situation; they signify, that is, being castrated, or copulated with, or giving birth to a baby. For this reason [writes Freud cheerfully] I have called this form of masochism, a *potiori* as it were (i.e. on the basis of its extreme examples), the feminine form, although so many of its features point to infantile life.

In addition, a guilt feeling arises. The person has in some way offended and this has to be atoned for with all this pain and torment.

Now we come to the third form: *moral masochism.* Here the connection with sexuality has become looser. Who is making the person suffer is less important. What is important is the suffering itself: "the real masochist always turns the cheek in the direction of a possible slap". The reason is that the urge to destroy (one of the forms the death-wish takes) is again turned in towards the person involved.

Again it is the Oedipus complex that is the source: originally the parents are sexual objects, then they lose their sexual charge and are displaced by the *superego.* Freud used the word *superego* for the part of the personality in which are found conscience, moral demands and similar aspects: it is the superego's task to keep the ego from sinking into its instinctual drives (which Freud calls the *id*).

The superego maintains, it might be said, the parents' power and discipline and their tendencies to control and punish. In the course of time, the personal importance of the parents decreases; their role is taken over by teachers, for instance, or other authorities, self-chosen images and socially accepted heroes. Now it is clear how moral masochism separates itself from a stern morality: in morality, the main stress lies on the sadism of the superego, whereas moral masochism puts the main stress on the ego longing for punishment.

This then is the secret meaning of moral masochism: conscience and morality arose when the Oedipal attachment was overcome and de-sexualised; through moral masochism, morality is given a new sexual charge. Moral masochism creates a temptation to commit "sinful" actions that have to be atoned for – whether through the reproaches of sadistic conscience, or through fate, the great parental power. The superego's sadism and the ego's masochism supplement each other.

But Freud says this also has something to do with the fact that we as people live in a *culture*. As this culture suppresses our instinctual drives, it also creates a sense of guilt about these drives, and the conscience grows sterner and more sensitive the more you abstain from aggression against other people (even if you would expect it to be the other way round).

Freud ends by emphasising the duality in masochism: it is dangerous because it stems from the death-wish; but as it is at the same time erotic, even self-destruction cannot take place without the urges being satisfied...

So:

No, I must admit I don't understand all this. But I think it is thought-provoking that Freud differentiates between various forms of masochism – one that is erotic and another that is moral. Only it is confusing of him to say afterwards that the erotic form is the basis of the other forms – because then they are not really different...

I also think it is interesting to hear that I suffer from an unconscious sense of guilt, although I would maintain as firmly as

Linda Lovelace that I have never noticed it. But Freud says somewhere else, that we must admit this sense of guilt may be unconscious, and that such an unconscious sense of guilt may play a decisive part in many neuroses, and is the most important obstacle in the way of cure:

> If we come back once more to our scale of values, we shall have to say that not only what is lowest but also what is highest in the ego can be unconscious.

The highest and the lowest. . . why should my natural urges be the lowest when Freud otherwise tries to see people as normal, that is, in agreement with nature? You are welcome to understand that if you can. But I do understand enough to know that he means I have an unconscious sense of guilt and an unconscious need to punish myself, and that it all stems from my superego, the finest part of myself.

I simply didn't think that as a woman I even had a real superego. That was something the boys got when they were afraid their fathers were going to castrate them – so they abandoned the father and replaced him with a superego to direct their morality and conscience. But girls were to keep their fathers and not exchange them for a superego; why then do I react with a sense of guilt? When Freud refers to the superego as "the highest", he cannot at the same time mean that as a woman I have a superego – naturally that is reserved for men.

In my naivety, I thought at the time that Freud had hit on something important in me when he spoke of moral masochism. I feel that as a woman, much of what I feel and do has been directed by a great number of "higher" destinies: I mean all the things I have done quite voluntarily, anyhow without having gone to an analyst (which was in fact unnecessary!), following the rules and developing into a "real woman". There are so many commandments (you should be a good mother, lover, kitchen maid, wife, and all that), as well as prohibitions (don't think you are anything!) directed at women.

But now I do understand Freud: the business of being a real woman has nothing to do with the superego at all. That kind of minor detail is no business of the superego's. The superego is concerned with *culture,* an expression by means of which in our culture we overcome "the lowest", namely, our instinctual drives, and replace them with morality. But my woman's role has, according to Freud, nothing to do with our culture – it simply belongs under *nature.* If I do not follow the course of nature, I am not just immoral, but sick, and the only thing I can be intimidated with is being *treated* until I am normal, by psychoanalysts, for instance, who have set themselves the task of seeing that the laws of nature are observed; not by the men, clearly a superior species who are to observe the laws of *culture,* but by the women.

And what then is a natural normal woman?

Well, I can read about that in Freud: a normal woman is me, provided that I have renounced my clitoris and my masculinity-complex, and provided my Oedipus complex has been liquidated as it should be. And first and foremost provided that I have transferred my love from my mother to my father, so that I won't end up a homosexual...

From my mother? Yes, for Freud was clearly not quite satisfied with his old theory about the Oedipus complex. He went on working on it and extending it, and the most important conclusion he came to was that the Oedipal stage was not the beginning of anything, but the end of something – that it had a prehistory, namely the period when the love life of the little girl was concentrated on the mother.

When Freud later on explains how the bisexually-inclined child develops into a woman, he names four prerequisites, four reasons why the girl turns away from her mother:

1. She feels her mother is giving her too little milk and thus too little love;
2. She feels her mother is giving to her younger brothers and sisters more love than to herself;
3. The mother forbids her to masturbate.

Finally, the fourth reason concerns only girls, while the three previous ones also hold good for boys.

4. She discovers that the boy's penis is much bigger than her own clitoris, and thus thinks it is her mother who has cut

off her penis. It is the shock of her life, and she envies the
boy his penis for the rest of her life.

This paramount penis-envy may again lead to various reactions in the girl:

a. The girl may develop sexual inhibitions or a neurosis. She
also discovers that her mother has also had her penis cut off; so
she despises her mother, just as she will go on despising women
in general;
b. The girl may work up a masculinity-complex, that is, try to
be a man to make up for not having a penis;
c. Finally she may be nice and cast her love upon her father in a
normal Oedipus-father tie; she may be nice and give up
masturbating her clitoris and adopt her normal passive female
role; and she may be nice and abandon herself to the dream of
having a child with her father. Naturally she is not allowed to
do that, but maybe she will be fortunate enough later on in life
(when she has married a man like her father) to have a son: and
then she will have the final compensation for the penis she
never had.

But – is it really necessary to bother quite so much with that
damned Oedipus complex when what we are really interested
in is masochism? Yes, it is. For Freud says emphatically that
the two things are related. He says that perversions are a kind
of negative, or imprint of neuroses; and he says that the
neuroses are tied to the Oedipus complex: when a part of
mankind's archaic heritage (i.e. what we all have in common
as human beings) is repressed, the sexual urges resist and
replacement-formations arise – such as masochism, for instance. Therefore repressed child-sexuality is the main driving
force behind neuroses – and the Oedipus complex is the central complex of all the neuroses. (Did someone say this was
complicated? Freud would have answered that if it weren't so
complicated, there would be no use for psychoanalysis.)
   If I now wish to attempt a criticism of Freud on some points
touching on the problem of masochism, then first and foremost
I have to tackle the Oedipus theory.
   But – can I criticise Freud at all – as a non-professional?

I suppose I cannot really do that, because I have no first-hand knowledge of what happens when psychoanalysis makes the unconscious conscious and reconstructs the forgotten past into definite patterns. I only know what I read in Freud and in the works of other psychoanalysts, and I cannot base any legitimate criticism on other people's authority.

All I can do is to say what seems to me to be inherently improbable – and what appears to me to be contradictory in the theory.

Here are some of the questions I am left with:

Why should my father's and younger brother's penis play such an overwhelming part in my life? When I can remember thinking little boys' penises very sweet, but not necessarily anything else? When I had no idea whatsoever what it was going to be used for later? When I didn't actually think an adult penis was especially nice, but rather frightening to look at?

And if I suspected my mother of having cut off my penis – why should my little brother be so afraid that my father and not my mother would cut *his* penis off?

Although I loved my father, did I have to hate my mother? Was I really so obsessed with a desire to *own* him and have him to myself, that I grudged her being loved by him as well? Is it I or Freud who was so hopelessly tainted with a sense of possession? Has that anything to do with the fact that both Freud and I lived in a place and in a period when society was full of violent contrasts between those who owned things and those who didn't?

And why didn't I hate my father just as much – for loving my brother and not only me?

Why should there be such a significant difference in the feelings I had for my father and for my mother? Was I really so obsessed by the differences in the *gender* of my parents that I had to react totally differently to them? Is it I or Freud who was so hopelessly tainted with patriarchal ideas? Has that anything to do with the fact that both Freud and I lived in a place and a period when society emphasised the contrast between men's and women's functions in the nuclear family?

And if it is true that these experiences have made me a psychic semi-invalid for the rest of my life, why just me? Why not my younger brother as well? And all the other people who grew up under those conditions?

And why is Freud so very much more interested in masochism than in sadism? Is it not really rather remarkable that we have so much cruelty and so much aggression in us? Is it certain that sadism is natural, while masochism isn't? Is it not possible that this "sadism" was a product of poor conditions of life, which in reality would appear only when the person is hard pressed – for material reasons, or from lack of human warmth?

And then our archaic heritage that he says we have in common with the whole of mankind, that makes each one of us repeat mankind's development in our own – our *nature* in fact – why is that always judged by conditions in the past? Why is more recent evolution not considered *real* evolution? Is it really because all life strives to revert to a previous condition?

Could it not also be because our nature is *changeable* – dependent on conditions in which we grow up and the society we are surrounded by and are part of? Is Freud afraid to admit conscious arbitrary changes in people around him, because that would upset his fundamental concept of an eternal human nature, an eternal family structure – and an equally eternal structure of society?

Is that why Freud speaks so scornfully of women in the women's movement of his time ("who want to foist full equality on to us", as he expresses it – well, you bet they do)? Is that why he thinks we are not only vainer, more envious, more rigid than men, but also morally inferior, in that we have a weaker superego than men ("feminists do not like to hear that", as he said – you bet they don't)?

If I tried to find a psychoanalyst to treat me for masochism – wouldn't he just pat me on my shoulder and send me home, consoling me with the assurance that it was only natural? As Freud himself might have done:

And you will scarcely have failed to notice that sadism has a more intimate relation with masculinity and masochism with femininity, as though there were a secret kinship present; though I must add that we have made no progress along that path.

What a typical Freudian manoeuvre: we know nothing. We must make all possible reservations. But *nevertheless*!

But nevertheless...I do not regret having tried to acquaint myself with Freud's thought processes as he himself formulated them. Despite the remarkable lack of agreement between high-flying imagination and the dry creaking house of cards that came out of it, he has taught me something.

He has told me something about how much of the past I drag around with me, and how early on in life the decisive things happen. He has told me what strange routes inner forces may take if they are not allowed to go the right way. He has told me there is something called the superego...although he did not think I would use that word for precisely the thing he calls my nature, let alone ever settle accounts with it and the forces that have created it, and which try to keep it alive.

8 Enter the Black Prince

Then one day he was there, my Black Prince – my dream lover, the sadist, just like in the fairy tales when someone waves a wand. Everything went of its own accord. I didn't even have to provoke him. He did everything I had hoped for in my fantasies. He spoke quietly and menacingly and he beat me, and while in bed, forced me to do humiliating things. I was taken up as high as never before.

But not quite to the top.

I was completely disorientated when this was repeated several times.

It didn't last long, because the hero of my dreams said goodbye and thank you and left, and I was very unhappy. Today I realise that he was frightened by the enthusiasm with which I received him; a strong chest is needed to stand up to such a warm welcome. But at the time it surprised me, because I thought men who talked quietly and beat you and were menacing were strong men who could take anything.

I was even more disorientated when shortly after that, I had my first orgasm. An orgasm within marriage, after nearly twenty years of active sexual life, after experiencing childbirth and achieving professional success, right in the middle of a good and secure life.

I kept wondering what it all meant. I think several different factors went into the remarkable pattern.

First of all, a colossal tension had been released. The miracle had happened and the prince had been there. There really were princes of the kind I had been waiting for. He had opened a door into that forbidden room for me. It was not full of all the lovely things I had dreamt about, and this astonished me, but afterwards I was able to relax a little and try to be where I actually was.

Secondly, I am sure that prince of mine took me to places where I had never been before, probably right to the beginning of the path and perhaps even quite a way up it – so high up that for the first time I caught a glimpse of the top for which I was aiming. Although I perhaps didn't immediately register it consciously, I think that glimpse etched itself in so that I did not forget it again, and so at last I had a course to steer by.

But why then was it so unsuccessful with him?

That was because figuratively speaking, I had to give up before I got to the top. What happened was far too violent and distracting, taking all my attention, so I could not achieve anything else. I had to concentrate when it hurt, and I also had automatically to absorb all the details on the way, so had no room for anything else. Although I had dreamt of this role for so many years, I also had to learn to *act* it. At the same time, in some strange way I was perfectly aware that it *was* a role. I also had to use my body in a different and unfamiliar way. There was nothing left over for climbing up the path. I think I was like someone who has been hungry for a long time and is then given a huge helping of food and throws herself at it with tremendous appetite – only to find it is too much and she brings it all up.

I found (which I should have known) that if physical pain is to be used directly as sexual stimulation, then it has to be on a defined and strictly limited level. Perhaps this is not true of everyone, but it certainly was for me. If anything hurts really badly, there is no room for pleasure. Then I cannot think of anything else except that it hurts and ought to stop, that I must get away. If it doesn't really hurt, nothing happens. The ideal pain should be governed by a computer that ensures it stops just within that tiny area when it becomes sexual pleasure. This hair-line balance is easy enough to achieve in the imagination, but in real life it is almost impossible. So in reality I had to write off pain as a direct stimulant.

But not as an indirect one. I got as far as realising that the coveted state was *outside* the actual pain. Pain is a necessary part of it, but because the mechanism is so finely graded and the balance so hopeless to achieve, the pain is active only outside the actual situation – before and after. It *has* to hurt at a certain moment (alas). The pain threshold *has* to be passed. There has to be a moment when I hate and loathe the pain, and only wish I could get away from it. But once you have been on the pain-level, it can be used sexually at another moment in time.

When it hurts really seriously, the sexual connection practically ceases – when, for instance, you're beaten with some
object or other. But before and after, there is plenty of
opportunity for sexual use of the situation. There is sexual
stimulation in the memory (you can remember what it was like)
or in the threat (''you know what to expect''), and perhaps
especially in combination (''Perhaps you want to try it
again''). This assumes that you *have* already tried out pain on
your body – whereas a couple of spanks from a friendly lover
is neither here nor there. It is only the pain you hate that can be
manipulated in a certain way so that it may become sexual
stimulation.

But I also found that as far as I was concerned, the psychic
side was decisive. In practice this meant that I could simply
hop over the physical pain and replace it with the symbol of the
pain – humiliation. There are all kinds of ingredients in
humiliation – terror and fear (but not of real maltreatment),
shame, powerlessness, the feeling of being dominated and
unable to do anything about it, the feeling of being dependent
on someone else – a feeling of having become nothing.

I made use of that when I went back home, where there was
no one who beat me, which I was glad about; and where there
was no one who humiliated me, either, which I had to make up
for in another way – and I had actually started doing that
before. There was simply more of a system in my fantasy
activities now.

When I returned home from my prince and at last had my first
orgasm (and many more afterwards) I seemed to have brought
some experience back with me. That was why I could go on
working at letting my fantasy transform normal intercourse into sado-masochistic intercourse, although it was really only
myself taking part in the two-person race.

I was mostly very frightened of expressing what I wanted.
But there were certain things I could cultivate without reveal-
ing myself too much: a slow tempo, for instance. A slow intercourse rhythm was something I could transform secretly – in
my imagination – into something I could then use: I could tell
myself I hated it, because it was slower than I wished it to be
(which naturally it was in a way); that its only purpose was to

keep me back, make me wait, extending my desire and thus dominating and humiliating me. The orgasm perhaps came at the very moment when we were lying quite still and I was saying to myself how grossly sexually starved I was.

I can do many other similar things to make reality adapt to my own puzzle, my own needs. If my partner becomes tired, I tell myself he only wants to demonstrate who is deciding the pace. If my partner comes too soon and then lies still, I tell myself he did it on purpose to torment me. If he does the opposite and plays with me, I tell myself he is hard and unfeeling and just wants to work me up until I almost explode. And so on and so forth.

Constant fantasies are required to interpret an innocent action as conscious sadism in this way; in reality it is very hard work. But it has worked for long periods. It is marvellously effective, despite the long series of deceptions and self-deceptions on which it is based.

Naturally this has not been so effective as being with a man who consciously used the same mechanisms and left me in no doubt that he was consciously playing on them; presuming he followed the rules of the game – my own!

For instance, many men think that rape or rape games automatically give the woman a feeling she is subjecting herself – and that she becomes even more stimulated the harder, the faster and the more violently it all goes. But that is a male wishful dream originating in the old concept of women as refined creatures with no sexual desires of their own – and *that* male dream does not work as far as I am concerned. Naturally I get a little out of it – if I resist with all my strength, for instance, and persuade myself my partner is stronger than I am. But if I am sexually aroused, I want exactly the same thing as he does, that it will end in intercourse, and my ability to fantasise is not so great that I can interpret intercourse as debasement. All right, I am dragged off by the hair – but in the direction of my own goal and not away from it. So rape games are not arousing enough to give me an orgasm.

Regular rape is not especially arousing, either. If I really find myself in a situation in which a man forces me into intercourse against my will, then the most rational thing is to close my eyes and get it over and done with. If against my expecta-

tions I then become sexually aroused, the result is very mixed.
Perhaps it concerns a man I feel real dislike for – if I've just
seen him hit a child, for instance. Then on the one side there
may be something arousing about how my will and feelings are
being annihilated. But at the same time it is simply a matter of
sexual arousal.

In this way, while I may re-interpret a normal intercourse
into sadism, I can also be prevented from receiving masochistic
yield from intercourse that actually contains real sadistic
elements. So it is not that simple...

Then there are more ordinary everyday situations that I can
use, that occur out of bed and when fully dressed. For instance,
a domestic – or service – situation of the kind that is found in
all couple-relationships, or as good as all.

Let us say I am cleaning a pair of shoes for a man. That in
itself can be degrading (why can't he clean his own shoes?), but
it may also be part of work-sharing that is very sensible. If I feel
it is a degrading situation in itself, I can react in different ways.
I can be rebellious and stop cleaning his shoes. Or I can go on
cleaning them, feeling bitter and wronged. Without really
understanding why, I can also turn my irritation in on myself,
transforming it into a feeling of inferiority – I'm not worthy of
anything else but to clean his shoes, while he does more noble
things.

This everyday female situation can be blown up into a real
sado-masochistic situation if played upon. If he sits in his chair
smoking his pipe while watching me cleaning his shoes; if he
comments on my work, criticising me, or handing out com-
pliments to the clever girl serving him so well, as a woman
should – then, a little while ago a free and independent person, I am suddenly processed and channelled into a role in
which my actions are no longer my own, but forced labour.

In that way, in the course of the day, all kinds of things can
be transformed into conscious power games, and conversations
can become an exchange of orders and humble responses:
Clear the table! Coffee! There's a button missing on my shirt!

Such examples may thus be everyday things for married
couples in a male society – or also cultivated sexual games,
part and parcel of foreplay. If the game is to function as a sex
game and not just ensure one partner of his daily comfort,

however, it must be played on the conditions of the other partner. So the slave must first instruct the master, just as Severin
teaches Wanda. Otherwise there is chaos and the game loses its
sexual content and I get furious and spiteful and throw his shirt
at him and say why the hell hasn't his mother taught him to
sew an ordinary button on.

I lived the role of slave in so many ways – in reality. I
washed up and addressed envelopes and was small and sweet
like the rest. I carried on in total invisibility, keeping quiet at
meetings, never dreaming I could change anything in the
whole world. (This was before the days of the women's movement.)

I was quite unconscious. I didn't know what was going on. I
experienced enjoyment at being a marionette being manipulated by my partner – I thought it was nice and exciting when
he pulled the strings like that, and my will didn't have a
chance. But if he happened to pull the wrong string, then
everything was spoilt – if he pulled a string that did not suit
me! Rather slowly, I realised how paradoxical this whole game
was. I gradually discovered that I was really being the consumer and he the supplier. I discovered how amazingly self-
centred a masochist is. Everything was to do with me, me, me.

Actually it is all one great self-deception. I am really the one
being served and waited on. I am really the main character. I
am the one who must receive the right service to enable me to
imagine that I am nothing.

It is not that strange that reaching a goal so full of inner contradictions should be such a difficult business in actuality. But
it can be done with the help of imagination.

In fact I reached the goal more and more frequently, though
I don't think I have ever had a single orgasm in my life –
either with a man or on my own – when my head was not
filled with fantasies about being put down. So in my fantasies I
have deceived a lot of men, by transforming them into
something they simply were not, and letting them act according to a pattern they knew nothing about, even perhaps
transforming them into quite different men. I am sorry it has
been necessary, and would think it reasonable if they felt
grossly cheated – if they knew. I myself feel I have cheated
them, anyhow. And myself as well, in a way. At a certain

point, my partner seemed to be superfluous, maybe even irritating – because he was disturbing me in something that was actually a kind of masturbation...

But the method was necessary to me if I was to function sexually. I have also found that many of my lovers probably deceived me in the same way – by making me into another woman, a woman they knew, or a film star, or a girl in a pornographic magazine. I could console myself with that, if that was any consolation. But I don't know whether I think it is.

The men I have met whose desires corresponded to my own can be counted on the fingers of one hand. So I always had to find fuel for my fantasies. In a way, it became easier and easier to build them up consciously with material from good medical books and literature and less good pornography.

But while the pieces of the puzzle began to fall into place and I began coming to terms with my destiny, I also started tiring of all this troublesome comedy. What was it all for?

9 The Fear of Freedom

Some of Freud's successors: Fromm, Horney, Deutsch, Bonaparte

At the end of the Danish novel *The Missing Clerk*, by Hans Scherfig, the author describes his hero Theodor Amsted in prison at Christmas, delighted by the inner security he has at last found. His ingenious plan has succeeded and he has been sentenced for a murder he has not committed. He has been fortunate enough to have been given a life sentence. At last his troubles are over. Never again will he have to express an opinion on anything, or support himself, or be independent. He has rid himself of the freedom which had frightened him so. In future, everything will be looked after in the same way that his authoritarian mother and stern father cared for him in his childhood home, when everything was in its right place and you ate *up* your food. At last he has returned home – if not to his mother's womb, at least to the safe haven of authority. All round him and his fellow-prisoners, the joyous message of Christmas is ringing out...

I don't know whether anyone has ever thought of calling this man a masochist. But there is only one reason against doing so and that is that Scherfig's book is laundered of all sexual overtones. On the contrary, it is full of humorous overtones and undertones – and humour and sexual perversion do not usually go very well together.

Otherwise there is not much difference between Theodor Amsted and Josef K and all the others who are attracted to non-freedom like moths to the light, and he could well be counted among what Freud calls the moral masochists. Except that the flame that consumes Josef K simply warms the little clerk up.

So the missing clerk is not really a masochist, and neither is he a woman. I mention him in this connection because he is an *authoritarian character*, an expression that comes from a book by Erich Fromm called *The Fear of Freedom*.

To renounce freedom, the individual has to use one or more of what Fromm calls "flight mechanisms", strategies for evasion. One of these involves assuming what Fromm calls an authoritarian personality.

This personality type seeks to replace the old primary bonds with new secondary bonds. This can be done if you allow your personality to fuse with someone or something outside yourself – if you submit to an authority. This mechanism is demonstrated most clearly in masochistic endeavours and with contrasting manifestations in sadistic endeavours. Both are a form of flight from intolerable loneliness.

Fromm describes how masochistic endeavours are usually expressed as feelings of inferiority, powerlessness and insignificance. When people afflicted with these feelings are analysed, it appears that although they consciously complain about them, they are unconsciously clinging to an urge to feel inferior and insignificant.

So some people like disparaging themselves, humiliating themselves and subjecting themselves to pain – they even find enjoyment in it. When the masochist lets himself be hit, or weakened "morally" by being scolded or humiliated or treated like a child, his feeling of insignificance is even further intensified.

But what is the explanation – is it possible that you can reduce a fear by increasing it? For that is exactly what the masochistic person tries to do.

Fromm responds with a kind of comparison. As long as I struggle with my wish to be independent and strong at the same time as I struggle against my feeling of weakness and powerlessness, I am a victim of a cruel conflict. If I manage to reduce my individual ego, and thus the consciousness of being alone, to nothing, I may be able to solve the conflict.

Feeling absolutely weak and helpless is one of the ways of achieving this aim. Feeling controlled by pain and despair is another. Getting drunk is a third, and suicide is the last hope, the last way out, when all other means of easing the burden of loneliness have failed. But common to all these panic reactions is the fact that they are means, not ends. The pain, the suffering and humiliation are simply the price that has to be paid.

In this book, Erich Fromm tries to identify the factors that gave rise to the authoritarian regimes, especially that of Nazi Germany, that led to the second world war. Fromm believes that we must investigate the conflicts within the individual in order to explain what happens out in the world.

That was also what Freud did, but while Freud regarded the individual human being as a more or less isolated unit, Fromm is primarily interested in the individual's relations with the outside world. While Freud sees the individual's relationship to his surroundings as determined for life by his early experience, Fromm says that this relationship is constantly developing.

He describes this development in the following way.

The foetus is bound to its mother by the umbilical cord. When the child is born, the umbilical cord has to be severed. In emotional terms this means that the primary bonds that gave the child security, safety and the knowledge of *belonging* must be severed before the child can become independent and free. When that has happened the child faces *another* task: it has to find its own direction, and a foothold in the world. It has to achieve security in another way.

Thus freedom acquires a double meaning. On the one hand the individual is strengthened, and on the other the individual is more alone:

> This separation from a world, which in comparison with one's own individual existence is overwhelmingly strong and powerful, and often threatening and dangerous, creates a feeling of powerlessness and anxiety.

Faced with this frightening freedom, the child has two possible responses. It can make a spontaneous connection with the world through love and work and by allowing its feelings, senses and intellect to find expression in an open and honest way, and thus achieve positive freedom – that is, it can once again be united with its fellow human beings, with nature and with itself without losing its independence. The other possibility is to renounce freedom.

It is possible to ease the burden of freedom by forming a neurotic relationship with another person. The masochist can do this by submitting, the sadist by dominating – the sadist's desire for power is also an expression of his inability to live alone with his ego, and his wish to dominate is nothing but a

attempt to gain secondary strengh in the absence of
strength.

The masochist – the slave – has to repress the hatred he
really feels for his master. He has to do this for two reasons,
first because the feeling of hatred is harmful and tormenting,
and second because he has to mitigate his own sense of shame.
He can do this by surrounding the person he is submitting to
with qualities that justify his own submission.

You do not have to seek out an individual person as a partner, either. The authority you choose to submit to may be an
institution with rigid rules as to what may be done and what
may not.

The authority may even be an inner one – a sense of duty
for instance, or conscience. Analysis would be able to show that
conscience can react with quite as hard a hand as an external
authority: the external authority has simply been replaced by
an internal one.

Fromm says the person who cannot bear living freely – the
authoritarian character – is not necessarily a person who can
be *called* neurotic. It depends on what the social situation is,
what task is to be carried out, and what the pattern is in the
culture surrounding him.

Two sexes exist, so to speak, for the authoritarian character:
the strong sex and the weak sex. His impulse to submit is
automatically evoked by power, regardless of whether the
power comes from a person or an institution. It is power for the
sake of power that fascinates him – he does not look at the
values the power stands for, and powerless people and insti-
tutions arouse his contempt correspondingly.

The authoritarian character is never revolutionary – but
could well be called a rebel. However, inexplicable swings can
occur in him, so that he is able to submit to extremely
authoritarian systems. Similarly, he submits to his own
destiny. He likes to maintain that it is destiny that brings about
wars and that one-half of humanity is governed by the other. . .

So Fromm says that if I am a masochist, then that is due to
the fact that I am afraid of freedom. He does not do much
about describing what I am like, but is interested in the
dangers inherent in my masochistic, or authoritarian, stance in
the fact that I give myself quite uncritically to another person

or to an institution or a party or a religion. Or to destiny. Or to my conscience or my sense of duty. To anyone or anything that is large and has power – the power I myself dare not take...

Karen Horney is a psychoanalyst who approaches the subject in a somewhat different way. She says Freud puts too much emphasis on heredity and constitution. She says masochism is to a very great extent decided by the social conditions one grows up in. She also says it is harmful to think that the past governs the human being. She prefers to put the emphasis on the present, and to help neurotic patients by explaining to them how they function here and now, and defining the inner contradictions that are stealing their energy and stopping them from functioning normally.

She also questions the actual concept of masochism. Freud differentiated between erotogenic, feminine and moral masochism. Horney thinks that these three should be further differentiated. She questions whether masochism is a sexual phenomenon, or a fundamental character structure expressed in all fields, and so in the sexual field *as well*.

Anyhow, like Fromm, she outlines a character type who feels *angst,* and therefore must use a great deal of energy in sustaining her security. The masochistic way of managing this situation is to abandon oneself to the grace and favour of another person. It is the same, she says, as when a small exposed nation hands over its rights and independence to a powerful and aggressive nation, thus achieving protection.

Horney concedes that this view does not agree with the usual definition of masochism, which regards it as the striving for sexual satisfaction through suffering. This definition, according to her, involves three unproven statements: first, that masochism is essentially a sexual phenomenon; second, that it is a striving for satisfaction; and third that it is a wish for suffering.

Before Horney questions whether masochism really is a sexual phenomenon, she divides masochistic characteristics into two main tendencies:

1. A tendency to devaluation of self. The person is not usually aware of this tendency, only of the result, which is

that she feels she is boring, insignificant, stupid, worth-less. She exaggerates her inadequacy and always reacts with a helpless "I can't". She is nondescript and creeps down a mousehole.

2. A tendency to dependency. This dependency is a vital necessity to her. She feels she can no more live without the other person's presence, benevolence, love and friendship than she can live without oxygen.

To simplify things, says Horney, we can call the person on whom the woman is dependent her "partner", whether it is father, mother, lover, husband, friend or doctor, or even a group of people such as a family, or a religious sect.

The woman feels she can do nothing whatsoever for herself, but has to receive everything from her partner – love, success, esteem, care, protection. Without knowing it herself and mostly in opposition to her conscious modesty and humility, her expectations are almost parasitic.

She has to cling to another person to such an extent that she is incapable of seeing that a relationship has certain limits. So she cannot have too much evidence of her partner's devotion and interest. Usually she takes the same attitude to life in general – she feels like a ball in the hands of destiny, with no means of taking her fate into her own hands.

Horney asks why a woman takes this attitude?

Through the interplay of unfortunate influences, the little girl's ability to take the initiative, and spontaneously to develop her own feelings, wishes and opinions has been warped. So she feels the world around her is hostile. Under such difficult conditions, she has to find some means of managing safely in life, so she develops what are called neurotic traits. One such neurotic trait is self-disparagement, another exaggerated conforming to the established moral code.

The safety she achieves this way is real security – a person who undervalues and disparages herself achieves the security of obscurity. She behaves like a mouse which prefers its hole because it is afraid the cat will eat it if it dares to come out. She has the same feeling about life as a stowaway who has to remain hidden, so enjoys no rights of her own.

Who enjoys no rights of *her* own...I must admit I have

cheated in this last section. Karen Horney does not write "woman", but "the masochistic person". But we have heard so much about women being masochists that I will continue to use the word woman in Karen Horney's description of the masochistic person, because I think it fits the traditional woman in traditional male society so well. We really do learn something about ourselves – ourselves before the women's movement.

Karen Horney goes on:

When her craving for self-abasement breaks down, when this whole pattern breaks down, anxiety appears. A woman who devalues her own abilities becomes frightened when she wants to offer her opinion in a discussion, and even when she has something valuable to contribute she does so in an apologetic manner.

In her childhood, such a woman has often been afraid of wearing clothes that are different in some way from those of her friends, because she felt they would attract attention. Neither can she understand that anyone could be hurt by her, or care for her, or value her. As she is not convinced of the opposite, she sticks to her conviction that she means nothing. She often feels shy and ill at ease when recognition is given for work well carried out, and she tries to belittle it. In this way, productive work can be distressing to her because it implies asserting herself with her own special views or feelings. So the woman can only carry out the work if there is another person there who can always comfort her and give her security.

If she is successful despite these difficulties, she does not experience it as success. A new idea, or a finished piece of work, is immediately disparaged. She runs a little car instead of a Jaguar, although she would prefer a Jaguar and can afford to run one.

She usually has a general sense of inferiority. These feelings are, however, more likely to be the *result* of her lack of self-appreciation than the reason for it. But she isn't even aware of the fact that she is trying to make herself unnoticeable...

Conflicts follow on from this way of releasing oneself from anxiety. In reality it is not helplessness the woman needs. Helplessness is only an unavoidable and undesired result of the procedure she uses to achieve security. The fact that she suffers constantly from her own weakness is one of the many reasons why she nourishes an almost uncritical admiration for strength and power. Everyone who dares to be openly aggressive or who dares assert him or herself can be sure of her unconcealed admiration. Someone who dares to lie or bluff appeals just as much to an undercurrent of admiration in her as someone who shows courage for a good cause.

Relationships based on this form of dependency are full of hostility towards the partner.

This is primarily because of the expectations placed on the partner. As the woman herself lacks energy, initiative and courage, she has a secret expectation of receiving everything from her partner's care, help, exemption from risk and responsibility, esteem and honour. But these expectations are such that hardly any partner can live up to them.

The woman is also in reality hypersensitive to the slightest sign of the other person's contempt or indifference, and she reacts with fierce anger which is not expressed. In this way, bitterness develops in her relations with other people, and inevitably her conflict worsens: on the one hand she forces herself on to people, and on the other hand she hates them...

The third main reason for her hostility lies far deeper. As she cannot tolerate any distance between her and her partner, in reality she feels cowed. She feels she has to agree to her partner's conditions unreservedly. She feels he dominates her and that she is imprisoned like a fly in a spider's web, the partner being the spider.

Some of her hostility occasionally slips out in explosions of anger. But on the whole, she never gets free of it, because she needs her partner and is afraid of being separated from him. So her conflict is in the end a conflict between dependency and hostility.

She is really in no state to love anyone, and neither does she believe her partner or anyone else could possibly love her. Her devotion is really simply a clinging to her partner with the object of receiving relief from her anxiety.

She also nourishes a desire to be a child, but that is a neurotic wish, forced out by circumstances and the stress her anxiety puts on her. A dream of being a child is not really a desire, only an expression of a desire to be protected, not to have to stand on her own feet but to avoid responsibility – an obvious desire, as she has developed her helplessness to such a great extent.

The woman's special way of expressing desires is to give other people the impression that because of her bad state, she is in great need of help. She acts being unhappy or helpless to achieve things. But in the long run, this is not much use, because the effect soon wears off. People round her grow tired and sooner or later start thinking she really is unhappy, and that in fact it is no use trying to help her. But she has to use this tactic because, consciously or unconsciously, she is aware that the world around her is hard and menacing, and spontaneous friendliness does not exist.

She always feels deep down inside her that she has no right to make demands and she must justify her desires to herself. So she uses her helplessness and needs to exercise pressure on other people...

Similarly, her special way of showing hostility is by suffering, being helpless, by making herself out to be a victim someone has done injury to, by allowing herself to be destroyed...However, she can also go into attack more directly, because in her basic structure, she has all the means of developing sadistic traits. For many reasons, she is weak. She is or feels humble and oppressed, and in her heart she puts the responsibility for her suffering on to other people.

Because of her compulsive humility and dependency and all that goes with that, she makes mountains out of molehills. There are some women who simply avoid every effort and react for instance by becoming exhausted at the slightest thought of extra work – such as Christmas shopping, or a journey. The woman's typical reaction to difficulties is an immediate "I can't". Sometimes she is afraid that the necessary effort will injure her. Often she simply becomes ill. The problems are pushed away. If she just sat down and tackled them actively, she would soon find out how to solve them, and then the matter would be settled. But she has a vague and indistinct hope that difficulties will go away by themselves after a while, and so she goes on letting them hang threateningly over her head. This means that again she feels weaker, and she does in fact become weaker, because she cheats herself of the strength achieved by struggling through difficulties.

To understand all these astonishing conditions, we must be aware, Horney says, that nearly all other ways of finding satisfaction are excluded for the woman. Every form of fruitful, self-assertive activity includes anxiety. So it becomes impossible for her to function as leader, to take part in anything new that might include satisfaction for her, or indeed to carry out any kind of independent work or any planned pursuit of a definite goal...

All this necessarily also involves a certain basic injury to her love life. She cannot do without other people to have her own demands and wishes fulfilled, but she herself is not in a state to feel spontaneously for others and their interests, their wishes, their happiness and development. So the satisfaction achieved by others through love and sexuality is warped in her.

She can actually achieve satisfaction only in the same way that she finds security: from dependency and self-deprecation. But a problem arises here, as these qualities do not in themselves normally give satisfaction. However, observations show that satisfaction *can* be experienced when this attitude is driven to extremes. In her fantasies and her sexual life, the woman is not completely dependent on her partner; but she is wax in his hands, she is violated, cowed, humiliated and tormented by him. Similarly, her self-abasement gives her satisfaction if it is so exaggerated that she loses herself completely in her ''love'' or devotion: losing her identity, losing her dignity and allowing her individuality to be swallowed up in general humiliation.

But, Karen Horney goes on to say about woman...sorry, about the masochistic person -- that

> every individual who - for non-neurotic reasons as well - is weak and oppressed may develop these traits.

Karen Horney makes this statement again later on about women, so I shall return to her later.

I have to admit that I re-wrote Karen Horney's text as I did because I was very forcibly struck by it - every line of it. She was writing about masochists, and I was affected as a woman. I recognised myself as a woman, and many others as well as myself – I was taken back to the old days before there were any women who found they could find security and free themselves from anxiety in a less contradictory and more reliable way, by making decisions themselves and taking responsibility for them.

But it was not women Horney was writing about.

There were however other female successors of Freud who would not have thought it in the slightest remarkable that I was thinking about women instead of just about masochistic character types. They would simply have thought it slightly superfluous to change from one term to the other, because fundamentally they assumed the two to be identical. For them, masochism is almost a matter of honour for a woman, a badge of honour.   .

Among those the most celebrated is a contemporary of Karen Horney, and her name is Helene Deutsch. She was writing about the problem as long ago as the twenties, but her book on *The Psychology of Women* was first published in the 1940s.

(To set the record straight – I have not "cheated" in the section on Helene Deutsch, which is what she says herself, even if it sounds unbelievable.)

Deutsch starts by asking, like Freud, how a small girl develops into a woman. She too sees this development as far more difficult than that of a boy into a man. The difficulties are due to the fact that a girl has to move her sexuality inside her own body. Deutsch says with that she has to re-evaluate her own genitals, so that "the male clitoris" surrenders its sensitivity to the passive vagina.

Something even more important follows from that – namely that the woman must experience intercourse as a masochistic event. For her, intercourse is really concluded only nine months later, since the real climax does not come until the birth itself, in an *orgy of masochistic pleasure*.

Thus Deutsch answers the question about how the girl becomes a woman: by accepting the path of masochism. Sexual and reproductive urges are linked by a "masochistic bridge", and

In the deepest experience of the relation of mother to child it is masochism in its strongest form which finds gratification in the bliss of motherhood.

Nature has given woman her masochism as a magical helper, so that she can get safely through her life. It guides and supports her from the first time she experiences a love for her father so strong that she wishes to be castrated by him: through the monthly bleeding of menstruation; through the painful defloration in which a part of her body is annihilated; through intercourse that is often experienced as painful and anyhow always as passive; to birth, which is painful and dangerous right through.

Masochism is woman's helper, because she can adapt to reality only by saying yes to pain. On the other hand, masochism is also a dangerous helper, because it *can* be too strong. By this Deutsch means here, however, not that masochism in itself can be too strong – no, the danger lies in that it can be so strong that the woman starts *defending* herself against it, and thus turning her back on her womanhood...

In the introduction to her book, Deutsch complains that there has been a steadily increasing tendency to explain the psychological behaviour of the sexes in terms of educational and cultural factors. Her own book is written from a biological and anatomical base.

In the quite young girl an active phase occurs that involves a risk:

> *That this activity contains certain dangers* for the future sexual development of the girl, that is, for her future passivity, cannot be denied... [My italics M.M.]

But with puberty, a sudden increase in her passivity occurs, which bodes well for her womanhood, but also involves her in possible conflict:

> Many girls are forced by the pressure of social conditions to work at some occupation, but they regard such occupations as provisional. Even today it is striking how many women engaged in active professional work await the moment when they will be supported by their husbands, and bitterly

reproach a husband who is unable to satisfy this demand. Many girls take up professions because it is the fashion to do so or because of their social convictions...

Even a girl who has hitherto been in every way promising, may come to a stop when her "inner world" overwhelms her. On the other hand she can use ambitions, conscience and dutifulness as an armour to cut herself off, so that she does not even develop feminine qualities:

Such a girl seems to me to be the most miserable feminine type in existence, for...she is often an excellent, but usually an incomplete *man*...

Strength will naturally be taken as a sign of illness by anyone who considers weakness and passivity natural healthy female qualities, and correspondingly intuition as the proper female means of dealing with life. So Deutsch also says it is only exceptionally gifted girls who can carry a "*surplus of intellect*" without damaging their emotional life. Unfortunately, she says, modern education does not admit this truth, with the result that girls are often "*overburdened*" intellectually.

Passivity and masochism also govern a young girl's sexuality, making her turn inwards on her intense inner life and imagination. Thus she defends herself against "gross sexual demands" and transforms them into a longing for love and poetry – in contrast to boys, who replace their imaginations with masculine activity directly aimed at reality.

However, masochism and passivity are not one and the same thing, says Deutsch, although they are intimately connected. The question is then, how does the girl succeed in accepting her masochism and directing it in a positive way? This is a process that starts in childhood.

Apart from her passivity and her masochism, the girl also has an active tendency represented by the father. Both the boy and the girl will at a certain point turn away from the mother towards the father. What do they expect of him?

They expect an ally against the mother and her world, for the father represents reality and the outer world, where the children want to live as adults. But it is a much more complicated process for the girl than for the boy.

She may overvalue her father to such an extent that later on she will make far too great demands on her husband. She may also identify so much with her father that she can store up and "sublimate" her activity – i.e. transform it to female objects – but her sexual behaviour thus becomes extremely passive and masochistic. So much so, that she will either live erotically isolated, or become a victim of a brutal man.

So the relationship to the father is difficult and divided: he becomes the object at the same time of the girl's active and passive-masochistic tendencies. Deutsch formulates this inner contradiction in an effective and almost poetic manner:

> The psychological effect is as though the young girl had two fathers – the "day-father", to whom her relation is conscious, with an active emphasis, and the "night-father", who brings all the dangers of cruelty and seduction in his train and mobilises nightmares...

Although the father has from the start encouraged the girl in her activity-compulsion, he now inhibits it as well, for he is also the representative of the outside world.

> In this function the father is a representative of the environment, which later will again and again exert this inhibiting influence on the woman's activity and drive her back into her *constitutionally predetermined passive role*.

Deutsch does not, however, go any further into her evaluation of the role the outside world plays in the development of the girl, but remains with her relationship to her father. This has a fairly definite masochistic character from her very early years:

> It is enough to observe the little girl's fearful jubilation when the father performs acrobatic tricks with her that are often painful, when he throws her up in the air, or lets her ride "piggy back" on his shoulders. When this seduction on the part of the father is lacking, the girl will encounter difficulties in her feminine development.

Deutsch has then, "for simplicity's sake", divided the child's closest surroundings into two halves, the mother who inhibits her child and wishes to make her passive, and the father who encourages the child into activity. If the girl also has brothers, her disposition will also make itself known in her life with them – if she feels attracted, for instance, to running round with gangs of boys:

> It is fascinating to observe how easily the urge to boyish activity is transformed into a masochistic trend. The boys admit the girl to their games as an equal if she allows herself to be beaten from time to time and is willing to perform exhibitionistic and humiliating acts. There are desperate cries and tearful complaints; soon afterward the boyish masochist is consoled and again engages in the same games. This is a simple example of double gratification.

In puberty, the girl's fantasy life reveals an unmistakable masochistic content, with fantasies about rape and humiliation and beating.

Often it is not the father who appears in the girl's masochistic fantasies, but a woman who ties her up and maltreats her. Deutsch says that this woman represents the mother and acts as a counter-weight against the mother's prohibitions. Thus the function of rape fantasies is to free the girl from guilt feelings that are the result of feeling pleasure, despite her mother's prohibition.

Deutsch says that many women store up their fantasies for years without a masochistic perversion ever arising, as these women are often unusually sensitive and negative towards both physical and psychic pain:

> *It is known that the masochistic perversion is less frequently found in women than in men.*

This extremely interesting piece of information is suddenly flung into the middle of it all. There is nothing to say where Deutsch got it from, and she just goes on as if nothing had happened.

A woman can also become *too* masochistic, and a "badly administered masochism'' is a serious problem. But how can the woman then control the dangers that threaten her from such a ''surplus'' of masochism, which may also be neurotic? Can she use her ''passive-masochistic energies'' in a harmless way?

She can, because she also has a tendency towards narcissism, that is, towards being in love with herself. When masochism thus comes ''under narcissistic control'', she can face the onanistic rape-fantasy with all the weapons against mastur-bation that she has at her disposal (year 1944).

This condition

> in which the distribution of forces between the narcissistic ego and female masochism leads to complete harmony

is the aim that fortunately most women achieve. For, as Deutsch expresses it:

> *The attraction of suffering is incomparably stronger for women than for men.*

The assumption is simply that the girl overcomes a surplus of aggressions and again learns to feel love for her mother. That is easy for the woman who is of the erotic masochistic type (who is different from the perverse masochist). For others it is more dif-ficult:

> Because of their very avoidance of direct masochistic dangers, their lives are empty, without content; their masochism asserts itself in the form of a renunciation of the positive values of life.

Deutsch includes among those who reject the positive values of life those women who are politically active:

> They often participate in violent anonymous protests and join revolutionary movements. Most of the time they are un-consciously protesting against their own fate. By identifying themselves with the socially oppressed or the nonpossessing class, they take up a position against their own unsatisfying role. In many women this expresses a kind of ''masculine

protest'' and their sublimated and socialised dissatisfaction with their feminine destiny...In the childhood history of these women we find tyrannical fathers, and their sublimated activity is unconsciously directed against those who oppressed their mothers and limited their own freedom.

It is funny how staggeringly close Deutsch comes to a real understanding of the experiences that combine to make women become political. But she does not mean the above positively, because she goes on with this striking description of the feminine woman, the one without the masculinity complex:

The little stenographer who worships her boss, whoever he may be, and who bears with him in his worst moods, allegedly in order to keep her job, the sensitive woman who cannot leave her brutal husband because she loves him ''despite'' (actually because) of his brutality, and the active and talented woman collaborator who devotes all her intuitive gifts to her master's productions, are all happy in these roles and repress their erotic longings. The Slavic peasant woman who lets her drunken husband beat her and declares sadly, ''He does not love me, he has stopped beating me,'' the heroine and the prostitute – all of them are happy or wretched according to the extent of their feminine masochism and the degree to which they can utilise and assimilate it.

In the sexual field, there is also a clear ''division of labour'', in that activity is the man's field and passivity the woman's. So it is utterly insane when in ''modern'' circles...

the view seems to prevail that woman's passivity in sexual matters is outmoded and that now it is the woman who chooses the object and takes the sexual initiative. What takes place here is not, as is believed, the ''liberation'' of woman from a social evil that condemns her to passivity. In the light of psychology, this reversal of roles can be seen in many cases as arising from the interplay of two anxieties: women use activity as a mechanism of defence against the fear of their passivity.

"The masculinity complex" is then an overbalance of active and aggressive tendencies that leads to conflicts with the woman's surroundings, and most of all with what is left of her inner values:

> Another form of the conflict between femininity and masculinity results from the fact that the woman's psychological interest is here turned toward aims in the pursuit of which femininity is felt as troublesome and is rejected.

This concerns not least the woman who has dared to attempt combining motherhood with work that interests her (Deutsch calls it her *career*):

> The simplest example of such a conflict is provided by the mother who, after each success she achieves in her professional activity, or after each ambition-gratifying situation, instead of feeling satisfaction, is tormented by guilt feelings with regard to her children. This category also includes those women who constantly waver between two kinds of duties – those of wife and mother on the one hand, and those of a professional career on the other – and who finds satisfaction in neither... The active woman actually does transfer to other goals psychic energies that she otherwise would spend directly on the objects of her environment, particularly on her children. Conversely, not all her psychic energies are available for these goals, because, as a woman, she has spent them emotionally on more direct object relations.

These "more direct object relations" are the husband and children in a nuclear family. It is on them she has used her feelings, and that is as it should be, in perfect agreement with her natural role in the natural male society. There is something about the fact that she has also used her energy on things such as housekeeping and child-minding, for her husband has not been so impressed by her career that he has taken it into his head to do any housework!

Deutsch refers to "the active woman". For a moment I was tempted to cheat as I did with Karen Horney and change the active woman into the active man – for what would one do with a man who after every success in his work, simply reacted with guilt feelings about his wife and child? I assume he would be treated for masochism. But I did not change the expression because I realised it would be slightly too fantastic to imagine a man in that situation, for how many men come home to the second half of a double job? How many men would be tormented by guilt feelings and think that there was something wrong with *them*, and not with the endless demands of coping with housekeeping, parental duties, appearance, sex and all the rest, apart from the actual job?

The reason Deutsch does not mention any of these things is that she thinks the natural difference in the man's and woman's working life originates from the fact that their abilities lie in different areas. If you neglect that, retribution awaits you. For instance, it awaits those women who –

have brilliantly succeeded in sublimating their masculine activity but are not aware of the fact that *they have paid a high price for it in their feminine values*. Woman's intellectuality is to a large extent paid for by the loss of valuable feminine qualities: it feeds on the sap of the affective life and results in impoverishment of this life either as a whole or in specific emotional qualities...For intuition is God's gift to the feminine woman; everything relating to exploration and cognition, all the forms and kinds of human cultural aspiration that require a strictly objective approach, are with few exceptions the domain of the masculine intellect, of man's spiritual power, against which woman can rarely compete. All observations point to the fact that the *intellectual woman is masculinised*; in her, warm intuitive knowledge has yielded to cold unproductive thinking. [Italics M.M.]

So there is not just a difference between men and women, there is a difference between their thinking, for she says nothing about rationality in a man being cold and unproductive...

But in this argument, for once, Deutsch does not use the word masochism. I would have done so. What else can one call an attitude in which as a woman you subject yourself to a mass of physical chores, rejecting men's privileges and oppressing yourself?

But perhaps that is not quite right. Deutsch suppresses other women, but not herself, for she has been trained as a doctor and psychoanalyst and has written a great many professional articles and weighty tomes.

So: Helene Deutsch says I should not worry in the slightest about my masochism – on the contrary. I *may* be too masochistic, but the risk is not very great, because at the same time I have tendencies to love myself, and that will save me. It would be very much worse if I were not quite masochistic enough or if I suppressed my natural masochism, because I have been given that by Mother Nature herself, a kind of gift from God that I simply have to manage as best I can.

If I had been a man, it would have been a different matter. Then she would have said that I suffered from *moral* masochism, and she would have treated me accordingly. But as a woman, the explanation lies in my erotic life, and so everything is basically all right.

I must admit, however, I cannot quite follow Deutsch in the way she discusses my physical sufferings. I found nothing like a blood-stained earthquake at the ripping away of my maidenhead. Menstruation was liveable with, especially after the invention of tampons had turned minus-days into plus-days. Actual intercourse was very seldom a torment. But, of course, there were births. I admit that it hurt like hell the first time, actually too much for me to feel I was in the middle of an orgy – even a masochistic orgy.

But I may have repressed all that. I will never be able to convince a psychoanalyst like Deutsch that her theories do not fit me, as long as she uses concepts such as repression and the unconscious against me.

Fromm and Deutsch have been more interested in my general functions and behaviour patterns out in life than in my sexual life, although Helene Deutsch does say that it is nature's intention that I be a masochist.

This aspect, on the other hand, is gone into by one of her female analyst colleagues, who seems almost obsessed by my most intimate sex life. Her name is Marie Bonaparte (a very suitable name for an aggressive major-general of femininity). She published a book on female sexuality in 1951; it came out in English in 1953, almost a hundred years after the birth of Freud.

How is it possible, Bonaparte asks in surprise, for a woman to take pleasure in intercourse, and to long for caresses that are not masochistic? Only because the female organism contains masculinity. Woman is in reality a male organism which has stopped developing – a kind of halfway-house between man and child. Nature makes use of the stunted portion of the woman's masculinity, she says, to lead the woman towards eroticism.

This stunted portion of masculinity – also called "in relation to the male penis, an abbreviated penis", also called "a crippled penis", also called "this organ of exquisite male origins" – is our old friend "the little clitoris". The vagina in her language becomes "a hollow penis".

When the woman gets something out of intercourse, this is because in reality she is slightly a man. But in order to become sensitive to the man's real penis, she must, consciously or unconsciously, accept her own masochistic fantasies. For, as Bonaparte briefly and tersely puts it:

Masochism is actually more feminine.

This concerns masochism in all its forms – from the desire to be eaten by the father in the cannibalistic oral phase, the desire to be whipped and hit by him in the sadistic-anal phase, and to be castrated by him in the phallic stage, to the desire in the adult woman to be penetrated and made pregnant by the man who has now replaced the father.

The little girl *desires* her father's assault, and "blows" from his great penis – and if she uses her beating fantasy and the forces of passivity that lie slumbering within her properly, she will succeed in achieving full female vaginality. Because it is all quite natural:

Beating, in fact, is an act preliminary to penetration, to effraction. One knocks at a door before entering. One shakes, if necessary, the lock or key.

. . . and it is necessary that the woman give up both her clitoris and her struggle against masochism. Otherwise her intercourse will be a "struggle between two men", in which the weakest (i.e. the woman) suffers defeat, and in which only the strongest can win the victory trophy: orgasm. She must learn to accept that a penis –

> is neither a whip nor an awl nor a knife nor a cartridge, as in her sadistic infantile fantasies.

But nevertheless, there is perhaps a little in the idea of penis as weapon, for:

> During coitus, the woman, in effect, is subjected to a kind of beating by the man's penis. She receives the blows and often, even, loves their violence.

Otherwise she might be suspected of never having given up her clitoris and thus of not being a real woman. It is masochism which,

> combining with her passivity in coitus, impels her to welcome and to value some measure of brutality on the man's part.

It can be put that simply. I cannot help thinking what a good time I would have had if I had landed on Marie Bonaparte's analytical couch in time. I would have loved not only my masochism, but also all those brutal and ruthless lovers – and they would have loved me. . .

All in all, both Deutsch and Bonaparte wanted to tell me how perfectly I functioned as a woman. This was all the more necessary, since I had just read Karen Horney and found between the lines an indication of exactly the opposite: that all traits called typically feminine, were in reality neurotic.

There are humorous moments in reading Helene Deutsch and Marie Bonaparte, and indeed one could almost die laughing if it were not all so sad. For they are not just two isolated originals. Their books are translated, re-printed, read and used. They are based on one male authority, Freud, and although they out-Freud Freud and paint a female picture that is a caricature, they do so with extra authority: they are women themselves, are they not? They must know what they are talking about.

But that is not so. They are women from a time when women accepted the dogmas of male science uncritically.

We do nevertheless have to take them to a certain extent seriously, because they are not alone. Although they are more consistent than many others, they are two of many who have contributed to the cementing of the old image of women, and are still doing so.

Authors in the women's movement have constantly argued against various cornerstones of the edifice of psychoanalysis, primarily the Oedipus and penis-envy theories. They have done so by setting these phenomena in the context not of our personality structures alone, nor even of "cultural patterns", but far more directly in the context of the patriarchal capitalist society we live in. But it is an argument they will never be able to win in the long run. Psychoanalysis will always have the last word, so long as it can put us down with the charge that we have not all renounced our masculinity-complex, and the promise that they will cure us all.

But what is it they are to cure me of? Not my masochism, of course. Nor my associated orgasm problems, either.

The people who helped me with these were authors of quite a different category. They did not publish academic theories, but extended their practical experiences and handed them on to me. In that way, I realised that I had been sexually oppressed. Why had I not known it before? Because I simply lacked concrete things to strive for. I started finding those when I read the feminist writers who began openly to proclaim that the woman's orgasm comes from the clitoris.

Then contemporary writers on sex told me that an orgasm was not something that came like manna from heaven, but that there really was a *route* up to the top – and that this route went via the clitoris. They said straight out that all women could have orgasms as long as they were stimulated in the right way.

It bolstered me so enormously that I stopped taking all the blame for my fiascoes. It also bolstered me to read in Kinsey that more women had orgasms in the middle of the century than at the beginning of it. (And in Hunt's report it stated that the number had risen even further by the seventies – remarkably enough, with the growth of the women's movement.)

I achieved orgasm. There was nothing wrong with me. Not much, anyhow. Why then bother with the Oedipus complex any more – except to counteract it in one's own children? And why bother about whether you suffered from a masculinity-complex or penis-envy? When it is possible to take things as cheerfully as Rey Anthony, who writes of her encounter at three years old with a little boy, who had ''the oddest bit of flesh protruding from the place where his pussy ought to be''.

10 Parallel Tracks

That slow, all too slow rhythm that I loved because it worked me up so violently, turned out to have a double effect; first and foremost, the psychic effect that enabled me to tell myself I was dependent on someone else's will; but there was also a second, quite different effect – I got a kind of elementary lesson in how arousal functions physically.

I quite simply got to know my own functions in a way I had never dared hope for, as I had never really had the courage to investigate my own body (by masturbating, for instance) – perhaps because I did not seem able to regard it as my own, only as something that was destined for a man. When you get to know your own functions better, naturally you are in a better position to direct your desires towards orgasm. You can try in vain for years to adapt to a hard quick rhythm, just because you think the best thing for a woman must be "what she deserves". Which is usually the opposite of what I need...

It is said that there are people who can achieve orgasm purely psychically just by using the imagination. But most people need physical stimulation. I had been stimulated physically for years, but in a diffuse, complicated way that for several reasons, I could not handle.

This was partly because "technique" had always seemed to me rather crude, anyhow something a hundred-per-cent woman would not need. It was also partly because, even if technique had to be used, under no circumstances could I dream of being the person who taught the technique (which I couldn't have done, either), since that was not in keeping with my ideals. And finally, also, because I had always concentrated my attention on my vagina. Many years before reading Freud, I knew that a real woman has vaginal orgasms. That was... well, that was just something you knew, not something to speculate about.

So my only experiments with my own body involved sticking things up my vagina, from which I gained nothing at all. When either I or a lover did try to stimulate my clitoris, we must have been very clumsy, because the effort always came to grief. The result was that I lost interest in that strange little knob.

On the whole I was incredibly ignorant, even long after adolescence. Once or twice, very hesitantly and solemnly, I confided in a doctor that I didn't achieve orgasms; one gave me hormone pills, which made no difference, and another mumbled something about "something psychological". I had also asked a couple of girls for some advice about how to achieve sexual release, but I never said a word to a living soul about my masochistic desires, because I thought they were the most shameful thing in the whole world.

After the meeting with my black prince, it wasn't only psychic experiences I took home with me, but also physical ones. That was probably the real reason why I made such great strides, for I learnt to combine these experiences with a slow intercourse tempo. When I first tried to float extended between excitement and release, it seemed as if the desire-mechanism was being shown to me in slow motion. So at last I could catch a glimpse of details and focus on what it was that worked for me. It was in spaces in between, in pauses, in waiting times during foreplay, that my sensitivity was sufficiently sharpened for me to be able to localise pleasure points in my genitals.

In fact I think this is a very common experience, probably much the same kind of experience men have when they watch a woman stripping slowly and provocatively in front of them.

That is also probably why "exciting rhythms" really can make music sexually exciting. This goes for music that teases – music in which the notes *don't* come exactly on the beat (as they do in a march), but just off it. What your body is prepared for doesn't happen, so you react as if coming closer to the music with your whole body. Swinging, as they say – meaning that you swing too, you yourself, supplying the rhythm the music cheated you of. That is how I have felt, anyhow, with a lot of jazz and South American music.

I have also felt the same with a great many pictures, in which a line stops or swerves away just as you thought it was going to form a perfect geometric figure. Also with films and books and happenings in which what you expect *doesn't* happen, in which you are put off and have to wait in vain until you notice it in your body.

This is also an experience the doctor-couple, Masters and Johnson, have used in their work with couples who have sexual difficulties. They built up a long carefully worked out programme, in which the teasing technique played a decisive part. They taught their patients to summon up their desire and let it grow and grow – but would not allow them to satisfy it. In that way, they taught many people how to use their sexual excitement.

But of course I did not know anything about that at the time when it concerned me, and although I had heard a few rumours about the importance of the clitoris, I did not believe them. I just thought it all sounded rather far-fetched. In fact, I was astonished when I began to realise that orgasm really does mostly come from the clitoris. I found out about it because at long last I learnt to masturbate. I discovered rather slowly what I had been doing wrong, and I found it hard to believe that I had given up so quickly. Just imagine what I could have spared myself if I had dared take a more thorough interest in the workings of my own body and had not thought of techniques as something "unfeminine"!

Today I can achieve orgasm, occasionally even vaginal orgasm (i.e. probably a mixed orgasm, in which the whole area is involved). But mostly clitoris-orgasms. I can achieve orgasm alone and together with a man. But not always. Often it simply doesn't work, and often it doesn't work without a certain amount of trouble, for one of two things has to be present for it to work, a good lover or some good fantasies. In fact, it has to be a little of both, for if I am with a bad lover, I can fantasise endlessly – but nothing happens.

I do not know whether a bad lover is a bad lover for all women. But I am sure a good lover is a good lover for a great many women. This has nothing much to do with potency, but with a kind of sexual intuition, which may possibly be inborn, like musicality (if it is not just a feeling for other people).

It also has something to do with a certain experience, something to do with knowing how that sort of instrument should be played, and something to do with registering differences from one instrument to another.

Not least, it has something to do with whether you think it is

exciting to get something out of *that* instrument in particular –
to make that person you are with in particular react as strongly
as possible, to make the instrument respond, or as is also said,
to master the instrument...there are many terms.

Together with a good lover, it goes almost by itself, because
he is able and wishes to use physical possibilities in a good way.
But all the same, even with a good lover, physical stimulus does
not work alone. At a certain point, my imagination starts working – and orgasm then comes within reach. It is a perfectly
rigid ritual: physical stimulus – fantasy stimulus – orgasm.
The better the physical contact between me and my lover, the
later the fantasies start, and the shorter the distance between
fantasies and orgasm. But masochism is constantly alive and
kicking.

But it is not like in the old days, when everything ended in
frustrated complaints about never meeting a lover sufficiently
sadistic to carry me into the forbidden room and *realise* my fantasies. Today I know it is enough for them to remain there in
the imagination, to think about, or talk about.

When I am an instrument that my lover masters, I am an
object – even if he does not hit me. But there is more to the
"bed-grammar" than that. What is decisive is that I am no
longer a subject, that is, I am no longer an active creature
acting of my own free will. This is the essential content of every
form of humiliation. I learned that gradually, as I ex-
perimented more and became more advanced, as they say.

It has something to do with the will, that the will is blocked,
or to be more precise, the will, desire, is worked up, but
without getting there. As with Tantalus.

As a masochist, I find myself in the tortuous contradictory
situation that I need an obstacle between my will and my goal.
The more effective the obstacle is, the more overwhelming my
desire becomes – provided the goal is in sight. A moment
arrives when the distance to the goal is the smallest possible –
but the obstacle, the separating chasm, is at the same time at its
greatest. Pleasure (or whatever it is called) is at a maximum of
intensity at that moment, and a short circuit may occur, so the
chasm is crossed and the desire becomes orgasm. This happens
most easily if desire is stimulated at the same time as the way is

blocked. To put it another way – the more I long for the goal, the more emphatically it is indicated that I may not reach it, and what is emphasised is the power-relation, the superior force.

If I am tied up by my lover, the will may simply be the will to be free. Then he can emphasise the sexual content of the situation by drawing attention to all the things I could do if I were not tied up. The situation is thus filled with symbolism, so becomes effective, because there is really nothing especially bad in itself about being tied up, unless it hurts at the same time.

If I am hungry, and at the same time tied up, he can stimulate my hunger by eating in front of me. In that way, he makes my hunger – my desire for food – grow until it too becomes sexual desire; a desire that becomes sexual because the possibility of it being fulfilled is nil, because I am tied up and robbed of the last remains of my subject-character.

The most effective way to use this mechanism logically is for my sadistic (or just interested) lover to titillate me sexually, while at the same time refusing to carry through the titillation in such a way that I achieve release. Thus he can take with the one hand, so to speak, what he gives with the other, and the result is sexual arousal in which I am kept on a level that is a few steps up that path that leads to the top. At that point, the tension between the two poles is so strong that discharge may occur almost without extra physical stimulus. The whole thing keels over and becomes orgasm. Is that a physical or psychological situation? All I know is that what is decisive is my awareness that I can get nowhere despite all my will and all my desire, and that it is a situation based on my being quite consciously degraded, put beyond the pale. I have become nothing.

The physical and psychological thus become two curves that rise together at the same pace, like two parallel lines meeting somewhere out in eternity, somewhere in my head or my body. The place or the moment where they meet is the uncontrollable moment of orgasm.

I can take one or the other curve, according to the situation – i.e. whether I am with a not terribly good (or just very self-absorbed) lover, or with a very good, sensual and physically

orientated lover, who finds part of his enjoyment in that I come
too. But I am unable to be content with just the one curve.
They mutually need each other – and they mutually call on
each other. It is an inbuilt automatic process that I do not control. It starts by itself and I cannot keep it at bay. All strong
physical sexual arousal creates images in my head – just as all
sado-masochistic pictures and masochistic fantasies create
physical excitement. It is an automatic process that works both
ways.

What kind of laws lie behind all this? Why do those two
curves react inevitably by sending signals to each other? Why
do fantasies become body and why does body become fantasies? Why and how? What kind of peculiar parallel system
am I caught up in?

Sometimes I feel like an instrument with several strings over
and under each other: when you touch one string, the others
also sound, and the other way round. It is like a double-
language, in which everything can be expressed in two ways,
and in which you can translate from one language to the other.
Or it is like listening to music smoking hash, when the notes in
the music produce images in your inner eye; every note produces a figure and every shift of tone makes the pictures
change. I hear a chord and am on my way into Aladdin's cave.
I feel two fingers against my clitoris and find myself in the
punishment cell. I hear the word whip in my inner ear, and
note my womb contracting in orgasm.

It is possible that there are many people who are disposed
towards this kind of parallel system, because many people use
fantasy material to extend their physical arousal. Presumably
they do this more or less consciously, or more or less unconsciously. But they seldom talk about it, just as I have never
heard anyone say that he or she is a masochist.

I would like to know whether people who systematically use
fantasies are all ashamed of doing so – or whether this only
goes for those whose fantasies are not included in heterosexual
normal pornography. Anyhow, I do know that I feel that in
itself (regardless of whether anyone in the world knows about
it) it is very degrading. Perhaps that is why I am often filled
with depression at the actual moment of orgasm. Perhaps it is
simply because orgasm is essentially limited when started in the

head in this way. I don't know. In any case, I find it desperate and hopeless that I have to resort to such mad and tormenting fantasies to achieve what should be the most natural thing in the world, sexual release.

So I had to go on investigating the way in which it all functions. To put it directly: what is the connection between domination and sex? Why does blood pour into my genitals when I hear those words – whip, slave, order, discipline, obey, humble, submission... all those terms, all those signals, why do they send the symbols of oppression down into my *cunt*?

11 Not a Word about Women

Wilhelm Reich

At one point, our old friend Marie Bonaparte divulges that she once received a letter from Freud about the "beating fantasy" on which he based his first thorough theory on masochism. It was a letter about the four women who had made up his material.

All four of them were virgins.

This was clearly nothing that gave either Freud or Bonaparte any special qualms. But there was another person who would have gone straight up into the air at that information: Wilhelm Reich.

Reich was trained as a doctor and psychoanalyst, and was as involved in the problems of masochism as Freud was. But he tackled it in quite a different way. Going from Freud to Reich is like going from a hot-house out into the fresh air. Yet for most of his life, Reich kept within the field of classical psychoanalysis, and in all his writings, his respect and admiration for Freud comes through.

Freud was thirty years older than Reich and was Reich's teacher, and Reich adopted all Freud's conceptual apparatus – that the child has a sexual life; that some of it is suppressed (though Reich did not place the responsibility on the development of mankind, but on the surrounding society); that the child must go through an Oedipal stage (though Reich does not say this would necessarily be the case in a culture with freer sexual mores); that the origins of neuroses lie in early displacement of sexuality (though Reich states his sexuality and its displacement in far more concrete and physical terms than Freud does). Reich even adopted Freud's expression "passive-feminine", though without making any more of the connection between the two words.

At a certain point, Reich's development took a different direction from Freud's, and there was an open break between the two of them. What started this break was masochism – or rather, the second explanation that Freud gave for masochism:

that it was due to the death-wish so that masochism was a primary drive and not just something that occurred when sadism was turned in towards the person himself, or when other causes hindered the free development of sexuality.

Reich could not come to terms with the death-wish as an explanation for actual life processes. He also bridled over the way Freud made out such drives to be almost supernatural – Freud says in one place that our drives are "our mythology". Reich did not want mythology as a starting point for his understanding of how mankind functioned. He wanted to find the explanation in basic principles functioning in nature in general, organic as well as inorganic.

It also occurred to him that Freud's death-wish was at variance with the actual principle of cure. For if it was thought that, thanks to the death-wish, people had a biologically defined need to suffer and be punished – well, there was nothing to do but sit and wait with your hands in your lap. Because they did not wish to be cured, then cure would be at variance with the most elementary principles of life.

This disagreement on the one hand gave support to Reich's independent theories and on the other hand led to an open break with Freud. Reich was excluded from the Psychoanalytical Society in Vienna, and at the same time thrown out of the Communist Party.

The latter is the more surprising. In contrast to Freud, who treated his patients as individual isolated people, Reich saw neuroses as inextricably tied to the social system. Society created the neuroses – and usually also made it impossible to cure them, for the number of successful treatments was actually not great. Freud's method was reserved for a small privileged minority. Reich realised this when he was in charge of a sexual advisory clinic for the less well-off, where he found insight into the incalculable part that the patient's milieu, living and housing conditions played in their neurotic sufferings.

Reich's life was like an exciting and tragic movie (a film has actually been made on him and his theories, called *WR – Mysteries of the Organism*). He fled from his homeland, Germany, after the Nazi takeover, fleeing from country to country. He was in Scandinavia for a while. Everywhere he came up against suspicion and persecution. He ended his days in an American prison. Before that he had time to experience the burning of his books, not only in Nazi Germany, but also in God's Own Country – and as late as 1956 and 1960.

So Reich, like Freud, was very interested in the problems of masochism, and many a time concerned himself with them. Like his own teacher, he was mystified by the circumstance that pleasure can be sought in aversion and pain. He tells how he made his first dent in the problem:

A drastic occurrence in my practice cured me from an erroneous formulation by which psychology and sexology had been misled. In 1928 I treated a man who suffered from a masochistic perversion. His lamentations and his demands to be beaten blocked any progress. After some months of conventional psychoanalytic work my patience wore thin. One day, when he asked me again to beat him, I asked him what he would say if I actually did. He beamed with happy anticipation. I took a ruler and gave him two hard slaps on the buttocks. He yelled loud; there was no sign of pleasure whatsoever, and from that time on such demands were never repeated. However, his lamentations and passive reproaches persisted. My colleagues would have been horrified had they learned of this happening; but I had no regrets. All of a sudden I realised that – contrary to general belief – pain is far from being the instinctual goal of the masochist. When beaten, the masochist, like any other mortal, experiences pain. A whole industry (procuring instruments of torture, pictures and descriptions of masochistic perversions, and prostitutes to satisfy them) flourishes on the basis of that mistaken concept of masochism which it helps to create.

So it is not the actual pain the masochist experiences that is pleasurable. Freud had long realised that – he said that naturally it was not the pain itself the masochist experienced as pleasure, but only something connected with the pain. Freud said so, but with his usual "but nevertheless". In a way he continued to make it his starting point that it was the pain that created the pleasure, and so the puzzle lay in how anyone can experience aversion as pleasure.

Reich was equally bewildered, but after speculating for a long time, he arrived at a concrete and vivid comparison, which for him became the starting point for an understanding of what happened. It was an image of a hog's bladder. How – Reich asks – would a hog's bladder behave if it were blown up from inside and could not burst? If the inner pressure made the surface expand, but without bursting it into shreds?

His answer is that if the hog's bladder were brought to such a condition of intolerable tension, (and if it had human qualities), it would at first lament, and in its helplessness, seek reasons for its sufferings outside itself. Second, it would beseech someone outside itself to stick a hole in it. What it could not make happen from within, spontaneously, it would passively and helplessly await from outside.

Reich says that to a very great extent the masochistic person can be compared with the poor hog's bladder that cannot burst. A person can be pumped full, so to speak, from the inside, if that person's sexuality does not develop freely, so the pressure becomes too high, sexual energy pressing from within and striving for release – but there is a surface that stops it and inhibits natural release.

What kind of surface is it that will not give way?

It consists of muscular tensions the neurotic person has built up, which Reich called character armour, because they surround the whole person like armour. They are for protection against attacks from outside – and also against attacks from within, from the forces and urges that for one reason or another are not allowed their free run.

The idea of character armour is one of the determining elements in all of Reich's understanding of the human being, both the psychically ill and the relatively healthy. He arrived at this through his practice as a psychoanalyst – when dead moments arose in the treatment. This often happened, and according to classical psychoanalysis, the analyst should then sit quietly and wait for the patient on the couch to produce free ideas and associations. If the patient said nothing, this was due to the fact that there was some resistance in action. The patient was resisting bringing out the material that should come out if he were to be cured. Perhaps the patient was filled with unconscious inner desire for punishment, suffering and death. In any case, there was nothing to do but sit and wait – often for hours on end. The analyst was waiting for *words*. The patient was to *say* something. The decisive experiences from childhood had to be transformed into words. They *were* verbal by nature and could not be separated from the verbal form the patient gave them. The analyst had to wait until the patient told him about the "primordial scene" that had started it all.

Reich tried sitting and waiting, too. Perhaps he was of a more impatient nature than Freud, or anyhow more practically minded. There had to be another way to progress further. Instead of waiting for the unconscious to show itself, he started concentrating on *the resistance*. Nor was he content with seeking out the resistance as it appeared in words or suppression. He transferred his interest from the psychic to the physical.

He discovered that even if the patients said nothing, something happened all the same, their neck muscles tensed, for instance, or their fingers drummed, or the patients smiled over-politely. Reich started working on these external traits. He drew the patients' attention to their peculiarities. He imitated them, to show them clearly what they did. He worked on their facial muscles. He got them to exaggerate their own peculiarities by teasing and provoking them – to get them to work their way through them in some way.

On one very instructive occasion in Copenhagen, he treated a man who was obviously putting up strong resistance against having his homosexual fantasies revealed. This resistance was expressed in an extraordinary rigid neck posture (a physical posture that Reich compares with psychic resistance by using the term "stiff-necked"):

After an energetic attack upon his resistance he suddenly gave in, but in a rather alarming manner. For three days, he presented severe manifestations of vegetative shock. The colour of his face kept changing rapidly from white to yellow or blue; the skin was mottled and of various tints; he had severe pains in the neck and the occiput; the heart-beat was rapid; he had diarrhoea, felt worn out, and seemed to have lost hold. I was disturbed. True, I had often seen similar symptoms, but never that violent. Something had happened here that was somehow inherent in the therapeutic process but was at first unintelligible. *Affects had broken through somatically after the patient had yielded in a psychic defence attitude.* The stiff neck, expressing an attitude of tense masculinity, apparently had bound vegetative energies which now broke loose in an uncontrolled and disordered fashion. A person with a balanced sex-economy would be incapable of producing such a reaction. Such a reaction presupposes a continuous inhibition and damming-up of biological energy. It was the musculature that served this inhibitory function. When the muscles of the neck relaxed, powerful impulses broke through, as if propelled by a spring.

What Reich had discovered was that resistance is not only an inner psychic phenomenon, but also something quite physically tangible. This is due to the unconscious being stored, so to speak, in constant muscular tensions. They are created in the moment in childhood when the child has to suppress a violent emotion, for instance, because it would be punished or treated coldly if it gave the feeling free run. Instead of screaming and kicking, the child tenses a part of its body so that nothing happens. So unconscious suppressions or "knots" of the past are at the same time emotional and physical; the muscular tension *is* the repression, the body remembers on its own.

So Reich was able to treat resistance not only by talking to his patients, but also by tackling their muscular tensions, because they had the same function – inhibiting the patients' basic biological reactions: anxiety, hatred or sexual arousal.

When he treated muscular tension correctly, the patient was taken back to the stage when the energy had been suppressed, so it was made possible for him to live out the old feelings – by screaming and kicking at last.

This often involved the patient simultaneously remembering the event that had started the whole thing – but not always. Reich considered conscious remembrance as secondary. What was decisive was not that childhood memories could be put into words, but that the patient lived through what had been suppressed.

Reich says that to a certain extent, especially under stress, we all generate muscular tension, which allows us to function in our milieu, allowing us to take a stand on two fronts, one against the pressures surrounding us, and the other against the pressures from within, from emotions, for instance, that we dare not release at the relevant moment.

In neurotic people, these inhibiting mechanisms can be so hard, rigid and chronic that they make the whole person stiff, both physically and mentally. All his reactions become rigid, says Reich, and he will always react in the same predictable manner. He becomes incapable of reacting differently to new things, because he has always been steered into the same few limited paths. A person may become so rigid that he can no longer react naturally. This may, for instance, cause his sexual energy, his feelings and aggressions to implode, like a hog's bladder that has been pumped up but cannot do anything with what is happening inside it, because it is surrounded by an armour of muscular tension.

As these muscular tensions have almost the same function as emotional inhibitions and repressions (Reich calls them *functionally identical*), it was possible to start in both places, to make mental life function by making the body function as well as vice versa.

Making the body function consisted quite basically of starting massaging, working through and loosening muscular tensions. Reich started from above and outside and gradually worked towards the centre. Psychic forces were released at each point – for instance, when the tensions were relieved round the eyes, in the neck or in the speech organs. This was not ordinary massage – he used all his experience and knowledge as a psychoanalyst, because he always had to be in touch with the violent and often dramatic events involved when muscular tension was relieved.

One of the last places he set about was the respiratory organs because neurotic patients were hardly ever capable of deep relaxed breathing. Last of all came the loins.

Reich had established that none of his neurotic patients was capable of experiencing a sexual orgasm. That was true for all women, but to start with he did not say it was true for all men. This surprised him – until he started differentiating between two kinds of orgasm in men: one a surface, technical orgasm with potency and ejaculation, and the other the real, deep orgasm that involved the whole person.

Reich thought the last and most decisive obstacle that had to be overcome was a patient's inability to experience this kind of orgasm. This was crucial not only for the patient to be able to live a normal sexual life, but for the organism itself to be psychically healthy. So orgasm became at the same time a *goal*, and the *yardstick* of whether the patient was functioning healthily and normally in general.

Reich went as far as considering orgasm as the actual life principle, which was not just a beautiful image to him. Orgasm energy could be measured. He found it in all living organisms, and he discovered it vanished when the organism died. It could be accumulated into tension that demanded relief – orgasm. The energy that Reich measured he called the vegetative or bio-psychic energy, or later orgone energy, life-energy itself. On this basis, he created his orgasm formula: tension-charge-discharge-relaxation. This was a psychic sequence of events, an electro-physical course of events, a course of events that placed the human being in accord with the universe; in orgasm, the human being swings together with the whole of organic nature.

The function of character armour was finally to inhibit energy which for one reason or another the neurotic person was afraid of.

It is necessary to understand these experiences of Reich's and the way he built them into his own theories, if use is to be made of his theories on what masochism is. For masochism is absolutely central here. Reich found a masochistic period in all his neurotic patients shortly before they approached their ability to experience full orgasm – and thus a cure. This moment was the most critical in the whole treatment, and also the moment in which there was the greatest risk of the patient committing suicide.

So masochism was not a primary urge, but an event. It was the patient's last rejection mechanism against orgasm, immediately before the armour was broken through. The forces about to break through were so violent that the patient had to guard against them, so that they would not sweep him away. They were too strong for him to bear. So he had to strengthen his defences at the eleventh hour – and he did that with masochism.

This brought Reich closer to a theory on the nature of masochism. Now it was a question of finding out first where these very powerful inhibiting mechanisms against natural development stemmed from, and second why the masochist reacted with his special form of defence, namely seeking pleasure in its opposite.

Freud had explained that masochism either was a primary urge in itself, or it stemmed from a primary sadistic urge that had turned inwards, so the sadistic impulses were turned inwards on the individual instead of towards the world outside. In addition it was generally accepted that the individual seemed to feel driven to repeat past experiences although they were of a painful, tormenting and unpleasant nature. But no one had yet explained why this compulsion to repeat arose – unless one took refuge in the theory of the ancient death-wish. But Wilhelm Reich produced quite a different theory.

It was wrong to say that the masochist experiences pain as pleasure. The masochist strives for pleasure like everyone else, but a disturbing mechanism sets in that causes his striving to go awry. So he experiences what other people find pleasurable as something repellent as soon as it grows to a certain intensity.

The masochist does not strive for pain at all. He suffers from a particular inability to tolerate psychic tensions, and also from an excessive aversion that is greater than in any other neurosis. To find the reasons for this particular characteristic, Reich does not start studying sexual masochistic perversion (that occurred only in a minority of his patients), but what he called the characterological basis, i.e. the particular way in which the masochistic person's armour has arisen.

The rest of this chapter is almost exclusively about one single male patient whom Reich used as the starting point for his research. His theories are based on men, so I have to use the pronoun *he*.

As a small boy of two or three years of age, the patient had been playing in the garden and had relieved himself in his trousers. There were guests and the father was furious, carried him in and put him on his bed. The boy turned over on to his stomach and waited for the beating with a mixture of curiosity and anxiety. The father hit him hard, but the boy felt relieved all the same. A typical masochistic experience, says Reich, and the first of that kind.

He goes on to say that analysis showed that the boy was expecting something worse. He had turned over on to his stomach to protect his genitals, which was what he was worried about, and that was why he found the blows on his backside a relief. Reich concludes from this that masochistic punishment is not synonymous with the punishment the masochist fears, and which has now been brought out into the light, but is a milder punishment-replacement and thus a special defence mechanism against punishment and anxiety.

Later in the course of treatment, there was a long period during which the patient provoked the analyst in every possible way. As usual, Reich used the "transference situation" in the relationship between patient and himself to try to retrieve the template for the patient's behaviour in general. So, why was the patient provoking him? Not to force out a punishment that would relieve his sense of guilt, but to put the analyst (and with him the patient's father) in a bad light. The analyst was to be forced to do something that would really justify a reproach of the following kind: "You are bad, you don't love me. On the contrary, you are cruel to me, and I have a right to hate you."

Behind this reproach lies a childhood experience – grief over the child's love being disappointed, or anyhow not satisfied. The masochist has a great need for love, so great that in reality it can *never* be satisfied. The child may have sought in vain to express his desires and needs in words, but the adults did not understand. Finally the child gave up, with a feeling of – it's no use. The result can be an inner sense of deadness.

To this is added a fear of contact with objects, experiences and people. Reich says later that

the core of this fear of genuine, spontaneous psychic contact with people and the world in general is the fear of orgasmic contact.

In other words, it is an orgasm anxiety, which leads on to the most important part of character analysis – and the most difficult.

Among the difficulties arising as completion of the analysis approaches are the following: the things the patient tells the analyst become more and more superficial; the patient dreams and fantasises about *falling*; he becomes more reserved; he avoids mentioning his sexual desires; he has fantasies about physical dissolution and mutilation (not to be confused with castration); he flees from sexual and other relations with the world; he re-experiences reactions from childhood, and renewed feelings of emptiness.

At this point, it is important to analyse the patient's attitudes and feelings during masturbation and intercourse. It appears that he inhibits or slows down arousal in one way or another, for instance by moving violently and jerkily instead of gently; he tenses his pelvic muscles without knowing it; he often stops when orgasm feelings approach, instead of allowing their arousal to grow in a spontaneous rhythm. He avoids giving himself up to the orgastic experience of anxiety because it would overwhelm him.

This patient complained a great deal – at the beginning of every session – about spending several hours every day masturbating with strong masochistic fantasies. The more this masturbation increased his tension, the more intense was his feeling that he was in a "masochistic morass". At the same time, he made indirect reproaches against Reich and provoked him with childish defiant reactions. Reich interpreted this behaviour as a demand for love. The patient needed proof of love.

But why did he make his demands in such a devious way? Why did he not demand love directly and undisguised? Why was he complaining?

Reich maintains that his complaints meant the following: "Look how unhappy I am. Love me. You don't love me enough. You treat me badly. You must love me, or I'll punish you."

Reich interprets the provocations and sufferings from imaginary or real disappointments as due to a need for love that is so excessive that it cannot be satisfied. A need for love of this kind is particular to the masochist and is not found in other neurotics. But what does it mean?

It means that the masochist is disposed towards anxiety.

Reich believes that the masochistic character is trying to relieve an overwhelmingly threatening anxiety with the aid of an inappropriate method – by making demands for love in the form of provocation and defiance. It is characteristic that this defiance and provocation are directed at the person the patient loves and from whom he is requesting love. This means his fear of losing love increases and his feelings of guilt increase. The more the masochist tries to get out of his painful situation, the deeper he becomes stuck in it.

But why is this particular combination typical of the masochistic character?

Reich says that excessive demands for love stem from anxiety about being left alone, which the masochist has experienced very early in childhood. So he cannot bear the thought of being left alone, and so cannot give up the object of his love, so cannot do without the person he loves as a protector. He tries to hold on to this person by being humble and wretched. Many of these patients develop a sense of being alone in the world.

This is also one of the reasons why skin-eroticism plays such a special part in masochism. Many people maintain that the skin of masochists must have a special quality, as they feel pleasure in being beaten. But Reich says this again is due to anxiety over being left alone. All of the masochist's need to be brushed, pinched, whipped, chained, to bleed, etc., have one thing in common – the skin grows warm. When a masochist desires to be whipped, the pain is something he puts up with, it is the warmth that is decisive. Cold, on the other hand, is the worst thing he knows. For the same reason, masochists love lying in bed – the warmth of the skin is a satisfaction in itself.

This has a physiological explanation, anxiety producing a contraction of the blood vessels so the sufferer feels cold, whereas heat and desire involve expansion of the outer blood vessels and a greater flow of blood through the tissues. The same thing happens with physical contact with a loved one. Why it soothes anxieties is presumably because the central tension is relieved as the outer blood vessels expand. This is synonymous with maternal protection and the opposite of being alone in the world.

On several occasions Reich found further reasons for this excessive need for love. Anxiety about being left alone set in at a certain moment in which violent aggression in the child and curiosity about sex was met with serious disapproval by the parents. As a child, the patient was perhaps allowed to eat as much as he liked (the oral), his mother was perhaps much interested in his faeces (the anal), but when sexual curiosity arose – for instance, he started taking an interest in his mother's sexual organs and wanting to touch them – then strict parental authority was enforced.

Incidentally, and without further comment, Reich finds that excessive need for love in the masochist may have its empirical roots both in the child who has been given too little love and in the opposite, the child who has been over-indulged. Both, he says, are the result of child-rearing practices characteristic of the patriarchal system.

From there, Reich goes on to concern himself with the sexual structure of the masochist in its proper sense. (This is still in discussion of the same man, although it includes experiences of many more patients in analysis.)

At one time during treatment, when the patient started functioning sexually and could, for instance, achieve an erection, he could not free himself from the feeling of inner struggle and of something peculiar when he approached a woman. He kept complaining that he could not get out of the "masochistic morass". The least difficulty meant that he fell back on his fantasies. Primarily, he felt himself still to be a masochist, despite all outward signs of success.

This was also the moment when one day on some excuse he showed his penis to Reich, who interpreted this as an exhibitionist manoeuvre – the patient felt compelled to show his genitals.

This is a trait Reich regards as something quite peculiar to the masochist – that the genital phase (i.e. the part of the child's sexual development directly connected with sexual organs) has started in an exhibitionist manner. The child has shown off his genitals. But this exhibitionism has been soon condemned and suppressed, with the result that development has stopped at that point. Because exhibitionism has been met with disapproval, the masochist cannot later bear being different from others.

He may, for instance, not be able to bear being praised. He

is usually unsuitable as a leader. He has a tendency to denigrate himself and talk about himself in derogatory terms. This patient expressed himself in the following way: "If I remained a good student, I would feel as if I were standing in front of a crowd showing my erect penis." The fact that the child had been stopped from showing his sexual organs has caused severe damage to functioning and self-reliance later on in life. This becomes yet another source of tension and suffering that once again reinforces the masochistic process.

Another patient said that he could not bear praise because it made him feel he was standing there with his trousers down. Reich interprets this as follows:

The child's sense of shame over his faeces is transferred to his sexual organs. As all forms of praise represent encouragement of exhibitionist tendencies, and as they are linked with anxiety over standing out, the masochist has to make himself small to avoid that anxiety. He then has another reason to feel set aside, and that again produces the need for love. Other patients dare not show their love openly, or dare not show themselves naked. They are afraid the women will be angry and punish them.

All this together creates a sense of a lack of inner co-ordination and often a painful image of one's outward appearance. So patients also often become "bureaucratic", as this neurotic expressed it – unnatural and stiff.

But the determining question for Reich was – how is it that the masochist regards an increase in sexual excitement as something he is averse to?

Reich gives the following explanation:

The masochistic character is based on a very peculiar cramped condition not just in the pyschic apparatus, but also in the sex organs. This cramp will in time inhibit every strong feeling of pleasure and thus transform it into dislike and aversion. To return to the patient, the first time he experienced intercourse, he had an erection but dared not put his penis into the vagina. The explanation appeared a short while later. He was afraid the pleasurable excitement would be too violent. After a few experiences of intercourse, it turned out that he found far less pleasure in intercourse than in his masochistic masturbation.

It now turned out in continued analysis that some time between the ages of three and six the patient had been afraid to go to the lavatory. He was afraid that an animal would crawl up behind him. So he started holding back his faeces and at the same time was afraid it would come in his trousers. For if you do it in your trousers, then father will come and beat you. He had learnt that when he was three.

The next thing was that he grew afraid that his rectum or his bladder would burst – in other words, he would not be able to hold back and so he would again be beaten by his father. A hopeless situation, says Reich, and a situation whose causes were clearly social, not biological. Because he felt relaxation and satisfaction in connection with the evacuation process, he also regarded it as something he would be punished for. Out of fear of punishment from his father, he started punishing himself.

This simple process was for Reich far more important than identification with the punishing father and the masochistic attitude to an anal superego. He says straight out that this story (like so many others) shows that it is wrong to take a ninety-eight per cent interest in the detailed work of analysis and only two per cent in current methods of child-rearing and the damage parents do.

Thus psychoanalytic discoveries led Reich to criticise the patriarchal family's way of bringing up children.

He says that typical toilet-training methods, usually practised too early and too strictly, inhibit the child from proceeding to the genital phase, in which the sex organs take the central place. The resulting fantasy of being beaten is clearly aversion-accented and at first stamped with anxiety. It would be wrong to say that this aversion to being beaten is transformed into pleasure. What happens, on the other hand, is that anxiety about being beaten stops the feeling of pleasure developing. It is a mechanism that has arisen on the anal level in connection with the rectum and which is later transferred to the genitals.

Even later, this mechanism joins typical puberty difficulties, in which it is reinforced by barriers created by society – anxiety, for instance, over evacuation at an unsuitable moment. The patient has to be on guard against these dangers all the time, and so never has time to relax.

When during the course of treatment, this patient began to develop normal sexual feelings, he had an erection – but this disappeared during intercourse. It was the same when he masturbated – at first he had normal sexual fantasies, but as his excitement grew, they were transformed into masochistic fantasies. As soon as what the patient called "the feeling of melting" started, he grew afraid. Instead of letting himself go, he produced a kind of cramp in the lower pelvis and thus transformed the pleasure into the opposite.

He described how he experienced this "melting feeling" very clearly – normally a pleasurable orgastic feeling – as unpleasant and anxiety-provoking. He was afraid his penis would melt. It felt like a sack filled to bursting point.

This process of pleasure being transformed into the opposite the moment it becomes too strong, Reich describes in the following way:

1. I strive for pleasure;
2. I begin to melt – that is the punishment I am afraid of;
3. I must kill this feeling, if I want to save my penis.

In the masochist, it is this very feeling of melting before orgasm that is regarded as a threat – in contrast to other neurotics, in whom the sense of pleasure is still pleasure, but is resisted by anxiety, and in whom there is a decisive difference between pleasure and aversion. The anxiety the masochist has acquired in connection with pleasurable feelings at evacuation, means that genital pleasure, which is far more intense, will appear to be a danger or a punishment.

In this way, the masochist moves towards the expected pleasure – and suddenly finds himself face to face with aversion. It looks as if he has striven for aversion, but what really happens is that the anxiety always obtrudes between, so he starts regarding the longed-for pleasure as a feared danger. The end-pleasure (a Freudian expression) is replaced by an end-aversion. So there is no such thing as compulsive repetition "beyond the pleasure principle"; what happens can be explained within the framework of the pleasure principle and anxiety over punishment.

Both during intercourse and masturbation, the patient avoided every increase in pleasure. One day he expressed it in this way: "It is impossible to let these sensations take their course. It is absolutely intolerable." So he had to go on masturbating for hours and inhibit the pleasure every time he approached a climax. Because of his anal fixation, he was only used to limited pleasure, of the same "degree" as that he could feel when he evacuated. He was not used to sexual pleasure that rose steeply to violent heights – that frightened him. So the inhibition is not only a result of anxiety, but creates anxiety itself, and thus the chasm between tension and release is increased.

But how can it be that the beating fantasy sets in or is reinforced just as orgasm is in sight?

It is interesting to see, Reich says, how the psychic apparatus tries to reduce the chasm between the tension and release with the help of the beating fantasy. The patient said: "My penis seems all boiled to me. With the fifth or sixth blow it is bound to burst, as will my bladder."

In other words, the blows (beating) will produce the release he had been hindered from creating any other way. If his bladder and his penis burst and he ejaculates, it is not his fault – because it was not he himself, but his tormentor who created the situation. So the desire for punishment means the following:

Despite everything, its function is to create release – via a detour and by shifting the responsibility on to the punishing person. This is the same mechanism as if the patient had said: "Beat me, so that I can get relaxation without being responsible for it." According to Reich, this is the deepest meaning in the beating fantasy, and it also involves two images, one the idea of anxiety and punishment, and the other the image of end-pleasure and release – and the two ideas are gathered into the image of bursting.

When Reich worked with masochistic patients, he aimed primarily at making the orgasmic function normal. Other elements in his therapy were also involved, but his experience was that once orgasm functioned normally, the patient very rapidly improved. None the less he did not say one could be sure of a cure until the patient had lived a satisfactory sexual and working life for some time. He continued to regard masochism as one of the most difficult maladies to cure.

In his eyes, the worst obstacles in the way were past explanations, especially the old Freudian explanation that masochism was due to a biological death-instinct.

As long as masochism is explained by a death-wish, this allows the patient to desire his suffering, and so nothing will ever improve. What was in question was the contrary, to expose the masochist's will to suffering as disguised aggression. Beyond restoring the orgasm function, masochism is to be transformed back to sadism.

Reich summarised his theories in the following way:

1. Masochism is not primary, but secondary;
2. The masochist's sufferings are not desired subjectively, but they do exist objectively;
3. The fantasies have the function of producing release without guilt;
4. All this does not occur outside the pleasure-principle, but within its framework, in that release is synonymous with pleasure.

But there was still something not explained. Despite everything, there was still a striving towards a "Nirvana principle", a striving for dissolution, unconsciousness, non-existence. Was this anything like striving towards death?

After Reich has exorcised the ghost of the death-wish, something strange, and impressive, occurred – he summoned it up again. He said without vanity that he was always prepared to revise his own theories, and that he had in fact found just such a death-wish in his patients.

Oddly enough, this striving usually appeared at the end of the treatment, at the point when the patient was about to overcome his anxiety over orgasm. He very seldom found it in "real" masochists, but more in patients with a few masochistic mechanisms, but who did not suffer from any unconscious "need for punishment". What was the explanation?

To answer this question, Reich tells about a woman patient at the time when her treatment was approaching its conclusion.

Her armour had been almost broken down and her orgasm-*angst* was dominating the picture. Just as she approached the dissolution of her anxiety, she described some feelings she had never had before. She described them as "streaming", and "flushes", and "sweet-like feelings", and finally as an exquisite pleasurable sensation of "melting".

At the same time she started having pleasurable fantasies about a painful operation on her genitals. She said: "It is wonderful. You're dissolved. You die, and at last are at peace." She felt she had become "one with the world", that she heard sounds and yet didn't hear them, that she had lost herself, had become dissolved.

What was decisive to Reich was that she experienced the orgasm itself with the same feelings as those she described in association with her longing for death. Both orgasm and death were expressed in terms of dissolution, losing yourself, melting away. Reich stated quite clearly that this striving for non-existence, Nirvana, death, is identical with a striving for the release of orgasm, in other words, for life's most important manifestation. In this way, he gave the death-wish a positive and life-giving role.

He does not say he has thus solved the problem, but he says the final answer has to come from the biologist not the psychologist. What is in question is what lies behind this striving for relaxation found in all living beings – what until then had been included in the vague concept of the "Nirvana principle". He gave his own interpretation somewhat later, when he had concluded his measurement of bio-physical energy. He set up his "orgasm formula" on a purely physical basis. Orgasm is the charging and discharging of the organism.

By creating this connection between orgasm and cosmic energy on the one hand, and neuroses such as masochism on the other, Reich superseded the common understanding of neuroses as individual problems that had to be treated individually. In the long run, his opinion was that sufferings were due to the way children were brought up in the patriarchal nuclear family, in which punishment was an integral part of upbringing. The nuclear family represents to him the starting point of neuroses, and people who suffer from neuroses are all those in our society who have what he calls "emotional plague'' – i.e., people who live enclosed inside their armour and put all their strength and energy into stopping natural life-forces from breaking through, both within themselves and in others, because they are filled with a boundless fear.

Thus he extends his criticism beyond the nuclear family to the society which has created it and keeps it alive, because the nuclear family is a necessary condition for the continuation of that society within its rigid armour.

Reich is not content to produce this viewpoint as a free floating theory. He tries to substantiate it with the help of anthropology. He was, as were so many researchers of his time, burningly interested in the anthropologists' descriptions of a Melanesian people called the Trobriand Islanders. In contrast to us in patriarchal societies, they lived in what appeared to be a matriarchal society – a female-dominated society. There were no punishments in their methods of upbringing, nor was there any sexual oppression of children and young people.

The salient point was that the Trobriand Islanders knew nothing of neuroses or perversions, nor of the Oedipus complex.

From this, Reich drew the conclusion that it is our society, our culture, that must take the responsibility for our neuroses – and thus for our masochism as well.

So:

Wilhelm Reich says the roots of my masochism lie a long way back in my childhood. But it seems that he is not so interested in my past, all the same. It is my present that interests him, and he really does say that there is a chance I will be cured, even if I do not succeed in remembering what happened that time so very long ago.

He says my childhood lives on not only in my head, but also in my actual body. I can understand that – naturally my sex-life is not just dependent on my head, but also on my body, my whole body, including my loins. It is remarkable that Freud had not thought of that. It means that I feel much safer with Reich. As my body is involved, it seems to me that I am allowed to look over his shoulder. I do not want to abandon myself to an authority which in some mysterious way reconstructs my childhood, in a way in which I seem almost to be left out.

The childhood Reich is interested in consists of some very concrete situations and has nothing to do with an intangible common heredity. I can certainly imagine a whole series of such situations.

Perhaps a stupid nursemaid left me crying because she was being visited by her lover – so I lost the belief that I was loved and then had to provoke people into proving they loved me: that *could* have happened.

Perhaps I was given a spanking at an unfortunate moment when I was very sensitive, or perhaps I was scolded for dirtying my pants, for perhaps it was a very important part of my up-bringing that I be a clean little girl in every way – so I had to pinch my buttocks together and tense my loins for ever in the future. That *could* have happened, and I even start noticing muscular tensions now that my attention has been drawn to them. I notice them when I am sexually aroused – in my loins and down my legs.

Perhaps I inhibit my sexual desires because I was inhibited – perhaps just by raised eyebrows – when I once played with my clitoris, so I never again forgot that that was a forbidden area. I have to tense up – and imagine tortures or punish-ments. Perhaps that is why my system depends on those two parallel curves that run separately and yet have the same func-tions: to give myself permission, although I am really not allowed to.

I also think I am beginning to understand that you can turn your aggressions in on yourself if you cannot express them. If I cannot kick the person who hurts me, then it always helps a little if I can kick a wall instead, although – or because – it hurts my own foot.

In any case, Reich would have liked to help me get my orgasm in order, and he would have reckoned with the rest coming by itself. For him the orgasm was clearly a kind of fuse – that which goes first when there is disorder in the system, and which at the same time, is essential for the rest of me to function.

When he tells me how, after having relieved my muscular tensions, I will feel drawn towards dissolution as if towards a revelation, in which life and death join together and I am dissolved, then I also think I have some idea what he is talking about.

But Reich is dead – so it is hardly likely that I will ever know whether he was right about it all.

It also strikes me that Reich has not said anything special about me as a woman. He obviously did not think of a woman – or women – as anything enormously mysterious. That pleased me – and also disappointed me slightly. For he says emphatically that "barriers created by society" may reinforce the neurotic muscular tensions arising in childhood, to maintain them as unreleased sexual tension.

But he mentions only those which afflict *men*, such as the anxiety over making a girl pregnant. I can imagine, on just this point, that there may be a whole series of barriers created by society especially associated with women.

But perhaps it is quite right that we ourselves try to find them out. Here are some:

The anxiety over *becoming* pregnant. The anxiety over appearing unaesthetic (because we never lose the consciousness of being objects, of being looked at). Anxiety over wetting the bed. Anxiety over tiring our lovers if we cannot achieve release quickly enough – so we are not good enough in bed. And perhaps the general anxiety over abandoning ourselves (because we are afraid it will be used against us if we lose all control of ourselves, for who says that we will then be accepted?).

12 Germaine's Answer – and some other women's

Alexandra and Wilhelm, Kate Millett, Simone de Beauvoir, Karen Horney, etc.

One day a meeting took place between Wilhelm Reich, the champion of the sexually oppressed, and Alexandra Kollontai, the champion of oppressed women, and they started tackling the problems of masochism and sadism together.

It sounds too good to be true, and unfortunately it is not true. The only place the two ever met was in a few pages under the title *The Unfinished Story of Alexandra and Wilhelm*. But the two young people who take on their names in the story really invest themselves in the struggle against their own masochism and sadism.

They live together and have entered a relationship, each with his or her own traditional erotic fantasy-layer. He dreams about tying up girls and smacking them, and she enjoys being held down and screwed.

Wilhelm and Alexandra enjoy each other in this way – until Alexandra joins the women's movement. Then things are no longer so good. They are no longer able to accept each other's roles, and they start losing interest in going to bed together. Alexandra especially can no longer enjoy what she calls her "average masochism" during intercourse, now that she has become aware of how the oppression of women works, and now that she has become used to being active and herself taking the initiative.

Alexandra and Wilhelm try in several ways to bring their sexual life up to date. Instead of Wilhelm being the superactive man on top and Alexandra being the superpassive woman underneath, they experiment with *her* lying on top. But she does not care for that – they should not just exchange roles. That is not where the solution lies. Neither does it lie in using the old roles simply as voluntary roles and making allowances for each other because now there *is* a discrepancy, a dividing line between the way you think and the way you act.

Not until they find out that by lying on their sides, the two of them, so that both can be active, do they begin to feel good together:

> Wilhelm began to see the love he had earlier only caught a glimpse of, especially on occasions when the rhythm became a truly mutual rhythm and not one rhythm being colonised by the other.

And Alexandra? To start with she had to suppress part of her sexuality and maintain a hold on herself if she wished to fight her slavish desires. But gradually things grew better as they became equally active:

> As long as arousal was still under control and movements slow and gentle, there were no problems. But when excitement began to rise, Wilhelm tended arbitrarily to increase the pace and hold Alexandra firmly beneath him. Then everything went awry for Alexandra. To achieve orgasm she had to overcome her resistance and abandon herself to her old passive attitude...

Alexandra and Wilhelm are carrying out an important experiment. They are trying to align their sexual practice with their political attitudes. The story has no conclusion – fortunately, I would say, as it seems almost too nice and simple. These two are also honest enough to admit that they constantly relapse. But they feel they are making progress, and images they previously held as the basis of their sexuality seem no longer to be valid:

> There were no images, and the lack of them was perhaps the beginning of something new and better.

The Story of Alexandra and Wilhelm is clearly autobiographical, but it is anonymous. The authors (there are evidently two authors) have obviously felt no compulsion to reveal their names, which may be a sympathetic attempt to get away from traditional author roles – unless it is simply a reflection of the way masochism has been ignored as a problem inside the feminist movement. In this case, this story is the exception that proves the rule, and with its anonymity confirms the idea that for some reason or other the new feminist movement does not *wish* to tackle the problem.

Even the best feminist books seldom contain anything serious about masochism. There is indeed mention of it here and there, but always from the starting point of Freud and psychoanalysis, always treated as an academic and fairly abstract problem, as if the feminist movement preferred to handle the subject with a pair of tweezers.

Those tweezers may be Freud and his successors, or they may be literature. Kate Millett, for instance, includes some passages from authors which she feels set the tone of sexual politics (and thus are unconsciously myth-creating): authors such as D. H. Lawrence, Henry Miller and Norman Mailer, in which there is certainly writing about experience of masochism. Or rather, about how men experience masochism in women. Or rather, how he-men provoke masochistic attitudes in women, how they wallow in images and fantasies about women who react masochistically to their aggressive-sadistic-male sexuality.

In books, that is.

What feminist authors say *themselves* about women and masochism is very seldom given expression, and then only in passing.

Kate Millett, for instance, includes a passage from Marie Bonaparte's description of how the girl wants to be whipped, beaten or castrated by her father, and how the adult woman wishes to be penetrated. After these quotes, Kate writes:

> Miss Bonaparte, whose own predilections one has little trouble in deducing from her work, takes a strongly prescriptive line with regard to female masochism.

A sharply ironic little remark, but unmistakable: Ha, ha, Marie Bonaparte is just *masochistic*! Forgotten is all sister-solidarity. Forgotten also is the attempt to prove how male society forces women into definite patterns...

There is no doubt that masochism is regarded as rather compromising by the feminist movement. This is quite clear in the anthology *Sisterhood is Powerful*, which includes a list of what stops women joining discussion groups:

Reasons for keeping away:

1. Anxiety over exposing oneself (anxiety that the group will regard you as stupid, immoral, weak, masochistic etc)...

Not because they think that is how things *should* be – but that is clearly what happens in practice. One *is* afraid.

And what did Germaine Greer actually reply to the young girl who asked her how we could start a feminist movement if deep down inside we were masochists?

Germaine was clearly thrown off balance when the question was translated for her. In fact she looked rather unhappy. She replied something like this: "Yes, we know women are masochists – *that's what it's all about*! We've been told we're biologically defined as masochists. But even if masochism exists, that doesn't mean it has to go on existing. And I know that if I'm to keep on dreaming of being raped, then I'd rather die!"

It was a pathetic outburst. You could tell that Germaine was discussing a conflict actually experienced by the girl who had asked the question. Yet I did not think her reply quite honest. She sounded almost as if she dared not take the subject up seriously.

She has not taken it up seriously in her books either, nor is her own question on why we may be aroused at the sight of a Nazi uniform in her book. And yet she says that that's what it's all about...

Why then does the new feminist movement not talk about it? Why are they afraid to touch on masochism?

I do not think this very remarkable. Naturally, women who become conscious of their own roles and the games they have colluded in may well be afraid of finding the remnants of their old state in themselves. For the new feminist movement is simply not one that touches only the intellect, that you can discuss quite dispassionately – it involves the whole person. That is why it may be felt to be necessary to keep masochism at a safe distance, because masochism is the epitome of the imposed perverted femininity women retreat from and struggle against with themselves as the stake. Women have become oversensitive to everything connected with masochism. It is clear to women that this concerns one of the most dangerous of infections, and therefore they are nervous of approaching the problem either from fear of contamination or anxiety over being suspected of being a carrier.

So Alexandra is one of the few people who dares talk openly (if anonymously) about her "average-masochism". She does not simply say how she struggled against it, but also how difficult it was to be wholly rid of it. Why is that? Naturally because it has also *given* her something... something she could use, if not something she can use all her life.

What then has masochism to offer? A little more about that can be learnt from women of the earlier feminist movements. For them, masochism was at least a problem that could be *discussed*. Now and again it even seems as if they were speaking from their own experience – although they say "he" or "him".

The grande dame of the feminist movement, Simone de Beauvoir, is a case in question. She tackles masochism quite resolutely in *The Second Sex*:

We must note first of all that attributing an erotic value to pain does not at all imply behaviour marked by passive submission. Frequently pain serves to raise muscle tonus, to reawaken sensitivity blunted by the very violence of sex excitement and pleasure; it is a sharp beam of light flashing in the night of the flesh, it raises the lover from the limbo where he swoons so that he may be hurled down again. Pain is normally a part of the erotic frenzy; bodies that delight to be bodies for the joy they give each other, seek to find each other, to unite, to confront each other in every possible manner. There is in erotic love a tearing away from the self, transport, ecstasy; suffering also tears through the limits of the ego, it is transcendence, a paroxysm; pain has always played a great part in orgies; and it is well known that the exquisite and the painful intermesh: a caress can become torture, torment can give pleasure. The embrace leads easily to biting, pinching, scratching; such behaviour is not ordinarily sadistic; it shows a desire to blend, not to destroy; and the individual who suffers it is not seeking rejection and humiliation, but union; besides, it is not specifically masculine behaviour – far from it. Pain, in fact, is of masochistic significance only when it is accepted and wanted as proof of servitude.

So it isn't pain itself that leads to masochism...only pain that becomes symbolic.

It is a relief to come across a woman who is just as distant from the paternalistic, apparent objectivity of the psycho-analysts as from the anxious rejection of the feminist move-ment. A woman who is able, and dares, to divide sun and wind equally – and on top of that to analyse such a complicated feeling!

Masochism can for instance become symbolic if it turns into a reflection of arousal at a man's strength, authority and superiority. Simone writes about the French prostitute who is beaten by her pimp and who "is said to like it"!

It must be noted that if for some reason the lover's prestige is destroyed, his blows and demands become odious; they are precious only if they manifest the divinity of the loved one. But if they do, it is intoxicating joy to feel herself the prey of another's free action. An existent finds it a most amazing adventure to be justified through the varying and imperious will of another; one wearies of living always in the same skin, and blind obedience is the only chance for radical transforma-tion known to a human being. Woman is thus slave, queen, flower, hind, stained-glass window, wanton, servant, courtesan, muse, companion, mother, sister, child, accord-ing to the fugitive dreams, the imperious commands of her lover. She lends herself to these metamorphoses with ravish-ment as long as she does not realize that all the time her lips have retained the unvarying savour of submission. On the level of love, as on that of eroticism, it seems evident that masochism is one of the by-paths taken by the unsatisfied woman, disappointed in both the other and herself; but it is not the natural tendency of a happy resignation.

Submission – but as Simone says somewhere else, to be able to forget yourself you must first be quite certain that you have found yourself. Women are not certain. They are still occupied looking for themselves.

This is because the whole of the woman's upbringing has the effect that she must find a man to love her. The girl has learnt that she must wait for love. But before she can have her young man and thus face a radiant future, she is often in the role of a victim:

> The stories of Genevieve of Brabant, of Griselda, are not so simple as they seem; love and suffering are disquietingly mingled in them; woman assures her most delicious triumphs by first falling into depths of abjection; whether God or a man is concerned, the little girl learns that she will become all-powerful through deepest resignation: she takes delight in a masochism that promises supreme conquests. St. Blandine, her white body blood-streaked under the lion's claws, Snow White laid out as if dead in a glass coffin, the Beauty asleep, the fainting Atala, a whole flock of delicate heroines bruised, passive, wounded, kneeling, humiliated, demonstrate to their young sister the fascinating prestige of martyred, deserted, resigned beauty.

A new element now comes into Simone's account; masochism can lead to other rewards ending in pleasure and peace, real privileges, prestige and power. But perhaps prestige and power are not what women are seeking, she adds. Perhaps it is even the opposite. When the woman feels herself tied to her father and strives to gain his love – or win back his love – this is *also* because the father represents her childhood, the time when she was protected by adults. Love would give her her mother back just as much as her father, for it would give her her *childhood* back:

> What she wants to recover is a roof over her head, walls that prevent her from feeling her abandonment in the wide world, authority that protects her against her liberty. This childish drama haunts the love of many women; they are happy to be called "my little girl, my dear child"; men know that the words: "you're just like a little girl" are among those that most surely touch a woman's heart... To become

like a child again in a man's arms fills their cup with joy.

The way she is brought up is the result of the teaching she has taken in with her mother's milk, that love is a woman's greatest self-fulfilment, and that it is her function to sacrifice everything for the man she loves. But:

> Man has no need of the unconditional devotion he claims, nor of the idolatrous love that flatters his vanity; he accepts them only on condition that he need not satisfy the reciprocal demands these attitudes imply. He preaches to woman that she should give – and her gifts bore him to distraction; she is left in embarrassment with her useless offerings, her empty life. On the day when it will be possible for woman to love not in her weakness but in her strength...

On that day it may happen paradoxically that she feels relaxed at allowing herself to be erotically dominated by a man – but it will be hard for her to find a man who can do it. For when she starts doubting the man's superiority, she also starts regarding him as childish, especially when he acts in his masculine role largely in bed:

> assuredly there are certain forms of the sexual adventure which will be lost in the world of tomorrow.

But that is indeed far in the future, Simone says – thirty years ago. And yet it all leads to a confirmation of male supremacy, and the woman only *feels* passive in the sexual act because she *regards* herself as passive beforehand.

This whole chain of frustrations, complexes and guilts is passed on from mother to daughter, and then again to her daughters. For there is an indissoluble link with the upbringing of women – which again has its fixed place in the structure of our society.

Simone, who is a Marxist, is one of the first to combine an analysis of the position of women with an analysis of society. But she is existentialist at the same time. She does not doubt that the woman will eventually break out, even if she cannot suggest a way of doing so, no direct strategy, not even one of urging women to stick together. For Simone, as for existentialism in general, the decisive word is *choice* – freedom of choice, and with that the responsibility for the way you live. "The moment of decision flashes from a cloud of generality and repetition," says Simone, continuing with pride as if she were a feminist of today:

> I shall place woman in a world of values and give her behaviour a dimension of liberty. I believe she has the power to choose between the assertion of her transcendence and her alienation as object.

In other words, she can *choose* whether she wishes to regard herself with the man's eyes as an object and become masochistic – or act herself, be responsible, becoming a subject.

By emphasising that we have the opportunity of choosing, Simone deviates sharply from psychoanalysis, which says we have an inborn biological nature that we cannot escape. But it is possible to be a classical psychoanalyst and yet reject the concept of a "nature of woman". One such analyst does, anyhow, and that is Karen Horney. At a certain moment, she undertook a revision that is almost a *volte-face* in her understanding of women, masochism and the connection between the two. In this way, she has earned herself a place of honour in the feminist movement.

Karen says that the question of female masochism is not simply of medical and psychological interest, but directly concerned with western culture and the actual basis of evaluation of woman as a *cultural* being.

She maintains that there are some things that are very seldom discussed in connection with female masochism (which she accepts as a fact); including the origins of this masochism, and its distribution. In this connection, she asks some questions:

Why is it that so much emphasis has always been put on the difference between men's and women's *genitals* – why have we not taken the other great difference into consideration, that women give birth to children and breast-feed them and men do not? Does motherhood mean nothing? Nor the unutterable happiness of anticipation before the birth of this new creature? Nor the joy when it at last comes into the world and I hold it in my arms for the first time? Nor the profound satisfaction of breast-feeding and the happiness of the whole period when the infant needs its mother's care?

She comments on the basis of many years' experience of analysis of men. She comments on how astonishing is the intensity of the envy men reveal over everything concerned with pregnancy, birth, breast-feeding and motherhood – and breasts. Men, she concludes, have a greater need to denigrate women than the other way round. She also says that in this envy is to be found the basis of one of the most essential things in the creation of culture; namely men's productivity. Men produce because they feel that the role they play, when it comes to creating living creatures, is insignificant.

She also asks:

To what extent has the development of women been accounted for and judged from a male viewpoint? And to what extent has this account thus given a distorted picture of the true nature of women?

She goes on with a third question:

Is masochism principally a sexual phenomenon that touches on "morality", or is it the other way round, a moral phenomenon that also extends into the sexual area? Is it a matter of quite different processes originating in a common process? Or is masochism perhaps a pivot term for a whole series of different phenomena?

The realization of this wide range of masochistic phenomena is more bewildering and challenging than encouraging.

She ends despondently. But it was good that she wrote it – that someone wrote it.

She also maintains that all studies of female masochism have hitherto been done on neurotic women, emphasizing the fact that the neurotic view of the role of women is widespread in neurotic women, but resulting also in finding the same traits in all women – including her good old Russian peasant. But the Russian peasant lived under Csarist and patriarchal sovereignty. Today her grandchildren are Soviet women, who might be highly disturbed at being beaten by their husbands, sign of devotion or not. That is a change that has occurred in *cultural* patterns – not in the *nature* of women.

If we now move from the origins of masochism over to the question of how widespread it is, it is not possible to avoid a whole series of sociological factors. Karen says we cannot study those on our own. We must have the help of anthropologists, as we have to compare our own culture with those of others.

By reading about the Trobriand Islanders, Karen realized that it was necessary to extend her perspective to other cultures. The Trobriand Islanders inspired her, as they had inspired Wilhelm Reich and many other people, because they lived without a number of phenomena otherwise considered part of our common human heritage – especially the Oedipus complex and all the sexual inhibitions, neuroses and perversions that go with it.

But she did not stop at establishing that these traits, and particularly masochism, were culturally and not biologically determined. She wanted to investigate further and outlined a plan for finding, with the help of anthropologists, the connections between culture and female masochism.

She suggested that the anthropologists first investigate the incidence of masochistic attitudes among women under various social and cultural conditions; then try to establish in which special social/cultural conditions such masochistic attitudes among women were common: and in which more common among women than in men?

She suggests specific criteria for such masochistic attitudes, among them whether or not the women appear to inhibit their own demands and aggressions: whether or not they see themselves as weak or inferior; and whether or not they use this "helplessness" as a means of wooing and controlling the other sex?

Karen gives some information on where in her opinion masochistic tendencies in women can be expected to be found – that is, in every cultural circle where one or several of the following factors are found:

1. Blocking of outlets for expansiveness and sexuality.

2. Restriction in the number of children, inasmuch as having and rearing children supplies the woman with various gratifying outlets (tenderness, achievement, self-esteem), and this becomes all the more important when having and rearing children is the measuring rod of social evaluation.
3. Estimation of women as beings who are, on the whole, inferior to men (insofar as it leads to a deterioration of female self-confidence).
4. Economic dependence of women on men or on family inasmuch as it fosters an emotional adaptation in the way of emotional dependence.
5. Restriction of women to spheres of life that are built chiefly upon emotional bonds, such as family life, religion, or charity work.
6. Surplus of marriageable women, particularly when marriage offers the principal opportunity for sexual gratification, children, security, and social recognition. This condition is relevant inasmuch as it favours (as do also 3. and 4.) emotional dependence on men, and generally speaking, a development that is not autonomous but fashioned and moulded by existing male ideologies. It is pertinent also insofar as it creates among women a particularly strong competition from which recoil is an important factor in precipitating masochistic phenomena.

All these factors overlap each other, says Karen. Fierce competition between women, for instance, becomes even fiercer if at the same time other outlets are closed (in professions and occupations, for instance). On the whole there will presumably always be interplay between the various factors. She continues with a section that makes you feel like distributing it in a mass edition, because it describes how masochism may be a necessary protection in cultural patterns that offer us an impossible role:

In particular one must consider the fact that when some or all of the suggested elements are present in the culture-complex, there may appear certain fixed ideologies concerning the "nature" of woman; such as doctrines that woman is innately weak, emotional, enjoys dependence, is limited in capacities for independent work and autonomous thinking. One is tempted to include in this category the psychoanalytic belief that woman is masochistic by nature. It is fairly obvious that these ideologies function not only to reconcile women to their subordinate role by presenting it as an unalterable one, but also to *plant the belief that it represents a fulfilment they crave, or an ideal for which it is commendable and desirable to strive*. The influence that these ideologies exert on women is materially strengthened by the fact that *women presenting the specified traits are more frequently chosen by men*. This implies that women's erotic possibilities depend on their conformity to the image of that which constitutes their "true nature". It therefore seems no exaggeration to say that in such social organizations, masochistic attitudes (or rather, milder expressions of masochism) are favoured in women while they are discouraged in men. Qualities like emotional dependence on the other sex (clinging vine), absorption in "love", inhibition of expansive, autonomous development etc., are regarded as quite desirable in women but are treated with opprobrium and ridicule when found in men.

One sees that these cultural factors exert a powerful influence on women; so much so, in fact, that in our culture *it is hard to see how any woman can escape becoming masochistic to some degree, from the effects of the culture alone*. [My italics]

Thank you, Karen.

But all the same there is still something missing. We still lack, I think, a thoroughgoing account of what masochism does to people. We have circled around it, from many directions, but we have not got right down to the bottom, not plumbed the depths. So long as we have not done that, we cannot quite clarify our own position towards masochism. We must try to find out why it is so dangerous – and so tempting.

For my part, I find this at its most clear in *The Story of O*.

13   The Story of O

The Story of O first came out in 1954 in Paris under the pseudonym of Pauline Réage, published by Jean-Jacques Pauvert, who was also the first to publish de Sade's works.

The first chapter is called *The Lovers at Roissy* and I cannot resist quoting the beginning of it:

Her lover one day takes O for a walk, but this time in a part of the city – the Parc Montsouris, the Parc Monceau – where they've never been together before. After they've strolled awhile along the paths, after they've sat down side by side on a bench near the grass, and got up again, and moved on towards the edge of the park, there, where two streets meet, where there never used to be any taxi-stand, they see a car, at that corner. It looks like a taxi, for it does have a meter. "Get in," he says; she gets in. It's late in the afternoon, it's autumn. She is wearing what she always wears: high heels, a suit with a pleated skirt, a silk blouse, no hat. But she has on long gloves reaching up to the sleeves of her jacket, in her leather handbag she's got her papers, and her compact and lipstick. The taxi eases off, very slowly; nor has the man next to her said a word to the driver. But on the right, on the left, he draws down the little window-shades, and the one behind too; thinking that he is about to kiss her, or as to caress him, she has slipped off her gloves. Instead, he says: "I'll take your bag, it's in your way." She gives it to him, he puts it beyond her reach; then adds: "You've too much clothing on. Unhitch your stockings, roll them down to just above your knees. Go ahead," and he gives her some elastics to hold the stockings in place. It isn't easy, not in the car, which is going faster now, and she doesn't want to have the driver turn around. But she manages anyhow, at last; it's a queer, uncomfortable feeling, the contact of silk of her slip upon her naked and free legs, and the unattached garters are sliding loosely back and forth across her skin. "Undo your

garter-belt," he says, "take off your panties." There's
nothing to that, all she has to do is get the hook behind and
raise up a little. He takes the garter-belt from her hand, he
takes the panties, opens her bag, put them away inside it;
then he says: "You're not to sit on your slip or your skirt,
pull them up and sit on the seat without anything in between." The seat-covering is a sort of leather, slick and chil-
ly; it's a very strange sensation, the way it sticks and clings
to her thighs. Then he says: "Now put your gloves back
on." The taxi goes right along and she doesn't dare ask why
Rene is so quiet, so still, or what all this means to him: she so
motionless and so silent, so denuded and so offered, though
so thoroughly gloved, in a black car going she hasn't the least
idea where. He hasn't told her to do anything or not to do it,
but she doesn't dare either cross her legs or sit with them
held together. One on this side, one on that side, she rests
her gloved hands on the seat, pushing down.

"Here we are," he says all of a sudden. Here we are: the
taxi comes to a stop on a fine avenue, under a tree – those
are plane trees – in front of a small mansion, you could just
see it, nestled away between courtyard and garden, the way
the Faubourg Saint-Germain mansions are. There's no
streetlight nearby, it is dark inside the cab, and outside rain
is falling. "Don't move," says Rene. "Don't move a
muscle." He extends his hand towards the neck of her
blouse, unties the ribbon at the throat, then unbuttons the
buttons. She leans forward ever so little, and believes he is
about to caress her breasts. But no; he's got a small pen-
knife out, he's only groping for the shoulder-straps of her
brassière, he cuts the straps, removes the brassière. He has
closed her blouse again and now, underneath, her breasts
are free and nude, like her belly and thighs are nude and
free, like all of her is, from waist to knee.

"Listen," he says. "You're ready. Here's where I leave
you. You're going to get out and go to the door and ring the
bell. Someone will open the door, whoever it is you'll do as
he says. You'll do it right away and willingly of your own
accord, else they'll make you, if you don't obey at once,
they'll make you obey. What? No, you don't need your bag
any more. You don't need anything, you're just the whore,

I'm the pimp who's furnishing you. Yes, certainly, I'll be there, sure. Now go."

Chateau Roissy is owned by a secret brotherhood, and there Rene abandons his lover to the inhabitants and their régime. Briefly, this aims to turn the women who come there into utter slaves, with the aid of force, whips and rape. These means are used according to carefully arranged and familiar rituals – performed sometimes by the gentlemen, sometimes by the servants – and in the course of a few weeks O has become what they wish her to be. She has learnt to obey the rules of the mansion, which are all concerned with her three orifices – never to close her knees or cross her legs or wear pants; never to close her mouth; always to be dressed so that she is freely accessible, including from behind. The three orifices are the only things of hers that are of importance, so they no longer belong to her, but only to the men. She may not use her mouth to speak with (except when asked to do so) and neither is she allowed to look on a man's face – she may not raise her eyes above the level of his genitals, her lord and master.

Everything goes according to plan. O is trained, and (thanks to an efficient system of expansion) becomes sufficiently open in her third orifice, so can now return home with her lover. The book might well end there, but it does not. Everything that has gone so well with the unreal dream-world of the mansion, now continues in sober reality. In Paris, O has her independent occupation. She is a photographer and lives by photographing pretty young women. But Roissy has not left her. An iron ring on her finger tells the initiated where she belongs, and she still has to obey the mansion's clothing regulations.

O is the property of Rene, and she loves him. But one fine day, he finds a new and sterner lord and master for her, an Englishman, Sir Stephen. Sir Stephen knows how to do everything Rene is too weak to do, and when O belongs to him, she concentrates all her feelings on him.

Sir Stephen treats her with a mixture of chivalry, contempt and cruelty. He mainly makes use of the orifice most subject to shame ("the one she has in common with men"), he whips her or has her whipped, he lends her to others and talks about her in most brutal terms to the others. He even brands her with his own initials – one on each side of his favourite orifice – and has her equipped with a chain fastened to a metal ring through one of her labia.

He has also given her orders to seduce Jacqueline, the prettiest of her models, and O obeys with pleasure, for she herself is much taken with the young girl. O also has a past. She has had women lovers before, though she had never given herself to them, only enjoyed observing their desire. She has also had lovers she has played with as a cat plays with a mouse. But she has never loved anyone seriously until she met Rene – and Sir Stephen becomes her great love. So she also enjoys satisfying Sir Stephen's desire to watch two women in bed.

But one day she realises the reason for the seduction is that Jacqueline is also to be sent to Roissy. The thought fills her with fear – but only at first. After a while, this seems quite reasonable and right to her.

Then one day the climax comes. O is masked like an owl and taken to an evening party. She sits there naked, wearing nothing but the mask, while Jacqueline's younger sister, Natalie, holds her by the chain. The guests look on her with fear, and no one dares speak to her, nor does she say a word. When the night has passed, she is placed on a table, after which Sir Stephen and the host of the party take her in turns.

The game has come to an end. There is no way back. It is hardly necessary to write an ending. There are only a few lines:

> There existed another ending to the story of O. Seeing herself about to be left by Sir Stephen, she preferred to die. To which he gave his consent.

The Story of O is the best pornographic book I know for a sado-masochistic public. Just listen to how O is shown the whip:

> Her hands were still pinioned behind her back. She was shown the riding-crop, black, long and slender, made of fine bamboo sheathed in leather, an article such as one finds in the display-windows of expensive saddle-makers' shops; the leather whip – the one she's seen tucked in the first man's belt – was long, with six lashes each ending in a knot; there was a third whip whose numerous light cords were several times knotted and stiff, quite as if soaked in water, and they

actually had been soaked in water, as O was able to verify
when they stroked her belly with those cords and, opening
her thighs, exposing her hidden parts, let the damp, cold
ends trail against the tender membranes.

– or how the carefully thought out strap system works when O
is to be chained to her bed at night:

. . . caught hold of her two hands. He slipped the catch of one
wristband into the other, snapped them shut, thus joining
the inside of her wrists tightly together; then, raising her
hands, he secured them to the catch of her collar. Which left
her with her hands, pressed palm to palm, at the level of her
neck, as when one prays. All that now remained was to chain
her to the wall, and the chain was there in readiness. He
unlocked the hasp at the chain's upper end and made some
adjustments, shortening it. O was obliged to move closer to
the head of the bed, upon which Pierre had her lie down.
The chain slid clicking through the ring until at last the
young woman could only move to right or left on the bed or
stand erect on either side of the headboard. As the chain was
pulling the collar round behind and as, at the same time, her
hands tended to pull it round to the front, an equilibrium
was struck, bringing her joined hands to lie upon her left
shoulder towards which her head was also leaning. The valet
drew the black coverlet over O.

That is very effectively thought out and very effectively
written. It has the advantage that no details are left to the imagination, so they are very useful to the reader, who can then
use them later on as ingredients in her own fantasies, herself in
the main part.

The same applies to various forms of intercourse, or rather,
forms of rape. There are minute descriptions of how the male
genitals force themselves on to O, how they force tears into her
eyes, when they fill her mouth with a gag that makes her choke,
and she is used by several men at a time.

But what does O feel herself – apart from feeling that she
can do nothing about it? We are not told much about that.
There is free play for every individual reader's imagination,

and this is important – for now it is no longer a question of instruments, or implements, but of most private feelings, and
those would only be weakened if they were bound to ordinary
descriptions. And also, a whip can be described, but how is
pain to be described, except by the pain? How can orgasm be
described, except by an orgasm?

Here and there, it can be read between the lines that O feels
a certain sexual excitement, but nothing direct is said about it.
The only form of desire described is the pleasure she feels in the
knowledge that she is allowed to satisfy the man she loves –
first Rene, then Sir Stephen.

Nowhere in the book is there a vulgar or taboo word. The
whole book is written soberly, as in the opening lines, and from
a linguistic point of view could well be given to any confirmation candidate.

But on another level, the language is used in a very arousing
manner, and that starts at the very beginning of the book.
There is a clearly pornographic effect in the way O is spoken
to. Almost every reference to her is in the form of a command
and is in the imperative form: Give me your bag. Take your
pants off. Get down on your knees. Stay there. Say thank you
to me. . . and so on.

O is the one who hear the orders and obeys them. Another
stylistic feature arouses equally strong sexual feelings in the
reader whose antennae are tuned in that direction. Nearly
everywhere, when O's thoughts or feelings or cries are concerned, she is in the accusative. She is the object in the
sentences – as an appropriate expression of her treatment as
an object by the men in the book. Or the sentences are in the
passive voice, so that the subject is again the object.

She was then drawn to her feet, and they were probably
about to detach her hands so as to tie her to some post or
other to the wall, when someone interrupted, saying that
before anything else he wanted her – immediately. She was
forced down upon her knees again, but this time a hassock
was placed as a support under her chest; her hands were still
fixed behind her back.

Those are O's two alternatives, to be an object or passively to suffer.

The book is the same all the way through. She is tied up, she is whipped, she is put on a table, or allowed to climb out of a car. They leave her lying imprisoned, broken...she is robbed of all independent action – she is dealt with, she is treated by them. Everything is allowed with her. She is allowed nothing. She is quite simply for free usage. They also decide on the details:

Rene was drinking his second Martini and O the grapefruit Rene had ordered for her.

At certain times, they are quite generous, as when O feels like ice-cream with crushed almonds and crême fraiche:

Her request for ice-cream was granted but to coffee they said no.

They are astonishingly considerate on the whole, and keep asking her whether she agrees to their whipping her – as evidence that her submission is voluntary. She signs no contracts, as Severin did with Wanda, but nevertheless it is understood as a contract, and O learns that she can leave. But like Severin, she *cannot* say no – she no longer wishes to say no.

And it was true that she would have to consent, in the true sense of the word consent, for nothing would be forcibly inflicted upon her, she would have first to consent; she could refuse, nothing obliged her to remain a slave, nothing except her love and slavery itself.

The Story of O is an effective porn-book because it is a masochistic pipedream. This is also true in the sense that all the external decoration and male participation in the last resort has only one single function – to set O in the centre, bound, maltreated, raped, yes, but still in the centre. The whole book is about her. She is the main character, and in the last resort everything is staged for her sake. The men are only supernumeraries in the pipedream, instruments necessary for O to give herself fully and completely. So it is not necessary to make the men – though they are the active characters in the book – into anything but flat cardboard figures characterised with features that make an impression on O.

Rene, her lover, is a weak youth, colourless and without will. He loves to see O moaning during the maltreatment of her, and to gaze at the fresh weals with which the whips and scourges ornament her. But he cannot take part in whipping her himself. He has neither enough initiative nor the temperament. He fades into obscurity as soon as Sir Stephen appears, and he sits on the outskirts, smoking and watching as the Englishman exploits O. He is clearly drawn to this authoritarian person almost in the same way as O is herself. It is implied that there is a homosexual link between the two men, but that is not followed up, and it is probably more true to say that Rene has a kind of father-fixation for Sir Stephen. He is thus faced with O in a relationship that has a sibling touch about it – they have their love for Sir Stephen in common, just as Sir Stephen and Rene have their sexual exploitation of O in common. Rene is attracted to power, but never consciously does anything himself; he is only the spectator. So O also finds it easy to change:

> But, objectively now, what was Rene next to Sir Stephen? Threads of paper, strings of straw – such in actual truth were the ties whereby he had bound her to him, and which he had so quickly severed; and that quick, that easy sunderance was what those so frail ties symbolized. Whereas what peaceful security, what reassurance, what delight, this iron ring which pierces flesh and weighs eternally, this mark that will remain forever, the master's hand which lays you down to rest on a couch of rock, the love of a master who is capable of pitilessly appropriating unto himself that which he loves.

We are never told what Rene looks like, and neither has Sir Stephen any kind of face. The only description we are given is of the hands with which he coldly and purposefully subdues. All we are told in general is that he is pale – often even corpse-like, giving him a romantic shimmer, like a Byronic hero or silent Athos, a shimmer which is one of the few banalities in the book, and is connected with a glow of infatuated passion blazing in his eyes, which at the same time grates against his coldness and sternness. Otherwise he is a monolith, like Wanda, unapproachable and unfathomable, and his impersonal rituals and contempt for women are what most appeal to masochistic fantasies. In the very precise description, for instance, of him making O sit and wait, her breasts bared, and quite by chance – either out of distraction, or intentionally – happening to spill ash on to her. Why not – why not spill ash on what is your property, something you can dispose of in any way you like, something you can lend out, especially after you have left your mark on it with your initials, as on any other goods?

It is worth noting that the men in *The Story of O* are not particularly sadistic. They are primarily men interested in making life as easy and pleasant as possible and whose practices work as intended. So they are not particularly interested in degrading O, for instance by giving her hard humiliating work, or dressing her in simple humbling clothing. Her corset is to be laced tightly, not to hurt her, but only because that emphasises her appearance of luxury, as her beautiful dresses made of expensive materials do. They like seeing her walking round looking beautiful, tending the fire and filling their glasses. On the whole, they are not interested in her sufferings, once she has been trained. On the whole, they are busy ensuring themselves a comfortable sex life at not too great a cost, either physical or emotional. Though there is a difference between gentlemen and servants, in that while the servants are satisfied with purely physical exploitation of their rights, the gentlemen also prize the symbolic confirmation of these rights every moment of the day. In this way, *The Story of O* is not simply a wishful masochistic dream, but also a pipedream for the men of our male society, and presumably one sadistic readers can also read with profit.

If the men in this book are pale and colourless, then the external decor makes up for it. Not only Chateau Roissy, which is a truly theatrical dream palace, with its ponderous portal, long corridors and exquisite salons illuminated by the fires in the open fireplaces, but also all the natural scenery. Trees and clouds, autumn flowers and dead leaves, and most of all the constant melancholy sighing of the wind are the inevitable accompaniment to the intense and contradictory but at root always melancholy, feelings obsessing O.

The Story of O is undoubtedly a pornographic novel, but it is also a book about feelings. It is prose, but poetry breathes on every page, sentences folding and unfolding in a long drawn-out lament, which also contains an inexplicable joy – a joy repeated over and over again, illuminated from every direction, so that O (the egocentric masochist) has to turn her feelings upside-down, full of wonder over the enigma of the apparently warring emotions within her.

For a long time, she cannot understand herself. The feelings that pour over her and carry her along are the opposite of everything a chic modern little independent Parisian with a taste for elegant clothes and beautiful women should feel. But gradually, as the story progresses, her amazement and doubts vanish, giving way to great assurance within her.

The Story of O is also more than a pornographic and lyrical book about feelings. These two levels are one with a third, for the book is primarily a novel, that is, an account of how a personality gradually changes. Or perhaps it would be truer to say that it is about how something that has lain slumbering deep down inside her is awakened and unfolds to its full strength – finally to lead her to destruction, to total annihilation.

This is in O from the start, for right from the first pages of the book she is described as a not particularly strong-willed person. From the moment she receives her first orders, she obeys silently and willingly, as if she had only been waiting for this happy moment to comply with a command. Not once does she object or protest. She may plead to be spared, but deep down she does not wish to be. She is never rebellious – although that theme might well have been considered for the book; that of a *will* being gradually broken through punishment for disobedience.

There is scarcely any need to punish O, only to tame her, shape her. When she is beaten this is done to make her position as slave and prostitute quite clear. So there is only one place in the book where instruments of *punishment* are directly mentioned, and that is when Sir Stephen comes back to O's apartment (Rene has given him the key without telling O) bringing with him a choice of whips and straps and putting them on the wall of her bedroom so that they are always handy – and also so that she is constantly reminded of her position. When there *is* mention of direct punishment, it may be because she has ventured to express a wish at an unsuitable moment, when for instance Rene alters an agreement, or because she refuses to touch herself while Sir Stephen is watching. For this is one thing she simply cannot do. She allows the men to rape her, but she cannot exploit her own body herself. That seems perverse to her.

Otherwise O is a born slave, which is also the reason why things go so badly for her, for it is a question of overstepping the boundary:

"You've never imposed physical restraints, for example tied her up?"

"No, never."

"Or whipped her?"

"Never. Though, the fact is —" It was her lover who was answering.

"The fact is," said the other voice, "that if you do tie her up, if you use a whip on her, and if she likes that – then no, you understand. Pleasure, we've got to move beyond that stage. We must make the tears flow."

O's sense of obedience to orders is so complete that she often anticipates orders. Nevertheless (or perhaps just for that reason) as early as during her stay in Roissy, she experiences the moment when she takes whip-lashes as a sign that she is guilty, a sinner:

She felt like a pillar of salt, a statue of ash, bitter, useless and damned, like the salt statues of Gomorrah. For she was guilt-ridden, a sinner. Those who love God and whom God abandons in the darkness of the night, are guilty, they are sinners because they are abandoned. What sins have they committed? They search for them in their memory of the past. She would seek for them in hers.

Just as Kafka's main character K (also a single letter of the alphabet) is driven by an inner force to seek out the court that will condemn him, because he accepts that he is guilty, in the same way O adjusts to her maltreatment as if everything were in order, as if it were logical and just, as if she were aware that she had something to atone for.

But that is only one example of how everything changes key for her. When she returns from Roissy, her friends in Paris can see that she has changed:

> She stood straighter, her gaze was clearer, sharper, but what was downright striking was this faultless immobility when she was still and, when she moved, the measure, the sureness in her movements.

One can read the book as a demonstration of how a person is turned into a masochist. That does not mean the whip-lashes stop hurting. They hurt O just as much as anyone else. No doubt O longs for the whip, but she also fears it as she longs for it, agonising beneath it, crying and begging for mercy – but afterwards she is proud and happy when she shows Jacqueline the marks:

> "He also had me stamped with his initials. The others are whip marks. He generally whips me himself, but he also has me whipped by his negro servant, the woman he has for a housekeeper."

And Jacqueline says in horror:

> "You look as if you were proud of it. I don't understand."
> "When Rene takes you to Roissy, you'll understand."

The first thing O is ordered to do in the book is to hand over her bag. She will have no more use for it, Rene says. Her bag – that is where she keeps her most personal property, her keys, the papers saying who she is. She sits back with no identity. She could be anyone.

That is only the beginning. The brainwashing works quickly, effectively, a process strengthened by its own procedure. She analyses herself all the time. Just as she has to sit in idle nakedness in front of the chateau mirror, looking at herself and her genitals, she has also constantly to observe her own reactions. What she finds is that she is becoming happier and happier, happy over the way she is being used, happy over being whipped, happy over not being allowed to speak and happy not to move:

> The chains and the silence which ought to have sealed her isolated self within twenty impenetrable walls, to have asphyxiated her, strangled her, hadn't; to the contrary, they'd been her deliverance, liberating her from herself. What might have become of her had speech been accorded her and freedom granted her hands, had the faculty of free will been hers when her lover prostituted her while he looked on?

How can she describe the joy, the inner peace and dignity and cleanliness she feels after being whipped and soiled by the sweat and semen of the men and her tears? How can she *explain* at all – do anything else but accept that her happiness is greatest when she is most maltreated, misused and humiliated?

Towards the end of the book, she feels that everything Sir Stephen does to her, he does exclusively out of his own desire. He hits her, so he loves her, just like the Russians who used the whip to show they loved their wives. This argument has its own logic. When O feels pain in her body and degradation in her soul, it is an insurance that he is not acting out of consideration for *her* desires. Only by suffering has she any guarantee that his only motive is his own desire. He makes me suffer, so he loves me. I suffer, so I exist. He misuses me, I see my reflection in his desire, so I am. With no desire of my own, with no bag, with no clothes of my own, with no name except a stray letter, with no other tie with reality except the strongest – pain, about which there is no doubt – then at last I am assured that I am...

At one moment, O is standing naked in a room, two men looking at her, and she is waiting obediently for them to give her orders. But something is wrong. She looks appealingly up to Sir Stephen:

> He understood what the trouble was, smiled, came up to her and, taking her two hands, drew them behind her back and held them pinioned there in one of his. She slid back against

him, her eyes shut, and it was in a dream – or at least, if not in dream, in the twilight of a half-slumbering weariness similar to that one when, as a child, only partially emerged from anaesthesia, but still thought to be unconscious by the nurses, she'd heard them talking about her.

Not until the moment O (I) becomes freed of her body, of the use of her arms, of the right to decide for herself, of the right to her own desires – not until the moment I (O) lose my identity, do I find my own identity. Not until that moment is there no longer anything to doubt. Not until that moment have I found my place in a system. Not until that moment can I be certain that there is a system, that the world follows a law, that it has its own order, and that I have my place – my rightful place – inside that order. At last I can be secure, strong, bold, proud, clean, filled with a great inner peace. At last I find myself – because I have lost myself. At last I have become – O.

O – a letter, impersonal, the name of anyone.

O – a hole, eternally accessible to men; O, a sexual symbol, a symbol that women are for men to empty themselves into.

O – an object, a creature that can only be dealt with.

O – a zero, a creature with no identity.

O – the complete form, the circle that encloses the world, that finally contains the world inside it; O, the vanishing-point, back to the womb, into the peace of non-existence – death.

The name O is a brilliant invention, but there is no doubt the author chose the pseudonym with equal care. The surname Réage also means several things at once. The word *réagir* or *react* lies in it – that is how you finally react when the right influence is there. The words *reaction* and *reactionary* are also there – for O's compulsive submissiveness goes against all the ideas we live by in Western democracies, in which every human being is born free and equal, and this freedom and equality must not be suppressed. *The Story of O* says the opposite, that some people, possibly all people, are born into inequality and bondage, and can only be happy by losing their false freedom and equality and giving themselves over to submissiveness and slavery.

The first name, Pauline, is probably not simply the name Paulhan, whom some readers guessed to be the author of the book, but also the word *pauline*, i.e. originating from the apostle, Paul. It was Paul who shaped the Christian church's anxiety-ridden, hate-filled and oppressive attitude to women, the attitude that still strikes hardest in Catholic countries such as the one O was born in, but which to a lesser degree lives on in all Christian countries, where women almost rhymes with sinning and women must therefore atone for being women, just as men have to atone for knowing them... "Wives, submit yourselves to your husbands, as unto the Lord. For the husband is the head of the wife, even as Christ is the head of the church: and he is the saviour of the body", as Paul says in his letter to the Ephesians, whoever they were.

Finally, the first name says quite clearly that the author is a woman.

I know a great many people who have read *The Story of O*. Most of them at some point or other (possibly to draw attention away from what has touched them about the book) start discussing whether a man or a woman wrote it. The publisher of the book does so, too. He argues that it is a woman, for who else but a woman would have thought up the down-to-earth little matter of Rene's slippers getting worn out and needing replacing?

Naturally that is silly and not what the argument is about. The argument is really about whether or not a man could possibly be thought to imagine himself into the soul of a slave – and the usual conclusion is that he could not possibly.

If I were to put my oar in, I would maintain that a man wrote the book. But my arguments would seem unimportant to those who usually discuss the matter. I imagine that the great interest in anal sex is especially masculine. I also know that men are traditionally interested in seeing girls fondling each other. A great many pornographic magazines profit from this curiosity: two girls in bed are better than one, so what matter if they're lesbians? Finally I think that men to a far greater extent than women consider the female genitals as something that stamps woman as a lower inferior creature, and so they use, for instance, the ban on wearing pants as the central symbol of their own power and woman's total subjection.

But never mind. The question is whether men or women are best at imagining that women are born slaves. I think they are

equally good, for men and women are equally deeply im-
pregnated with the idea that that is what women are like deep
down inside. And that is the determining factor here.

So we can go on arguing until Doomsday about whether *The
Story of O* was written by a masochistic woman or a sadistic
man, by a sadistic woman or a masochistic man, by a homosexual of either sex, or just by a man or a woman in a *male
society*. For *The Story of O* is simply the story of woman as male
society sees her.

That female image has been built up through the centuries,
over thousands of years, like an enormous collective work of
art. But there is one place where the rays seem to focus into one
burning point and then spread out again into a radiant spec-
trum of colour – in psychoanalysis. If one looks a little more
carefully, it turns out that O is in such complete agreement
with the theories of psychoanalysis that one might think she
had been model for Freud, Deutsch, Bonaparte and the rest.
What they didn't manage Pauline Réage did, turning theory
into flesh and blood. That does not mean we have to presume
the book was written by a psychoanalyst, only that it is
evidence of how systematically and decisively this view of
women has been drummed into our heads.

O has everything. She is the unaggressive, passive, penis-
less little creature adapting to the role offered to her. She
accepts all pain as part of her condition. She has an unconscious need for punishment, connected with the fact that
her original sadism has turned inwards to become masochism,
thanks to the correct method by which she has overcome her
Oedipus complex: a father-fixation all her life draws her
towards father-figures, whereas she despises her mother and
with her all women, whom logically she must betray. She is
faithful to her feelings, and she has no especially strong
superego, which is demonstrated by her accepting no morality
except what at any given moment she feels most fits the occasion. She is basically a narcissistic creature reflecting her body
and feelings, but she has learnt that she is forbidden to touch
her clitoris. She can play with women, but only give herself,
and thus know fulfilment as a woman, with men.

O has probably been led astray by a masculinity complex for
a while, into living an active, independent self-sufficient life,

but is happily cured on the way. So as a reward for curing her, the men can enjoy her new ego, an uncomplicated little sexual creature who does not start arguing with them, and whose charming purity they can go on sullying, so they can have sexual intercourse with her – which they could hardly have had with an equal liberated woman whom they respected, but could not enjoy as men.

O becomes the image of the *natural woman* and many readers will feel (whether they dare admit it openly or not) that it is good and right that Jacqueline also goes to Roissy and that little Natalie is developing healthily, as she so clearly longs to be there, and that all genuine women belong there – and O too must go back. Readers will feel all that, and trust their feelings, for feelings are natural, and anyone who doubts feelings, and starts talking about feelings being influenced by external forces, is at best a cold and bloodless creature in the clutches of the intellect.

When I first read *The Story of O,* it filled me with a mixture of sexual excitement, horror, anxiety – and envy. I read it many times, each time with the same feelings. But gradually, as I had the good fortune to plunge to some extent into acting out an "Imitation of O", my envy, anyhow, lessened, because no one imitates O without overstepping a boundary into a state which is not particularly enviable.

But I must still say that Pauline Réage is right – the description is correct and I understand O. I understand her pride in the weals from the whip (the same as pride in a bruise on arm or throat, only more violent, more serious. He owns me. I'm worth owning. Look what he makes me put up with. Look how strong the man who loves me is. Look I'm valuable. I *exist*.) I understand that O comes to feel an inner peace, strength, dignity, security and psychic energy in this peculiar way, an energy that is nothing like anything else I (O) know.

But in contrast to O, I have long been sharply conscious of what the game is *also* about and what price has *also* to be paid – that it is a game with high stakes, and you never get anything for nothing. O does not know this. But Pauline Réage knows very well, which is why *The Story of O* is such a strong book, because she shows both sides, the gains *and* the losses.

How does O pay?

She pays with herself. O sells herself.

She sells her own body, the right to her own body, her own pleasure. She sells her ability to speak – when only once she is asked to, all she can produce is a few cliches. She sells her relations with other people, for she lives isolated from the world about her. She particularly sells her relations with other women, for she can only betray them, just as they can only betray her. She sells her ability to stand on her own. She sells her ability to act, and her will, her responsibility and her individuality. She sells her emotions and finally her own death. She has nothing left.

And what does she get for it? Is her story one of a mystic experience, a consciousness-expanding trip? Is it a legend of martyrdom – a religious paradox? Is it the old old story about having to lose yourself in order to find yourself?

Beneath those stares, beneath those hands, beneath those sexes which raped her, beneath those lashes which tore her, she sank, lost in a delirious absence from herself which gave her unto love and loving, and may perhaps have brought her close to death and dying. She was – who? Anyone at all, no one.

On the way, O feels a security she cannot do without and cannot acquire in any other way. But at the bitter end, she is alone, disguised as an animal, chained by her genitals, dumb, without feeling. If it were ever a good trip, it ends as a bad one. She has given herself up and has received nothing in exchange. Only the rest of them have gained. O has been cheated, by the men who use her, by the women who (like Natalie) hold her firmly by the chain in her genitals, by herself – by me. By all of us who in glorious unison listen to our feelings in the firm conviction that our feelings are our own, and define her as Woman.

I have kept back *The Story of O* for so long because I know no other book expressing so well all the contradictions involved in our image of womanhood. It features them so sharply and intensely that we cannot avoid feeling them in our bodies and deep down in our souls. What shall we do about those contradictions?

O gives us a kind of answer, for she lives out what many of the rest of us have vague dreams about. Her story can teach us something about ourselves – what we must expect if we join in on male society's idea of what a woman is. It is a *fable about women*. But it will never come up with an unambiguous answer. If offers no solution, only a question mark.

So we shall have to continue concerning ourselves with *The Story of O*, and I know no book that should be more central for the feminist movement to commit itself to, among other things, to be able to answer the young woman at the meeting with Germaine Greer.

PART III

14 Masochism is Several Things

Dear unknown and anonymous young woman, whose face I could not even see – I only heard your voice, and that this was important.

You asked the feminist movement a question. Did you benefit from the answer you were given by Germaine Greer?

That would surprise me. If Germaine would rather die than go on dreaming about being raped, perhaps you feel you too should prefer to die? Or anyhow keep quiet next time. But neither of these is a particularly constructive solution.

Germaine's reply bears the stamp of a reaction to one who enters a forbidden area. I think you must consider the possibility that the whole feminist movement has always been secretly afraid that one day someone would come and ask that question in public, thus exposing us, like the boy in *The Emperor's New Clothes*. Exposing the fearful truth about the feminist movement.

For of course, you are right: how can you maintain that you desire freedom and equality, when fundamentally you are a slave?

We have all been frightened of what would happen if we started admitting to ourselves and to others that a great many of us are masochists. We do not seem to have been able to afford to face the question in a period of mobilisation, in case it might recoil on our morale. But I am no longer so afraid, so I wish to try to answer you, because I think we are in an untenable situation involving far too many hidden conflicts.

Not because I have found the solution to the "riddle of masochism" that no one else has been able to solve. This is no story with a happy ending. But nevertheless, perhaps you can make use of it.

Anyhow, I do not think we have finished with masochism yet, despite all that we have learnt about it.

Masochists . . .

What did you mean exactly when you used that word? What

did Germaine mean when she answered you? Are we using the word in the same way? Have we made it clear what we mean by it? Or are we simply continuing to use a word we have been given?

Once long ago, I found out there was something called masochism, and simply being given a name was liberating. Today I hardly know whether I wish to endorse the concept of something definite we can call masochism. It seems to me to move and change all the time.

What have we learnt about this "masochism" – except that it concerns a deviation, a speciality, a perversion, a neurosis; except that it is something to do with a desire for pain or subjection, psychically or physically, in reality or in the imagination? We have been given many different theories:

Masochism arises from a need for punishment. It is an expression of guilt. It is due to a very high orgasm threshold. It is due to a very low orgasm threshold, so that everything becomes sexualised. Our senses have become blunted, so we need strong nourishment. We inhibit ourselves because we are afraid of orgasm. We are afraid of freedom. We need to return to our childhood, because we once received a psychic shock. We once received a physical shock that remained in our bodies. It is just as normal as everything else. We are simply natural women. We share a destiny with all oppressed people. We have an excessive need for love and warmth. We are afraid of being left alone. We dare not let our aggressions loose, so have turned them in on ourselves. Like all living beings, we strive towards annihilation and death. The word masochism is a pivot term...

It is not very remarkable that we have such mixed feelings about our masochism and such an unstable sense of where we actually stand, when masochism, as distinct from most other deviations, is proclaimed to be both good and bad. We cannot even say masochists of the world, unite, or form a masochists' liberation front. We have enemies everywhere, both those who wish to throw us out into the cold, and those who pat us on the shoulder and tell us not to worry about it. As well as those who profit from our masochism.

But with so many quite different theories, there must be something that does not fit. So I don't think there is any point now in studying any *more* theories on how masochism arises. That is why I stop here, instead of burrowing further into any more research. I believe it would be far more useful to clarify how masochism *works* – how it affects us in practice. For I think one thing is certain, and that is that in one way or another it harms us.

I think we can go no further without tackling the actual *concept* and examining it.

So:

Does the concept of masochism involve different elements?

If this is so, we have to examine its individual parts separately instead of allowing them to cluster under the same umbrella, and then discover the function of each one. What place do they take in our lives? Is it a reasonable place?

If it is not a reasonable place, to whose advantage is that? What are the consequent disadvantages? And what can we do to change the situation?

Could it be that we can be masochists and still form a feminist movement?

To systematise these elements, I suggest we start by distinguishing between two *main forms*: sexual and authoritarian masochism.

We are used to mixing these two forms together. I have done so myself when writing this book, but I had to describe how I experienced things. Now I would like to say what I think today. The most important conclusion I have come to is that it is this *confusion* of the two forms that makes masochism so harmful to us.

An authoritarian masochist is a person like Scherfig's missing clerk, and Kafka's main character, K. You are an authoritarian masochist if you pay homage to an authority that puts you down, making you into a cipher, a letter, a zero; if you do everything in your power to observe the laws against you and if you seek out subjection and bar all ways that lead to freedom.

Then you love your own subjection, and the proof is that you protest if anyone calls it subjection, that you maintain that this is how it should be, that you personally actually like it best that way.

But – are there really people who love their own subjection? Are these not just words?

Probably no one does so consciously, but there are a great many people who unconsciously cling to their own servitude. There are a great many people who prefer to live in that mousehole, shuddering with anxiety at the thought of sticking a nose out into the sun.

In everyday speech, they are perhaps not called masochists but martyrs, which means that they irritate us, because in one way or another they always ensure for themselves a great deal of extra attention. Everything is about them, them, them...

They pity themselves – in order to be pitied. They apologise for themselves – so that someone will protest and praise them. They make themselves small and weak – and get someone to help them. They stay in the background – so that someone will feel bound to push them forward. They seek impossible situations in which they are *bound* to suffer defeat, and preach almost exultantly that they are always persecuted by fate. They always turn the other cheek – especially when someone is looking.

But they dare not plumb the depths to find the real reason why they need the attention of others so badly, which is that they do not believe in themselves and so do not reckon others can either. When they do not believe in themselves, it is because they dare not stand on their own two feet, or choose for themselves, or act themselves and take responsibility for what they do. They have to put that responsibility on to other people, whom rightly or wrongly they regard as authorities they can adapt to. That involves a certain convenience – but comes back on them because they thus become weaker and more uncertain than ever. That makes them trust the evidence of love and respect they receive from others even less. It is a vicious circle.

Despite all their self-pity, they would protest violently if anyone said it was true that they were sick, and should, for instance, go to an analyst. That would be far too risky, and so they prefer to creep further into the mousehole and leave it to others to decide for them – a spouse, a church, a powerful organisation, a law-and-order system.

Are they sick? Should they seek treatment?

That depends who they are – and who shall determine it. A businessman or a political leader in that condition would be declared ill and sent for treatment. A bank clerk or an industrial worker would be quite a different matter, for they would cope with their jobs well enough. What is necessary for the one is not considered necessary for the other, because people can be treated differently. So you may easily believe you are healthy but just unlucky, or for some purely personal reason inadequate – even if in reality you are sick, judging by the yardstick that is used for individuals of another class.

But authoritarian masochism is not simply a question of individuals. Authoritarian masochists seldom appear alone, they generally live in groups. So there is little point in sacrificing a great deal of time and money on patching up the health of an individual, because then it is never clear whether there is a collective cause for the sickness.

Naturally the individual is sick, presumably barricaded inside an armour that prevents free movement, and presumably incapable of coping with freedom, because the individual is not accustomed to freedom – *because it has been forbidden and still is so,* both for the individual and the group.

But which whole groups of people are collectively afflicted by authoritarian masochism?

They are the oppressed groups, groups that are defenceless – or imagine they are – because of their race, their colour, their class, their sex, because they are a minority, because they are ruled by a colonial power. Or because of their age – because they are children, for instance.

Who has not been a child, and what child does not live in an authoritarian system? The nuclear family is still a system in which some have rights and others do not, and where the differences are clearly marked, not least because the ruling group – adults – has the physical strength, the money and the support of the law, i.e. the power. When you have power on your side, you also have right – and in matters of doubt, power steps in.

The heads of families, generally without making it clear, teach their defenceless subjects how the power system will function later, out in society. Bringing up children is essentially training in obeying authorities. The person who does not obey will be punished, or perhaps just ignored or loved a little less, while the person who is well behaved is rewarded, or perhaps noticed or loved a little more. Praise and punishment are similar means of upbringing, for both indoctrinate the child that it cannot expect to be judged by its own norms and desires, but from above – according to the norms of the authorities.

It is said that children love authority and need it, and that is probably not entirely untrue. You love what you know – as long as you know nothing else. Security and protection also often follow on the subject-relationship (although power can also be used so conditionally that the child simply has no idea where it stands).

But when a child brought up in an authoritarian way grows older, conflicts often arise, because it may rebel against just those points on which authorities make the sternest demands. It is said that that is quite natural and simply puberty. It will pass.

Some become rebels, others drop out, others become normal active people as they should – all according to their dispositions and the system they live under. But there are also those in whom subjection has got into the bloodstream to such an extent that it becomes necessary to choose new authorities – a righteous father-boss, a firm mother-wife, or a law-and-order system in which everything is in its right place, including themselves. They live with their obedience and precision. They become good at saying thank you, and lying there tidily when the consultant does his rounds. They become dutiful officials and silent workers on the assembly line. They take life as it comes, and never dream of protesting, despite the fact that the good things in life are so unevenly divided. There are the authoritarian masochists who voluntarily seek to be put in a pocket.

Whole groups of people – races, minorities, classes – may also arrive at the age of discretion, but that is not considered a natural transition. This is something the authorities have foreseen, and they do what they can to prevent the oppressed from becoming too dissatisfied. They ensure that people have other things to do. If their actual work does not tire them sufficiently, their leisure is occupied with entertainment. The object is to prevent the oppressed from thinking too much and talking to each other so they risk finding out that they have sufferings – symptoms of oppression – in common with a huge number of other people.

There is also a good chance that they will not be seriously dissatisfied. In every power system that has functioned sufficiently long, power ends up rendering itself superfluous, for it has achieved the most effective means of maintaining the status quo – this is collective authoritarian masochism and is also called *false consciousness*.

False consciousness functions with the help of a mechanism that makes the oppressed take on the oppressors' ideals and values quite voluntarily – which is not that difficult, as they have taken them in with their mother's milk and then in kindergarten, school, training and through the mass media, which are all shaped according to the needs of the ruling group. Everywhere it is drummed into their heads that the rulers are the great ones, strong and admirable, and that they themselves are less admirable and weaker and almost by nature eternal children, who would never manage on their own. Just as their labour is exploited by the ruling class, so will their culture also be that of the oppressors: the history books are never about them, nor are portraits ever painted of them, nor are they heroes in films, and the law and police are not theirs either, but are used against them. There is nothing else to do but fit into your place and believe that is the place you like above all others. You even end up believing you have had the same chances of being successful as your rulers – but purely personally you have not been quite so lucky.

So you voluntarily introduce a series of symbols for your acceptance of oppression, which you do not call oppression, but *life*. The symbols vary according to what kind of group you belong to, but their meaning is the same.

You roll your eyes and bare your teeth in an Uncle Tom smile that confirms that you are pleased to be a slightly stupid, but hard-working and humble slave, and when you have to say thank you politely, you say: "That's mighty *white* of you!", even if you are black. You buy picture magazines and read about upper class parties, so you can confirm your conviction that people are different. And you subscribe to the paper that presents your employer's case.

Every oppressive system obviously has advantages for the oppressors, but there are also advantages for the oppressed, as long as they react with authoritarian masochism and identify with their own oppressed status. There is not much to speculate over. Things will be arranged for you, for there are rules and policing systems for everything. As you have nothing to say, you do not have to speculate on what you should say. When you have no choice, you need not choose. That can also be quite a comfortable existence (apart from having to toil away for your daily bread). You avoid stress and stomach ulcers anyhow (or get them from other causes than your superiors do...).

Oppressed minorities also often have some special privileges that their superiors do not have. They are allowed to wear colourful clothes, while their oppressors usually resemble people in uniform. They are allowed to clown and even make jokes about the ruling power, thereby ensuring that they work off steam, and so need not be taken seriously. Or they are allowed to sing and dance and even cry when they are sad (about being oppressed, for instance), while the rulers must ensure they do not lose face. So there are certain advantages – particularly if you have a good and kindly oppressor, which you often have as long as the oppressor sees the advantages of being relatively good and kindly, which means as long as it pays to be so.

However, even among oppressed groups where everything apparently functions as it should, disorder in the system may arise. This happens when rumours that there are other systems in the world and that this is not freedom penetrate right through everyday toil and evening entertainment down into the mouseholes. Then the oppressed will react as they have been trained to do – they will enforce law and order and attack the rumour-mongers to keep them quiet, for there is nothing that strikes the oppressed so hard as being told they are oppressed and not free. They must distance themselves from the jail-breakers. Are we no longer good enough? Are our life styles and mouseholes no longer good enough? Are you going to make people *dissatisfied*?

Thus the authoritarian masochists defend themselves against every tiny seed of rebellion. It is necessary to maintain the last shreds of self-respect, for how could you bear being told that you have been living a lie and have been a puppet in the hands of authority?

But should the information spread and the rumours about

there being another freedom grow stronger, and should they be followed up with training in living in the sun, with a growing internal solidarity and with renewed self-respect, then authoritarian masochism can be cured and be succeeded by a political struggle for freedom, and then the forces that were previously used to reinforce oppression can be used against it.

So the cure takes place both on a theoretical and a practical level. It demands *knowledge* of how your own system works and where in reality you are placed in it. It also demands *training* in thinking, speaking and doing things yourself, together with other people, from the slightest everyday thing that is filled with new meaning, to joint common actions. Then authoritarian masochism can be transformed into its opposite: rebellion. The first step is decisive and is in reality a cure:

Admitting that servitude is not freedom; and feeling that freedom is better.

Then you stop talking about something being "mighty white" and instead start saying black is beautiful, or talking about sisterhood, or about solidarity of the workers.

But it is kill or cure, for when the rulers can no longer rely on the false consciousness of the oppressed which saves so much money, trouble and police energy, they must bring the whole of the power apparatus into action. What happens then is not only a question of solidarity and the will to fight in the oppressed, but also a question of arms and the balance of power.

It may end with the rebellion being crushed, but that does not mean authoritarian masochism again sets in. When the will for freedom is once awakened, it survives, if only in an underground movement.

But in those people who have never got as far as tasting freedom, masochism may be strengthened, so they are forced to creep even further down into their mouseholes and to talk even more loudly about how they like it best down there. So they die, more or less, leaving behind a bundle of gaudy clothes and a few beautiful laments about life that divides good and evil so inscrutably – life, destiny, the greatest authority.

Do you think I have cheated – that this has nothing whatsoever to do with masochism?

But it has. It is masochism when you *choose* servitude and oppression – perhaps from resignation, as long as there is no choice; perhaps from ignorance, because you think there is no choice; perhaps from indolence, because rebellion is difficult and troublesome; perhaps because you have got used to being held down, so your neck has grown so stiff it would be painful to raise your head. The result is the same: oppression has got into the bloodstream and servitude has made you into a slave.

That is what they say about us. They say we have always lived with bowed heads, and so we *must* have been created to be put down. It must be something *in our nature* that makes oppression our special form of freedom... because we are created for masochism. It is a very common logical failing – it begs the question. But it is clearly very usable...

You can be cured of your authoritarian masochism and nevertheless suffer from regular sexual masochism. That is quite a different illness.

While authoritarian masochism attacks the head and heart and presumably a number of precise places in the body, and is difficult to cure on an individual basis, it is hard to imagine how to treat sexual masochism collectively – because that lies in the genitals of the individual person. Neither is there a definite cure for it. There are various possibilities – though how good they are is unfortunately another matter.

What then does it mean to be a *sexual masochist*?

It means that I feel *sexual* excitement, ultimately crowned by orgasm, from pain, compulsion or degradation – whether occurring in my imagination or in reality. It is largely secondary whether I am sexually aroused by being whipped, or by thinking that I will probably shortly be whipped, or by imagining that I have just been whipped, or by the sight of a whip, or just at the word *whip*. They are all one and the same thing. Fortunately, I almost said...

But there are some distinctions that must be made. There exists for instance a purely sensual enjoyment in slight pain – a nail scratching your skin or sharp teeth nipping your shoulder. Isn't this a form of masochism, if I enjoy something that hurts? No, not necessarily. I think it is a purely sensual pleasure of the same kind as when I drink something bitter, or have a lot of pepper on my food, a different and slightly acrid flavour that makes me feel more awake. It does not become masochism until the feeling takes a short cut somewhere up in my head, where it is sliced in two by a sharp knife and sent down to my cunt: then it has become a symbol, not simply a sensual feeling. Then it suddenly concerns two people, myself and another pair of eyes watching me: look how he treats her (i.e. making me into an object); look how she can't do a thing (i.e. stopping me from being a subject).

Whose eyes? My own? No, that is not enough. Another person must be involved, not necessarily the person I am with, so it is possible we become three. The third person may be a man I have seen on the bus, or Marlon Brando, or a fantasy figure. It may also be the person I am with, but then he usually has to be embellished slightly. For it first becomes a matter of masochism the moment I either experience or myself invent *another person's conscious awareness* of what is going on.

But what is it I feel then – is it really pleasure? I don't know, and perhaps this is a linguistic problem, for in reality language is poverty-stricken. Pain is not pleasure, nor is shame or anxiety. It is nothing to smile or be free and light and joyful about – on the contrary. But perhaps you could say it gives me a safer feeling that I *am*. It hurts me, so I exist. When I cry, I am in no doubt that I am alive. I wish I could be so certain in a less complicated and life-denying way.

I think there are two main ways of experiencing sex. One I imagine as a beautiful, organic, sensual form unfolding like a flower, growing like a wave and bursting into fireworks. The other goes the opposite way, has to be scaled and narrowed down and compressed, as it can only find release if it goes through the eye of a needle.

Both ways can be used and both methods are effective. Perhaps I should not think so much about whether I use one method or the other. There is at least an advantage in my masochism, in that it gives me orgasm. Perhaps I should try to create a more functional relation to it, cultivate it with slightly lighter mind, and instead of feeling it an enormous burden, manage to regard it as a chance as good as many others, and try to give it the conditions to flourish.

In any case, I think I have a duty (or desire) to experiment, instead of pitying myself. I could try putting an advertisement in the paper or a pornographic magazine – imagine if a real live sadist were waiting just round the corner!

Sadists and masochists should be able to live happily together, the experts say, but the condition is that they meet. It will no doubt be a long time before the state undertakes a contact-agency, even in liberated Denmark, the pig-sty of Europe.

Unfortunately. For it is a fearful burden to have to make such a contact yourself. Imagine the risk. Naturally the sadist also runs a certain risk – that I don't come back again. But that nevertheless is slightly smaller than the risk I run, if I am lying there tied up and he actually *uses* the whip and I find it horrible and unbearable and simply not what I had imagined.

Quite apart from the risk that he might run off with my money, or take photographs which he can later use for blackmail – because I'm so deathly afraid of being exposed as a masochist...

Also is it really true that a proper sadist is what I need? Is it perhaps more of an "erotic samaritan"? Or would it be even better if there were a brothel where I could buy myself a couple of hours in a torture chamber in safe circumstances?

I don't really think so. A man who does that for money or out of friendliness would certainly lack the inner glow needed for it to be serious – without it becoming too serious. It would become nothing but a half-hearted game, lacking the spark of mutual honesty.

Another question is whether the sadist has any use for me at all. It would be more logical if he preferred someone who hated it, rather than one who liked it. Presumably the truth lies somewhere in between, that he prefers someone who is in agreement – so at intervals he can overstep the boundaries of the agreement.

But that boundary does not tolerate being overstepped too far. If I did dare initiate such experiments, perhaps I would get a stomach ulcer from wondering whether I *dare* take this fantasy into reality. On the other hand I would guarantee myself a great deal of new material for my fantasies, and then perhaps using *them* would suffice alone or together with a partner who extracts just as much out of fantasy games as I do.

On the other hand, if I do venture to leap, I will perhaps find that the distance between my fantasies and reality is so great that I lose my illusions, and thus also my fantasies.

So I risk being left with neither one nor the other... well, I'll face that when the time comes. There must be some way out even from that situation, if it results in sex becoming less terribly important than it was, then there are fortunately other things to do in life.

It is easy to say what advantage my sexual masochism has to offer, it gives me orgasm. But what about the men I am with – is it also an advantage to them?

Not much, I think. Even the men who are sadists are usually so in a different way from the way I am masochist. The chances of my finding one tailor-made for me, so that our mutual neuroses for once "fall in line", are negligible. For all the others, it is bound to be a mixed blessing to be with a woman who tries to force them into a rigid pattern in which they do not feel at home, and who is constantly taken up with herself.

It also entails some distinct disadvantages for me – apart from being troublesome and dangerous, and possibly hurtful and unpleasant in other ways, which must not be forgotten.

It is not enough simply to have an orgasm. Orgasm is necessary, but insufficient. I almost think it is not only on the men's side that there are two kinds of orgasm – a technical superficial one, and one that is real and all-embracing. All too often I have found that what ought to be end-pleasure becomes confused with end-aversion, so in the actual moment of orgasm I catch myself thinking – never again. Never again, if it has to be this way... But you always forget that soon afterwards.

I most often have that kind of dispiriting orgasm if my partner has not been a particularly good lover physically, so I have had to run mainly along my mental track. Whereas I can *approach* an unmixed end-pleasure, when sexual arousal does not need to draw so much on my fantasies that it approaches an intellectual achievement to obtain orgasm.

In the course of time, I have had so many experiences of that kind that I have become certain that I miss a great deal because I am a sexual masochist. So much energy goes into overcoming the resistance I myself build up inside. Why must I keep on being Tantalus? Why should I be forced to build up this alien-ation from myself and my own sexuality? Why must everything be so against nature – so perverse?

When I feel desolated by that kind of degrading ending of something that is otherwise lovely, I ask myself why I do not try to find a cure for sexual masochism. How should I set about it?

But is that not a question I ought to leave to the experts, to the doctors and psychologists?

No. I think the time has now come to try to find the answer myself. The experts do not seem to be all that much better at it than I am. I have the advantage of knowing about it from within, while they talk about it like a blind man talking about colours, and muddle everything up.

Also, I am accustomed to being able to decide for myself how I want to be cured of my maladies. If I have a stomach-ache, I can go to a doctor who prescribes a diet, or one who refers me to a consultant surgeon, or to a psychiatrist, who then prescribes some tranquillising drugs. I myself am the one who decides which of them to go to, and the matter is settled. But to whom, I wonder, should I go to be rid of my sexual masochism?

A gynaecologist? A relaxation therapist? A priest? A psychoanalyst? A hypnotist? A man? A woman? An astrologist? Uri Geller? An acupuncturist? A guru? A yoga teacher? A homoeopath? A sensitivity group? Zone therapy? Group Dynamics? An anti-psychiatrist? Jazz Ballet? Primal Therapy? Transcendental Meditation?

I am sure I would be given help in most of those quarters, but that does not mean I would stop being a sexual masochist. The risk is that I go to the gynaecologist and wonder whether I ought to have gone to a guru instead.

If it were only a matter of ordinary "average masochism", then I think I would start by following Alexandra's and Wilhelm's example, trying to change my sexual habits and experimenting with new intercourse patterns. That is, after all, a feasible method. But I am afraid it would not affect a genuine sexual masochism like mine, that has been through so much.

That also entails my having a good lover to do it with – and perhaps finding one in itself would be the best cure of all. By a good lover, in this connection, I mean among other things one with good clitoris fingers or a good tongue. For one of the problems, I think – in contrast to Freud – is that it is necessary to go the whole way back and shift sexual feelings away from the nerveless vagina to the real centre of pleasure, the clitoris; the clitoris, whose only function is to give me feelings of pleasure, not to receive semen nor to provide a passage for babies nor provide friction for a man's penis. Those are all excellent functions, but my clitoris is all my own and I can rely on it, so what could be more logical than to give it the best conditions possible.

Not because all intercourse has necessarily to end in a purely clitoris orgasm, but because normal intercourse so often leaves the whole lovely area round the vagina lying fallow and unheeded, as if it were a minefield left over from the war... Perhaps I would be fortunate enough to find such a lover. Perhaps it doesn't even have to be a man, now that it is no longer quite so forbidden to make love to women; anyhow they know from their own experience what men seem to find unbelievable. Then I would have a chance of extracting so much from my physical track that the parallel psychic track might dwindle to almost nothing. And just imagine if one day it vanished altogether...

I have noticed the extent to which, under that kind of circumstance, I can afterwards be liberated from my masochistic fantasies, and stay so for a long time. Perhaps it would be possible to transform full-time masochism into quarter-time masochism, if nothing else. But during masturbation periods, I think it would come back.

Then, of course, there is the possibility of psychoanalysis. But that costs a great deal of money, and can be reckoned on taking several years. I have neither the time nor money for that, and I do not think you have either, you, the young woman at the meeting. And imagine if I were cured of what they call my "masculinity complex" instead of my masochism – or they managed to transform my masochism into sadism!

I would also have to be very careful in my choice of analyst. Should it be a Freudian, or a post-Freudian, or perhaps a Jungian? How do I find an analyst who has the same ideas as myself on what is normal and what abnormal? An analyst who doesn't work from a rigid plan? An analyst who can get through to some "me" behind all those fantasies?

But if you and I should go to an analyst, then there is sure to be a whole host of other people who also should, and I just can't imagine so many psychoanalysts at once. Generally speaking, taking everything into consideration, it is a luxury solution that is of use only to privileged individuals. And what use is that?

Then there are the more recent forms of psychotherapy that make use of consciousness-expanding drugs such as LSD. That has the advantage that it is quicker and involves the patient more actively. The drug may take the patient straight back to the dramatic moment in childhood when the repression and thus the neurosis arose. You meet your opponents alive, so to speak, in the form of dragons, trolls and monsters, and you have an opportunity to fight them and perhaps kill them, or, alternatively, to discover they are simply not worth being so frightened of – they may dissolve and vanish into a cloud of smoke. You are helped by a therapist who sits beside you to advise you on how to avoid the dangers of the trip.

But this method has been fiercely criticised (also for irrelevant reasons) and is not permitted in many countries at present, although reports say that it is very effective when it comes to drawing repressions and resistances out into consciousness, and living through the anxiety and getting it out of your body.

Out of your body? Or out of your head?

That is one of the salient points. Psychiatry largely concerns itself with the head. But what if I prefer to start with my body?

Then the whole general practitioner trip starts, and I may be prescribed some hormone tablets. The point is that my orgasm threshold is to be lowered, so that I do not need so much extra stimulus, according to the theory that masochism is like an exotic spice and I am simply too fussy to be satisfied with ordinary everyday food. The hormones are to teach me that spring-water is the most intoxicating drink in the world by making my sexual tastebuds more receptive. Spring-water may well be that, too. But the hormones I have been given on various occasions have not made the slightest difference.

This could be because doctors are not all equally good at informing their patients of the real purpose of hormones, which is to heighten one's sexual feeling by making those functions slightly clearer – for instance, because the clitoris becomes slightly larger. If that had been explained to me in a sensible way, I might have made use of the hormone cure (if at that point I had had a good lover to use it with...)

Otherwise it might work against what is intended, and make the sexual masochism it is supposed to be curing worse. I think Reich is right in his belief that, like all other neuroses, sexual masochism stays alive because of a surplus of sexual desire that you cannot get rid of.

And Reich himself – well, he is dead...

Otherwise I would have rushed to consult him, even if that had meant waiting for several years.

I think it is obvious that, if there are experiences that have lodged in my loins and absorbed my energies in a constant and apparently successful attempt to inhibit me in my pleasure ever since I was a child, it would be a good idea to work directly on those tensions.

Some of Reich's successors can be seen at work in the film called *W R – Mysteries of the Organism*. If you don't know what is going on, the people lying there crying and screaming and twisting about seem grotesque and horrible. But what you see is how some of the repressed emotions of anxiety or rage or despair are at last being let out. This does not happen through a lengthy process of talking, nor with the help of drugs affecting the psyche and breaking down barriers, but quite palpably by attacking the hardened muscles that have long been guarding those dangerous experiences.

Although I have begun to take note of these tensions, I don't think I can bring them to life on my own. That would require a pair of hands that have learnt a special sensitivity, and a person who knows how the body and the mind react when resistances are washed away and what has been repressed pours out.

But Reich is dead and although there are people all over the world continuing his work, most of it remains on the fringe of therapy.

Until these people are more plentiful on the surface of the earth, perhaps the yoga teachers may be the ones with knowledge I could use. They also work with crossover points between body and mind. Perhaps I should try them – or some of the others?

There are so many things I would like to try, and perhaps I should have waited to write this book until I had tried them all, and eventually been able to report on a successful cure for sexual masochism. But who says that the story will end before I am eighty? Who says that it will ever end? And you asked the question now, and now is where we are at.

To be honest – I doubt I will ever be cured. Although over the years I have managed to escape some of my authoritarian masochism, and prefer to fight, instead of submitting to the inscrutable will of destiny and authority, this has in no way whatsoever affected my sexual masochism, which seems to be incorrigible.

This does not mean that sexual masochism is "only" a kind of sub-division of ordinary all-comprehensive authoritarian masochism, including a desire for subjection at all levels and so at the sexual level *as well*. It is clearly a very much more independent illness.

It is clearly also independent of the sexual life you live as an adult woman in a male society. No doubt there are people who say women become sexual masochists because the men they go to bed with are aggressive and dominating – so you have no choice but to take up the submissive role and love it. But that cannot possibly be the right explanation, for my sexual masochism was fully developed before I was seven years old.

Undoubtedly men in our society were brought up to be dominating and aggressive – but that is obviously not enough. I had to search all over for my black prince. I could not find a man who was dominating in the right way and to the right degree. So I am largely a sexual masochist *despite* the lovers I have met, and not because of them.

Also – I am addicted to compulsive masochistic fantasies almost independently of whom I am with. Even with the gentlest and warmest and most considerate lover – yes, even when I have been with a woman – my fantasies have been there and followed up my excitement and provided my orgasm.

That is possibly the greatest obstacle to being cured, for it is so tempting to give in to them. I sometimes try to see if I can do without them. But where can I get the strength from, as long as I dare not ask anyone to support me in the long frustrating struggle that is bound to occur, if I were to try to find my way to my own new sexual images?

So perhaps there is nothing else for it but to go on living with my sexual masochism, as I have done hitherto. One thing is certain, though, and that is I do not want to die for its sake. It is not that terrible.

Who would it help anyhow, if I died for it?

Yes, it would help someone, because there would be one woman less who was a sexual masochist, and not only that, who also talked aloud about it. There would be one person less to be used as evidence that women and masochism belong together. Every woman who is a sexual masochist does damage to the whole female sex – for sexual masochism is used against us, to add insult to injury. A man who is a masochist is so because he is a masochist. But a woman who is a masochist is so because she is a woman.

That is what lies in the air all the time. What was it Siv Holm said in her interview:

As a human being I wish to be self-sufficient – as a woman I want to be ruled.

That is briefly and clearly formulated. But Siv will not be let off so lightly, and she knows it too, because she added what life had taught her:

Many men find it so hellishly difficult to understand such a simple thing.

Perhaps it is not so strange that men find it difficult, when we ourselves can't keep authoritarian and sexual masochism apart from each other. For that is what makes us feel our sexual masochism as in itself shameful and compromising and not just troublesome and deplorable.

Why Siv is so easily misunderstood is just because sexual masochism has quite different consequences in a woman's life from those in a man's. If a woman is a sexual masochist, it is simply assumed that she is also an authoritarian masochist, that is, that she also loves her own subjection, and all talk of freedom and equal rights in her mouth is an expression of betrayal and self-betrayal, at most a fashionable whim, a need to be in on that trip.

But *Severin*, for instance – he is not misunderstood, although he has really entered into a slave-relationship, and afterwards he can continue his life as if nothing had happened. He is still a rich count, who just has an eccentric sex life. He can still exchange his slave role with the opposite. Whereas we others are expected to die like dogs, more or less − like Kafka's Josef K, the authoritarian masochist who could not resist his own need to subject himself to the law and abandon his independence.

And *Justine* − no, she is simply not a masochist. She is only a poor victim of a number of lecherous men. She is also stupid, as she goes on letting herself be raped and tortured without getting anything out of it herself. But Kate on the other hand will only be a victim for a time. She has backbone and loves freedom, and she will not be broken for life. No one becomes a genuine masochist that quickly. Kate will rebel one day, for subjection does create masochists − but it can also create rebels.

But it is possible that Kate, just because of her appetite for life and love, will still be called a masochist, anyhow, if she meets men like the heroes in the writings of Henry Miller, Norman Mailer and D. H. Lawrence, who deep down regard intercourse as rape. And there are a great many of them.

They feel this to a marked degree when it concerns forms of intercourse involving other than the gentlest rhythms and the most cautious caresses. But even normal intercourse is regarded by many men as a form of rape or punishment, and as something in itself degrading for women − and for the same reason arousing for themselves. If her sexuality is stronger than they had reckoned with, they tell themselves (or her) that after all, she has asked for it, and that she will get what is good for her. Naturally she must be a masochist if she likes it, and as a result no holds are barred.

That stems from the days when the church maintained that we simply did not have any sexual feelings. The power of the church is not what it once was, but we still talk about our sex in terms of shame, and shame is still included as a stimulating element in our sexual life; sexual life that should be regarded as natural and good for both partners, but which still contains the idea that one person gives herself to the other.

It will no doubt be a long time before justice is seriously done to our own sexuality, and it is no longer excused as a freely invented sexual masochism. That is one side of our sexual oppression.

The other side of the same coin is the fact that we are constantly judged by how our sexual organs function – for the church's understanding of us as temptresses of men still lives on in the understanding of women as itinerant cunts.

The fact is that a man can quite easily be a leader or a revolutionary or a business man or active in some other way – and nevertheless in between allow himself to be whipped by a woman (or a man) without anyone questioning for that reason the justification of his work; for it is work and not sexual life that is important in a man.

But men guffaw and make scornful insinuations about how people ought to know about what certain feminists are like in bed – implying that if a feminist is sexually aroused by being beaten or dragged around by the hair, then her work and her ideas are worthless.

Why should men and we ourselves adhere to this implied common definition of us; that our true selves show themselves *in bed* and nowhere else, and that we shall be judged by our sexual life – because we are in the long run *sex-beings*?

I am sick to death of that, which is why I say it is important to separate sexual masochism from authoritarian masochism, so that at last we can get used to the thought that our sexual life is a part of us, but not the whole.

15 He Who Catches the Bird Catches not the Bird's Flight

Very early one morning, not long ago, I experienced something that clarified certain connections for me better than ever before.

I was in a house in the country, looking out at the trees. I had not slept much that night, and had had a little to drink the evening before. The sky was blue and the air clear, the barometer at fine. I mention this because it is under just those kinds of circumstances that you become receptive to impressions, seeing and hearing more than usual. You might say I was slightly high.

I must have looked down, because when I looked up again, suddenly there was a lovely blackbird perched on the rail outside the window. It was looking round, and then just as suddenly, it took off and flew away.

It was fantastic to see and caught me unawares. With a shock I registered that the sight of the bird had caused a special sensation in my legs, as if I myself had grown lighter, and it was a feeling of pure delight.

I could not help trying to analyse the feeling in my legs or rather, in my thighs. I noticed that it was the same as when you are in a lift and it goes down quickly. When a lift goes up quickly, your body becomes heavy, but when it goes down, your body seems to become lighter, although in fact you are falling.

I also realised that I had noticed this feeling in other circumstances, whenever I saw or heard anything exceptional – an unexpected meeting between two things, or saw a specially lovely flower, or heard Jimi Hendrix or Bach, or when bathing and feeling elevated by the water, or on a bicycle at the top of a hill just about to fly down. Also when some words suddenly became charged – like a line of poetry that struck me at that moment.

He who catches the bird catches not the bird's flight.

They were all feelings of pure rapture, making me feel free

and happy so that I actually smiled, something to do with being just about to solve a riddle, as if a wall between me and life had vanished for a brief moment.

In short, it was like being high, and not very different from being slightly tipsy. When you say you are high, it is because you seem to have been raised aloft or drawn upwards, as if physically. In a way it is like the flight of a bird. On the other hand it can seem like losing your contact with the earth, or losing yourself, and that can make you afraid.

So I came to think about what Wilhelm Reich had said about his patients, just before they were cured:

They described some sweet, rapturous, melting feelings in their bodies – feelings that were almost too strong to bear.

That was at the same time as they dreamt they were falling.

It was just at the moment all his patients were living through a masochistic period.

I thought also about another feeling I knew in my body that was perhaps the opposite of being high or elevated: a kind of inhibiting muscular tension that occurred when I was sexually aroused. Sometimes it felt almost as if I were on a rollercoaster and pressed back because I was scared, or high up on a tower and had to put a brake on myself because it was tempting to jump, as if the void tempted me just because it was so dangerous.

But why does that kind of feeling arise in sexual situations? The other kind of feeling, the good weightless feeling of being lighter, does not. Is sex dangerous – forbidden?

Am I afraid to throw myself into the sexual void? Am I afraid that some law or other will be abolished – only inevitably to come into force in the end, and crush me in the moment of catastrophe?

Have I become like a bird that has sold its flight, so that it no longer dares fly?

Do my muscles function like a brake, quite literally? Is the way to my cunt blocked by muscular tension in my thighs and perhaps elsewhere, putting a brake on sexual desire that is also at first pure delight, but which perhaps must not flout some law or other and transmit itself to my genitals, my centre? Because I would then be overwhelmed by a lawless, uncontrollable orgasm, which for some reason I fear as a catastrophe?

I really do think that I had a kind of understanding of what Reich means when he writes that the masochist puts his foot on the brakes before orgasm.

So perhaps there is *reality* behind the images I used to describe my sexual excitement: there really are two tracks, one psychic and the other physical. Naturally that should not be so. Naturally a person should be whole, not divided. But it clearly may involve something that seems to be an insuperable danger. So it seems to be myself creating the distance between the two tracks – for safety's sake, because I am frightened. I dare not allow them to approach each other and melt together. I resist my own natural unity by putting sleepers in, an endless series of sleepers, as far as control goes...

Nevertheless, my sexual arousal steers me in the direction of release. Connection between the tracks *must* be made, and when it cannot be done in the lovely organic way, I have to ensure that the tension is so powerful between the tracks that a spark can leap over.

If release – discharge – is to be able to come, both tracks must separately receive the biggest possible charge. The physical track is charged by my genitals being stimulated in the most expedient way; and if I had never learnt how that could be done, no spark would ever have occurred and I would have remained unreleased and frustrated, as I did for many years.

But what about the psychic track? Is it the task of the painful unclean fantasies to protect me against these delightful sensations? Do I seek refuge in a kind of anti-pleasure – do my fantasies function as a brake on desire? Are my fantasies my special form of inhibition and in a way *functionally identical with* muscular tension? I rather think that is so.

That is also why they have to become masochistic, i.e. are concerned with punishment and shame, for then I am still obedient to some old prohibitions. I distance myself from my own lovely pleasure by putting a brake on it. In that way I remind myself it is prohibited.

When a prohibition is impressed on you, desire increases – something that is forbidden increases your desire for it, as in teasing techniques when you are aroused with the one hand and held back with the other, creating an artificial distance and thus showing your desire the way and tempting it and summoning it up even more powerfully – until the charge in the field of tension becomes so great that the spark can leap over where permission and prohibition are made powerless, and discharge comes right across the void. Perhaps you could even say that orgasm is the body's rebellion against the law and order oppressing its freedom.

When there is a need for masochistic fantasies, this must be because sexual pleasure is experienced as a dangerous breaking of the law. So it must also have been forbidden from the start, from when I was a child – in contrast to other forms of experiences, poetry, music, nature and so on.

There are many things forbidden to children, but a particular characteristic of the prohibitions that affect the person who later becomes a sexual masochist must be that the prohibitions – regardless of what they are aimed at – store themselves in the area round the genitals and stay there, blocking the way into them.

What has created these prohibitions? I think many things may have happened.

Like so many other people, I grew up in a secure and loving and peaceful home – slap in the middle of a patriarchal authoritarian society with an inhibited relation to sexuality.

Perhaps someone scolded me or just reproved me with raised eyebrows, or simply showed me slightly less love, or once pretended I was invisible when I played with my clitoris when I was very small, so that I had to shut off a good sensation and keep on shutting it off. It is not that long ago that small children were threatened with having their fingers cut off if they did such things; but less fierce measures can surely have the same effect.

Perhaps the prohibition was not of such a direct sexual kind. Perhaps I kept on wetting the bed or messing my pants or farting – and then made far too great an effort to hold back by tensing my loins, so that I never again managed to relax them.

Perhaps I really was spanked once, with the best of intentions of course, although I don't remember it; and no one in my family would have dreamt of tying me to the dining-room table or locking me in the wardrobe or anything else of the kind people still do to their children. But less than that may well make you tense the muscles round your behind so that from then on the area never again becomes soft and receptive.

Perhaps something happened during the period Freud calls the anal period, in which I lived most strongly in my loins. Perhaps in that period I not only had to learn to be clean, but also obedient, behave properly, be seen but not heard, like a nice little girl. Perhaps I had done something that was not quite proper. Perhaps something I had done was misunderstood. For some reason, I may have been sent to bed without dessert, a mild but symbolic punishment. Or I was simply rebuffed or overlooked or overheard at a critical moment. A thousand things may have happened to make me desperate and unable to show my feelings, so that I had to cramp up internally and never again managed to loosen those cramps.

That kind of thing can happen in the best of families, and probably happens in most families in which children – especially girls – are brought up as they are in an authoritarian male society with an inbuilt law-and-order system and an inhibited relation to sexuality. That upbringing creates both authoritarian masochists and sexual masochists. But there are some concrete differences. An authoritarian masochist may develop muscle cramps round the speech organs or in the back of the neck or in the respiratory regions, so that later it is difficult to breathe and speak and act freely. A sexual masochist is affected in the loins and later cannot give him or herself freely over to his or her own natural sexual desires. Some people are presumably affected in both places; indeed there must be a great many people who suffer from both illnesses at once.

It is possible that if, like me, you are a sexual, but not (any longer) an authoritarian masochist, it was purely a chance event that gave rise to it: perhaps I was once frightened of falling out of the pram; perhaps I was given an enema that frightened me; perhaps I once really did stand on a little look-out tower that I thought was fantastically high, and start braking with my legs. There is no knowing.

It is also irrelevant what gave rise to my private illness. What is decisive is that it happened early on. People are made into masochists of one kind or another in early childhood. Some people never rid themselves of their double masochism, others overcome the authoritarian but never get rid of the sexual, and perhaps there are some who do it the other way round, although I doubt it.

But if it is easier for us to become masochists because we are women, this is not due to the fact that we are *biologically* women. Anatomy is destiny, Freud said, but he should have said *Family is destiny* – anyhow, the nuclear family in the patriarchal male society.

For what are the characteristics of that family? When as children we observed power and perhaps violence, we most often saw it in men – first and foremost concentrated in our fathers. For even the father who had never spanked his child, could do so, and perhaps even threatened to, or was used as a threat: he or another man. Just you wait until your father comes home! Mind the policeman doesn't find out! Mind the conductor doesn't put you off the bus! Mind the milkman doesn't come after you!

All these men in their uniforms, their caps, with their brusque masculine behaviour, their rough strides and air of command – all the men we only knew from their work and their position of power, who were seldom gentle and weak, and who were never sad, but only angry, who were not even spontaneously upset when they slapped our faces – they functioned as an objective and absolute confirmation of the fact that our own place was at the bottom of their system, and that our rights, like our own will, lay in their pockets. Just you wait until your father comes home!

The pervert who enticed children was a man. The person hiding down in the dark cellar was a man. All bogeymen naturally belonged to the kingdom of men. Soldiers were men, not just living ones, but also tin soldiers and the soldiers in picture books – and dolls were little girl children, although that could be seen only, for decency's sake, by their hair and clothes. Thus, from the start, men became analogous with power and violence. Women literally found themselves in no-man's-land, and little girls found themselves right at the very bottom. While the boys were soon trained in sports and fighting, so that they could learn to master the main virtues of the masculine world – aggression and dominance, we became the ones on whom they practised their domination, the ones who were chased in the street and the playground, only on special occasions allowed perversely to pretend to chase them. It was not our lovers who made us sexual masochists. It was not even they who made our sexual masochism flourish. That had happened long ago. It was the fathers, brothers and playmates of male society, the *men* of male society, who dominated us from the start, and perhaps that is the reason why our masochism received sexual overtones. But we as women, sisters, mothers, dolls, may have then had it strengthened and maintained because *we* were taught how to react to hard aggressive male signals.

Or we may not have been directly instructed, only indirectly reminded that from the start we have always been the weak ones.

In his memoirs, Casanova says he once saw a spider devouring a fly – and it gave him sexual feelings. He did not identify himself with either creature; it was the actual scene of violence that fascinated him. Both men and women are said to be sexually excited by boxing matches or fights, so perhaps it is the actual *violence*, the ever-present violence, that reminds us of our children's hidden or all too visible violence, giving our mutual fascination a sexual stamp. Perhaps we as women are apt to put ourselves into the role of victim – as masochists – and men do so in the victorious hero's role – as sadists – because it used to be so.

It is impossible to know with certainty how masochism arises, and I am afraid it will be a long time before we have any real firm ground beneath our feet. Unfortunately, for what about our own children? Who knows whether things will be any better for them? For we carry on traditions of upbringing in society, and we do it quite unconsciously. It is usually quite a time before you realise that you yourself have used a certain set of principles of upbringing. Neither do we bring up our children alone – all society is visibly or invisibly there every moment of the day, and our society is still authoritarian and patriarchal, although not so markedly as before. Then before we know where we are, our children are reading *Uncle Tom's Cabin* and playing punishment games which they stop the moment we come into the room.

Even if we haven't done our children any direct harm, how much have we helped them – physically speaking? How many of us have dared teach our children that it is a pleasant feeling caressing your own sexual organs, so that they have the greatest possible chance of counteracting the anxiety and faith in authority that threatens to settle in their loins?

Well, imagine if the children ran out on to the street and shared their knowledge...that would never do.

Of course I know that the majority of all women have not become sexual masochists to the extent that I am one... although I also know that I am by no means one of the worst afflicted.

It could be a question of the extent to which surrounding society has affected the family; this could be dependent on time and place, and things are presumably not so bad as they used to be in my childhood. But the old attitudes have not gone away, or you would not have been able to ask in the way you did, and there would not have been so many women reacting with such great distaste when someone touched on masochism.

Alexandra herself, the freedom-loving modern young woman, would not still have to struggle with her masochism – although she modestly calls it ordinary "average-masochism". These words alone show that she considers it fairly common, and presumably she has dared talk about it with many more people than I have. How many women do not still find themselves compelled to respond to men as hard beings, aggressive and dominating, sweeping away their objections and putting them down – as men do everywhere in our entertainment industry, not to mention in daily life?

For Alexandra too, childhood was the meeting place and common source of sexual and authoritarian masochism. But in Alexandra too (as with me) the two later became separated from each other. But they did not disappear like dew in the sun, and both Alexandra and I still run the risk of reacting sexually against our will to everything in a man that we loathe and detest, and can't even *respect*.

Naturally the other side of the law-and-order system of up-bringing is that children are given a safe sense of where they stand. They don't catch the flight of the bird, but in exchange they perhaps catch the bird.

Once, after one of the more drastic experiments I had plunged into, in which for a few moments I shamelessly tried

out what others are involuntarily exposed to every minute
somewhere on earth, I experienced being put down more than
I had ever been before. It shook me profoundly. But there was
also something elevating about it – afterwards. I cannot come
any closer to it than that I felt like the tigers who melt in *Little
Black Sambo*.

I particularly remember one thing quite clearly, because it
surprised me! I did not feel myself to be more of a woman as a
result of that experience; but I did feel like a child.

A tiny little child.

Is that what it is all about – becoming small again, being
punished and comforted and tucked up...being small and
weak and meeting yourself somewhere deep down in some
layer which you do not usually inhabit, but where you at last
know you *belong*? Is it like reaching a refuge, in which you are
freed from the pressure on you – men and women – to be
always big and strong, taking decisions, taking actions, being
responsible? Is it the same as creeping down under the safe
quilt, or into a dark autumn cave, or perhaps into the armpit of
a lover, who becomes father and mother to you, warming and
protecting you – and keeping you down to earth, so that you
cannot leave the ground?

Is masochism in the end my false sexual consciousness, well
preserved from childhood, the prohibition time – a weapon
against what is called lawlessness, against the flight of the bird,
against the release of the body in orgasm?

In many ways it is like a good trip. But I think it is a bad trip,
for we end up like the spider or the fly, and I wish to be neither.
I do not even wish to be forced to choose between the bird and
its flight. I want to have, to be, both.

If we do not persist in that demand, we risk not being given,
not becoming either: for even the good things in laborious
masochistic self-abandonment are taken away from those of us
who are women. The men have included that in the contract
they have with us, which we ourselves have signed. When we
melt, like in *Little Black Sambo*, a man comes and collects up the
tiger-butter and goes home and has pancakes made from it.
Easy and cheap.

16   But They Like It That Way

Female Masochism

In a way, you are right. We cannot start a woman's movement as long as we are masochists, for the women's movement is rebellion, and masochists are simply not able to rebel – masochists are the opposite of rebels, by definition. But that in a way is a question of words – or time; the time that it takes for us to stop bowing our heads in humble female masochism.

Female masochism?

Yes, because I think that was what you meant that evening, not sexual or authoritarian masochism. I am not talking about what Freud so gallantly called feminine masochism, but a great many women suffer from it – O and Marie Grubbe and the Russian peasant woman, and millions of women all over the world. The question is, how many of us can say we are quite free of it?

It is our particular illness. We cannot be said to have dealt with masochism until we have tried to clarify what the function of female masochism is, in our own lives as well as in a wider social context. We must also look first at how society – the economic and political system we live in – contributes to steering our thoughts, emotions, actions and our most private life in the direction of masochism.

Otherwise in an excess of masochism we risk – masochism squared, so to speak – taking on all the blame for our own oppression.

But do others really oppress us?

Many people bridle at the very word oppression. Perhaps we could use another word – self-aggrandisement. 'Their' aim is not to oppress anyone, but to exalt themselves, to acquire privileges and advantages at the expense of others, in the form of services, cheap labour, prestige, self-esteem – power.

Female masochism is so perfectly adapted to meet this aim, that you might think it was created for it. If female masochism did not exist, 'they' would have had to invent it – which they

did. They foisted an illness on to us that is deadly dangerous –
and dead clever.

They – who? Who invented female masochism? That is not
so easy to define. Naturally the church had a finger in it – the
church that loathed and denied our bodies and forbade us to
speak in public. But there are other forces exploiting female
masochism today, for of course it is an advantage for one half of
the population of the world to persuade the other half that they
are created by nature to be – well, oppressed.

That is what has happened. There is no need to go through
the whole syndrome again. Female masochism plays the same
tune as sexual masochism and authoritarian masochism. The
mechanisms are the same, the only difference being that they
concern only us – because we are women.

Briefly:

Oppression creates masochism, and oppression of females
creates female masochists. We are stuffed with the idea that we
live best in a pocket buttoned up from the outside, or in a
mousehole. Our false consciousness as women is imposed on
us, that is, we are persuaded that by nature we are worth less
than men, and so it is best for us to live a slave existence. This
entails a series of commands (look what he gets her to do), as
well as a series of prohibitions (look how she cannot do
anything). We are dulled by an entertainment industry that
addresses itself particularly to us as women, and we are given
privileges that are appropriate to us (like that of dealing with
children and growing things), or are harmless (emotions, love
and gaudy clothes). This condition gets into our bloodstreams
to such an extent that we protest when someone calls it servitude. We are the first to call our more rebellious sisters to
order and ask them angrily whether our way of life is suddenly
no longer good enough; we are the first to crush the seeds of
rebellion.

Rebellion – yes, for oppression breeds masochism, but
under certain given circumstances it can also breed rebellion.
That demands that we take the first step and admit we are oppressed: we cannot start a feminist movement as long as we are
female masochists; but we can do so the moment we start calling the condition by its right name and declare it an *illness*, not
our nature incarnate. Then at last we shall be speaking with

our own voices, not the voices of others. Then we can be cured
– collectively and individually.

Although we need not go through the whole mechanism
again, we must look at how female masochism is constructed.
It is an artificial product, a wretched and unnecessary illness.
That can, of course, be said about all forms of masochism, but
female masochism in particular is surrounded by such an incredible sense of what pays, and has such a feeble hold on reality,
that it seems an especially superfluous source of suffering.

"They" have constructed it by taking sexual masochism in
one hand and authoritarian masochism in the other, then
kneading them together into a dough and slapping it on to our
heads so that we can neither hear nor see. In other words:

They maintain that if we are excited by being beaten or
dragged about by the hair, this is not because there is anything
wrong with our sexuality, but because in the depths of our
beings we are slaves – *because we are women.*

They maintain that since we have been so good at playing
second fiddle in society's symphony orchestra, and since we
have taken such a subordinate position in political life, then we
can also be kept down in bed – because we were clearly
created to be put down. *Because we are women.*

They set an equals sign between the slightest tendency to
sexual masochism and the slightest tinge of authoritarian
masochism, making us regard these two things as a higher unit.
As we have for so long lived under a double oppression, they
maintain (with good old circular logic) that our female nature
must itself have been created for darkness and oppression.
That is – it has been said – the very best and most feminine
thing about us.

If they had admitted that it was an illness, they would not
have been able to evade taking responsibility for it, and that
would have been too shameful. If it was our very nature, things
could go on as they have always done.

They could continue to rape us, beat and maltreat us in bed,
or at least neglect our pleasure in intercourse – i.e. oppress us
sexually.

They could continue to keep us down economically and politically, at least by not giving a damn about equal rights in
society.

Briefly – they could continue their double oppression.

They – who? Who are these people exalting themselves at our expense?

First and foremost it has been men in a male society. The dream of the masochistic woman who can be used for this and that and kept away from areas in which men have no use for her, is primaeval and surrounded by mystique and sacrificial smoke. There is one point where it can be seen in its purest form – in what we have started calling the *female role*. Now we are at last clear that this is a matter of a social and cultural role, not a natural condition. But even if *we* call it a role and try to work ourselves out of it, it still goes on living in excellent health, if nowhere else, in men's heads – like a pipedream.

We are fortunate enough to have this old pipedream in a brand new authentic edition. In Danish papers there have recently appeared advertisements appealing to wishful thinking in men, urging them to send for information about young girls from Sri Lanka (Ceylon):

Would you like a young, stylish, good-looking, well-educated woman, who for us has an unusual charm, gentleness and devotion? She is a virgin, does not smoke and has never been to a dance. She would never dream of opposing her husband, and her great interest is to make life as pleasant for him as possible. She waits on her husband all day long. When he comes home, she hangs up his clothes, brings his slippers, serves up lovely food. She never nags and never says a cross word. In short, she is an amazing housekeeper, a faithful friend, and not least a good lover...She is brought up to be a good wife, which according to Sri Lankan custom is almost the same as a slave...

She would never dream of leaving her husband. You can always rely on such a wife under any circumstances. Even if you work a lot in the evenings, she will never go out. She sits waiting at home and receives you with open arms when you come back. She does not talk nonsense, but shows that her husband is the master in the house. A Sri Lankan wife always looks up to her husband, so is the best in the world. Her husband is like a god to her.

Naturally, there is money in acquiring women (for middle-aged men) with these qualities. Such sales promotion must be based on an efficient evaluation of the market, at a time when that kind of woman is beginning to disappear in western countries. It also confirms the male view of the psychology of oppression, for the clever slave-dealer says the Sri Lankan girl *is* a kind of slave, regarding her husband as a god, implying that it would be stupid not to exploit her.

On the other hand, the text goes on to betray the fact that behind all this is a power apparatus. The girl is portrayed as a female masochist, but the reasons for this may lie in the social, economic, legal and physical circumstances of her upbringing, not in her female nature:

> The family protects her so that she has no chance of going out and amusing herself. Her parents decide whom she may marry, and they also have to pay for her dowry, which is often considerable. If she formed a relationship with a married man, it would be catastrophe. She then has to resign herself to a life as a bar-girl and prostitute. She is prepared to marry a European man and become his wife for the rest of her life.

Yes, you can bet your life she is; her situation could hardly be worse. The question is what does *she* expect, this girl from Sri Lanka (or from wherever it may be easy to find such girls – India, Thailand, Korea, Formosa, Burma, Malaysia, Borneo, Vietnam or Singapore)? Is she prepared for a marriage with a traditional husband from western society?

The list of her hobbies indicates that this is so. Almost all of them fall between the four walls of the home, concerned with music, parlour games, flowers, cooking, cleaning, reading, letter-writing. So she is prepared to fulfill the female role in a nuclear family – and it is to be hoped she has no objections to accepting the slavery that goes with it.

There *is* a huge difference between conditions offered a young modern European woman and a dark-eyed Suneetha, Charmalia or whatever – the woman whose parents pay money to get rid of her. We do not regard our husbands as gods or ourselves as slaves. But we do what we can to make it seem like that.

We constantly choose a husband who is taller (so we become the small one), who is stronger (so we can be the weak one), older and more experienced (so we remain sweet little girls), more active (so that our passivity becomes clearer), better situated financially (so we become more dependent) and with more social prestige (so everyone can see that we keep in the background) – anyhow someone who can "manage us" should we become wayward. We voluntarily adhere to the symbols of our lower status.

Lower status is what we actually *have* in the female role – it is not just a matter of symbols. We are not slaves like the women from the East, but what should we honestly call the way we serve our men? We do a great number of things that have nothing whatsoever to do with our natural functions.

We give birth to and breast-feed children – that is our natural task and great privilege. But we also give them bottles, and change them, and take them to school and to the dentist. We cook food for our children, but also for our husbands and their friends and bosses. We wash up and clean, make sure there is beer in the refrigerator, wait for the electrician, clean the lavatory, and talk to mother-in-law on the phone. We do all this voluntarily and punish ourselves with guilt feelings and self-reproach if we don't live up to the woman's role in the nuclear family. That is because the *orders* have got into the bloodstream, just as the *prohibitions* have – all the things we must not do, if we wish to be reckoned truly feminine women.

For we are not free. We stand literally with our backs to the wall, enclosed in a semi-circle so small that we cannot move. We ourselves have helped draw the semi-circle that woman's role is, the female role, that is a masochistic role – which *is* our female masochism, with all that that entails in the way of humility and submission.

We have obediently handed on this role to our daughters – as confirmation that it is the right place for a woman. We have taught them to be pretty and neat in their clothes, to wash up, not to put themselves forward, to be seen and not heard. Then they can be sure to carry on the traditions, when the right man comes along and chooses them, because they are so small and sweet and so good at looking up to him and down on themselves.

This is not just a psychological problem. We can do many things, but what do we know that is valued so highly that we can make our living from it? What do we do the day we have to manage on our own because we have broken out or been discarded? We have got used to being dependent – because we have not earned money ourselves, because we voluntarily gave up our education.

But is this not all nonsense? Isn't it the woman who decides how everything is to be? Isn't it the wife who is ready there with the rolling-pin when her husband comes home late? Isn't it we who bring the children up and keep the whole enormous apparatus that is a home going?

Yes, it *is* nonsense in a way. It *is* we who run the home. If we had been devoid of will, responsibility, breadth of view, activity, and all the other unfeminine qualities, we would never have managed the job. But we have got used to living in the shadow of our husbands, calling ourselves by their names, using their titles, sunning ourselves in their social prestige and mixing with their friends, while they pay us back with praise and speeches for the ladies. For outside the home, we have had virtually nothing to say.

In any case, if we did at last manage to stick our noses out of the nuclear family mousehole, we discovered that things functioned in the same way outside as inside – for us, because we were women, for the nuclear family is a mirror of society.

So many of us, when we get a job, take our woman's role with us to our place of work and transfer it to a new family. A woman in an office, for instance, adorns meetings and receptions, she makes coffee for the men and in a motherly way makes sure they keep their appointments and protects them from unwanted phone calls. She listens when they speak, she notes down what they say and rewrites their muddled prose for them. Their time is too valuable for that kind of routine work – in contrast to hers, which is far worse paid.

The jobs we traditionally get are mother-jobs (such as looking after children, the sick, the old and the weak), housewife-jobs (like cleaning), markedly routine-jobs in factories, and lover-jobs (such as photographic models or air-hostesses). The latter are comparatively well paid, but strictly limited to a short period of our lives. All the others are reckoned women's jobs and paid accordingly. Small swift hands are paid less than strong arm muscles...why?

Well, why not, as long as it saves money to employ women, and as long as we "feel" that it is the natural order of things that our husbands earn more than we do, are promoted to more senior positions than we are, and generally have greater influence and status. We ourselves have declared that we prefer male bosses (just as we go to male doctors and vote for male politicians). Our natural place seems to have been *under* men, and if our pay-packets and our careers threaten to approach our husbands', we become nervous on their and our own behalf, and start backing out. It seems that an important balance must not be disturbed. For what would happen to their masculinity and our femininity, if we started making ourselves out as being as strong and important as men? It seems that we have only been able to function when we have clearly been defined as inferior.

Then when we do get a job – perhaps particularly when it is one we are pleased about, because it also satisfies some ambition is us – we feel that we must make extra efforts to show that we can live up to the woman's role. We have to keep the home extra clean, make extra-specially delicious food, and be model mothers to our children. It seems that the actual double-work which keeps us down, at the same time works as an extra spur to "womanhood", extra reinforcement of our female-slave-role. We are caught in a vicious circle. It is a good trick anyhow, because in this way we are further chained to the nuclear family, where we do most of the work so that men can function out in society. On the other hand, even when we don't work outside the home, the system still works the same way. By being kept, we become financially dependent, thus strengthening the nuclear family that keeps us down. We leave all functions except domestic ones to men: directing and allocating labour, making the decisions and receiving the money, prestige and political power that goes with it.

Thus the merry-go-round goes on round. We go on working for lower wages *when* we work outside the home, it is we who interrupt our education when the children come, and give up our jobs when the children are ill, because it is cheaper for the nuclear family. We cannot do without the men, the main breadwinners, and they cannot do without us in the home.

No one is interested in whether we might think or feel differently. No one is worried that we seldom ask for unemployment benefit when there is high unemployment – we are not in the unemployment statistics because we just go *home,* and yet we are prepared to be a kind of eternal reserve of low-paid labour, not to say sweated labour, for the free use of employers; we are like an army of foreign workers in our own country and we seldom cause trouble. Most disturbances and strikes occur in the men's places of work, as we have no time to go to meetings. We always have to hurry home.

We think deep down inside that it would be unwomanly and also slightly superfluous if we went on strike and we know that even if we did say anything at union meetings, they would rather see us and not hear us. Thus, we have even less to say, and when we look at the ruling organisations in our society, you would think we lived in a community where women were a vanishing minority, not half the population.

So just as woman's role does not exist isolated in the world, but is firmly placed in the nuclear family, so in the same way the nuclear family does not exist in a vacuum, but in a political context. And just as the woman's role is a masochistic one, the nuclear family is an instrument of oppression – and those two cannot do without each other. Unfortunately we still have not really learnt to do without the nuclear family. We still have not learnt how to find anywhere else the security and warmth it *also* gives us, even if some new models have begun to appear.

The nuclear family is of irreplaceable importance to the society we live in, because it divides us up into small isolated cells that are easy to control. In the nuclear family, the authoritarian law-and-order system is passed on undisturbed from generation to generation. In the nuclear family, children are formed according to the pattern society can use, and women are formed according to society's needs. For the nuclear family is not just the mirror of society, it is also society's school – society's school for women, with all its orders and prohibitions.

Through the family our female masochism is strengthened and exploited, and we fortify the nuclear family as we fortify our "womanhood". All that hangs together so well: woman's role and thus female masochism are in reality not turned just against ourselves. Our own oppression is a thread in a more comprehensive system of oppression.

We draw other women into oppression, and children – and men – as long as we are prevented from using our strength in things other than those within the four walls of the home; as long as we are set not only against other women (if they try to change our role) but also against men, we are a reactionary rearguard, instead of the opposite, an active aid to the women and men who are struggling to change the system. We have to face it squarely: if we ourselves take care not to overstep the semi-circle of woman's role, we remain not only female masochists, but also oppressors ourselves, for the divide-and-rule strategy has our collaboration.

But the nuclear family has yet another function in capitalist society, one of whose greatest needs is to dispose of the surplus of superfluous goods produced to keep the wheels rolling – and that is the function of consumer. Consumer goods have to be sold, and a large number of small nuclear families buys more consumer goods than fewer large families.

Women are the nuclear family's chief buyers, so it is expedient for capitalism to turn to us as mothers and housewives and to insist our main interest in life should be home and children. Thus we become hostages of the family. We strengthen the nuclear family, that weakens us by chaining us to the woman's role.

Simultaneously, we are appealed to as individuals – sex objects! Although it could be said that men's oppression of us is not conscious – indeed is blind, deaf and dumb – and although it would be difficult to put your finger on exactly where capitalism's *conscious* exploitation of female masochism lies, there is an area in which it is carried out with super-conscious skill, and that is in advertising.

Commercial advertisers know just how to play on all the symptoms of our oppression, our anxiety over not living up to impossible demands for eternal youth and beauty, our guilt over being unable to be the living heart of the family as well as manage a job, our frustration when we cannot fulfil the difficult task of finding happiness isolated within the four all too thin walls of the home.

We try to allay the complexes inflicted on us and relieve our anxiety by buying what they maintain will make us perfect and happy. But for each thing we buy, we find ourselves set more firmly in the trap.

The system is barefaced – capitalism profits from our guilt feelings over not being able to live up to incompatible ideals, while at the same time men acquire ever more delectable consumer goods (us), better care in the home, and buttressing for their own self-respect. Advertising thus once and for all exposes whom we have to thank for our double-oppression: a dual system in which male society and capitalism go hand in hand. And that kind of double-hand-clasp squeezes hard.

Whatever male society – the patriarchal system – cannot manage on its own, capitalism helps it with. What capitalism is unable to manage, male society helps it with, a co-operation that works so well and is so carefully balanced that it is tempting to give it a label, for why use two words when one will do? I would suggest the word *patriarcapitalism*, if it were not so difficult to say.

We cannot get away. It is our female masochism they have caught, our silent acceptance of the role of the inferior, *because we are women*. It has always been like that, they say, rubbing their hands, so it is the way you prefer it, so why object?

But the days of the happy slave are on their way out, which can be seen from the statistics on alcoholism and drug-abuse among women, if nothing else. Perhaps we have simply not seen those figures before. Anyhow, a great many people are discovering that something is very wrong.

The system itself has been partly involved in that. Its need for good active consumers has been so great that a far-sighted advantage has been sacrificed (our total female masochism) for a more short-sighted one (increased consumerism). They felt so safely in the saddle that they thought they could give us a slightly longer rope. But they were mistaken.

They thought it was necessary to tell us that we were free and had equal rights with men. They launched an era in which we became independent and could earn our own livings and buy beautiful clothes and cosmetics, and acquire expensive habits – before we were chased back into the nuclear family fold. Of course this new pattern was not something the advertisers could invent on their own; it coincided with the genuine liberation brought by "the pill", and the more ambiguous liberation of a new sexual morality, as well as with the rising prosperity of a better-informed society. But we suddenly started hearing from every direction that we were free, our happiness lay in our own hands, and women could achieve whatever they wanted.

The result was that we discovered we were oppressed.

We realised that the statement that we could achieve whatever we wanted was a double-lie.

First we discovered that it was almost impossible for us to *want*, that our actual will was sick, so that we were in no position to want anything except what they told us was in our nature.

When we at last learnt to use our will and want seriously, and started choosing a new role, we discovered that only a tiny minority of us could *achieve* what we wanted. This was not all pure self-made masochism. The symbols were real enough. The strong boy *was* stronger than we were. There *was* a wall behind us. We *were* in fact trapped in a tiny little semi-circle.

We also realised that the patriarchal capitalist system would not change just because we changed our consciousness. The first step is the decisive one – the one that takes us out of the old female masochism. But from then on we can reckon with a lengthy struggle claiming all our imagination, strength, co-operation and will-power – and presumably some money. For we shall face all the opposition that can be mobilised, as no one willingly gives up his privileges.

We can also predict which weapons will be used against us. From capitalism's viewpoint, they will of course be largely economic weapons. It is women who are vulnerable if child allowances are reduced and rent and rate rebates lowered, the number of places at day-nurseries cut or the fees raised. The principle of equal pay may be accepted, but seldom enforced; work is easily transferred from the low-pay area at home to other countries where wage demands are more modest – all with the effect of keeping us firmly in our place in the home and thus maintaining our feelings of inferiority everywhere in society. Perhaps one day, on some excuse or other, our meeting places, our organisations and our projects will be sabotaged, in the hope of propping up the remains of our authoritarian masochism. For capitalism will gain no advantages from our liberation. But for that I think it is too late.

From the men's side, the war will first and foremost be of a sexual nature, and we are all familiar with those weapons. Some of them will boycott us. This may be possible in a transition period when there is a reserve of the "old kind" of women left – here and in other countries. Those women will face a golden time, and let them enjoy it. Some men today declare loudly that a real man would not think of touching a feminist. "Those frustrated bitches are only longing for a good old fuck", they say (their tone of voice implying preferably from behind), or "they need a couple of good hard slaps", if we object. The object of both tactics is to give dear old sexual masochism an extra spurt so that everything can be as before. For this, it is not necessarily too late...

Even if we are cured of our authoritarian masochism, we may still suffer some sexual masochism. As long as we do, it will also be used to keep us down, and it will be interpreted as evidence that inwardly we long to submit ourselves to a ruling power. And many women may retain their faith in the link with authoritarian masochism. So if for no other reason, we should do something about it together.

We should try to analyse the origins of sexual masochism, and even if we cannot, still try to find out how to cure it – in ourselves and in others. We could set up self-help groups with the aim of mapping muscular tensions that arise when we become sexually stimulated, with or without masochistic elements. We could try to divert sexual arousal so that it does not have to take the route through the head, enabling it to spread unhindered to our soft relaxed receptive sexual organs, without being soiled by fantasies that we feel are destructive and degrading.

I think we should plump for the physical way, because the psychic way is so intangible and complicated that it would demand too much of us. But together, in groups, we might be able to cope with the physical track, in the way we have learnt to cope with so much else.

If we do it together, we may learn to cope with the violent

physical dramas that would presumably take place when resistance is swept away and orgasm threatens to break right through. For we know each other and we know ourselves, or we are beginning to know each other and the way we function. And even if men who suffer from sexual masochism do not suffer it under the same conditions as we do, they also might be able to profit from such work.

Naturally we will also be met with opposition in that field. But the strongest opponent of our liberation is the collective patriarchal capitalist system. That will polish its mightiest weapon, ideology, and strike up a beautiful unanimous hymn of praise to natural woman. To Woman with a capital W, to the weak little girl with strong feelings and large breasts, to the wife, the old woman, the missis, who knows that what fathers do out in the wide world is always best, and who sits faithfully waiting in the warm little nest; and to Mother, so much more necessary to the children than the father, and without whom they would never be real boys/girls.

Then we will have received what is our due, and all we will have to do is to keep our hands off the rest. They will have done what they can to keep the embers of female masochism alive and glowing.

For those tactics, it is not necessarily too late, for they are so damned clever at playing on all our old ingrained symptoms of oppression.

They will say with deep reproach in their voices and without us noticing they are again trying to set us against each other:

How can you make other women dissatisfied with their lot, if you have nothing else to offer them instead?

The system might then play a trump card and summon child-psychologists to testify that our children will pay for our liberation – with the more or less conscious aim of hitting us in our weakest spot, our ever-present guilt. For there *are* the children, and they belong in our semi-circle. For the nine hundred and ninety-ninth time, we will start asking ourselves what will happen to the children if *both* parents want to be human beings...but we must also deal with that tape that records instructions from the system's police force and remember that two people are involved with those children.

If they cannot use other women and our own children against us, they will try the last and strongest argument – nature. They will hold up biology in one hand and animal behaviour in the other, telling us that every single cell in a woman's body is different from every single cell in a man's, and that doing violence to our nature will not go unpunished. In that way, they will try to use animals, anatomy, the psyche and heaven knows what else against us.

For nature is the secret weapon they have to keep us in our place. It seems to represent something like the highest authority, the infinite law-and-order system, in which we have a fixed place we must not abandon, except that we do not know what kind of place that is. We do not know which law is genuine and which is false. We do not know where we are. We should not enter into any more discussions on just what our nature is. No one will ever be able to prove anything and it will end with us playing one animal off against another and seeing who can shout the loudest.

Instead we must investigate the ways in which *society* influences every cell of our psyche, and confront the society that exploits us. We can also deal with our own inner resistance to *seeing* the mechanisms of oppression that have made us what we are.

We could also use a little psychology in that field, but I do not think there will be much use for it elsewhere, as psychology and psychoanalysis are not ours, just as biology is not, nor history, nor culture, just as our bodies and our feelings have not been our own.

Take Freud, for instance. What else could we use him for, when he spent his life constructing houses of cards to show what "woman" "is"? As he himself once wrote:

"What does a woman want?"

He had no idea.

How could he possibly find out, surrounded as he was by women who were so oppressed that they themselves did not know what they wanted? Women who could only identify themselves negatively – as second rate editions of men, an intermediary thing between man and child, a hollow penis, whichever way their analysts expressed themselves. Or by running after the strongest male – just to be put down. Today the situation is different, because times change – anyhow when someone makes them change. Today we are surrounded by women who know what they want.

The women's movement alone is clear evidence that our nature is not predestined, and that we have a choice. We are not condemned to remain passive and masochistic, but can equally well be active, and vigorous, and full of strength, initiative, solidarity and political will. It is not a matter of a small handful of women who can be dismissed as abnormal and unnatural. We have become large numbers all over the world. Who dares say the new women are not part of nature?

But to us, it is not just on a theoretical level that the feminist movement can be used – we live not by discussions and theories alone. We live by our practice. The women's movement is not an anti-man movement – it is a liberation movement, directed at the united patriarcapitalistic system. So at the same time it will also become our cure for female masochism.

It will become that by curing the part that consists of authoritarian masochism. It has given us what the women in Freud's time did not have, a new image to live up to, a new image of women we can use, because it calls on our strength, and makes it possible for us to find women we can act with, find places where we can meet, projects we can work on together – a great political labour which is in full swing. It is the best strategy, the best cure we could dream of.

Do not say it is simply a new form of masochism – that we are simply undertaking this work because we need a new strong authority to look up to. That is nonsense, and quite out of keeping with the actual structure of the woman's movement, which is structured with the authoritarian system as a frightening warning. The movement is organised to give the small group, and thus every single one of us, opportunities to take part on an equal footing, which we women have never had before.

To quote the Norwegian feminist paper, *Sirene*:

Not all women feel oppressed. But we know that they are. No one feels oppressed as long as they do not have a dream – a vision of something else.

We have that vision today. If only we could get men to grasp
it, too, instead of being content to listen with half an ear and
continue as before. Naturally, men will have to give up some
privileges, and of course they are in a difficult position, because
they are losing their old identity, while we are struggling to find
a new one. Now it is their turn to set up defence-mechanisms
against facing up to what they have been living on. They
become frightened or aggressive, or both at once, and they try
to ridicule us, telling us yet again that it is much worse for
them, or that we are much better and simply quite different
from them.

All this means that for the moment we are growing further
apart as sexes, and it is very difficult to achieve a proper
balanced relationship with a man these days. But it's a transition, said the fox...

It is a transition, despite everything. Many of the "new"
men understand clearly that we do not want to liberate
ourselves in order to oppress them, but so that we can be equal
under all conditions. Many of them understand that the new
pattern will also involve advantages for them.

Imagine, as a man, being told that you look nice. Imagine
not having to go through the pressures involved in being the
seducer. Imagine being chosen yourself and being able to say
yes or no, or being allowed to be gentle and warm and sensual,
instead of having to live up to the "average-sadist" ideal; or
being allowed to be lazy and fickle and easy-going now and
again, instead of always having to be *father* making decisions
and taking responsibility. Imagine being soft and weak and
crying, instead of always having to be as hard as stone so that
we can lean our heads against you, or living slightly more
emotionally, without fear of losing face...

Imagine sharing the stress of being the breadwinner, escap-
ing the career rat-race that has to provide for two.

Imagine also living with the children!

Imagine having good active partners in bed for everyday
and in political work. If I were a man, I would do what I could
to help women release some of the forces that lie slumbering
within them...

Imagine, too, I nearly said, being allowed to be openly
masochistic occasionally – without it having the fatal conse-

quences it has had for us. Perhaps it is not just we who should be liberated from our masochism, perhaps masochism should be liberated from its women, for perhaps there is something in it we can use when we have cleared up all the muck it is mixed with...

But how shall we ever achieve the two things necessary for the whole system to be changed – *consciousness*-raising and *action* – as long as we have to spend so much time and energy on something that haunts us like a skeleton in the cupboard? Something that gives us bad dreams about creeping off to reveal in public the fearful truth, thus exposing ourselves and the whole women's movement?

17 The Fearful Truth

I think one of the greatest dilemmas of the feminist movement is reflected in the two quotes from the book *Sisterhood is Powerful* which I have put at the beginning of this book:

> We regard our personal experience, and our feelings about that experience, as the basis for an analysis of our common situation...The first requirement for raising class consciousness is honesty, in private and in public, with ourselves and other women.

> And Sister, if you can't turn on to a man who won't club you and drag you off by the hair, that's yours (hang up). Keep your hang ups the hell out of this revolution.

But, my friends, that does not work. Neither is it necessary. We must stop putting our heads in the sand. We must put our cards on the table at this point about what we think so terribly painful and compromising, that we hardly dare say the word – except vaguely scornfully and somewhat aloofly, or like something we have read in Freud – out of fear of the consequences to our movement.

We are afraid for two reasons: first, because the women's movement involves us so much on a purely personal level, and second because we realise its political significance and so are afraid of undertaking things that might damage it. But for just those reasons, we cannot live with that kind of taboo, not even in a time of mobilisation.

Neither should it ever have been so that I felt bound to write this book quite alone and in complete secrecy, worrying terribly about whether I would ever dare publish it – much less put my name to it.

But I have done so, all the same, and finally I would like to anticipate some of the things I predict will happen.

Some people will say that it is against the very core of the woman's movement to carry out this kind of one-woman project, and we must stop being navel-contemplating individualists. But I don't think you can put things like that.

I think there is still a place for some of us to do things alone – so that perhaps later we can work on them together. I think that through our most intimate life, we can arrive at some general structures, and I feel strongly that some general structures must lie hidden in my private experiences, although I would not dare say whether they apply to three-quarters of us. Even if this is an I-book, it is also thought of as a we-book and even if it is navel-contemplating, the aim is that in future we will not have to be the navel-contemplaters we have been forced to be.

Some people will say that it is all right to ask feminist questions, but that it is important for us to produce Marxist answers.

I think it a good thing to produce as many Marxist answers as possible. But I think there are also other answers – for we are not products of class oppression alone, but also of male oppression as well as of several other kinds.

So it is not any use either saying that the problems I have tried to set out touch only a small privileged minority with the time to concern themselves with their own private problems, and that I should have spent my time concerning myself with working-class women's problems. It is true that I am privileged, that is that my own oppression is "only" due to my place as a woman in a male society. But because working-class women are doubly oppressed, it does not necessarily follow that they are not *also* oppressed as women in male society, so why should we hit one form of liberation over the head with the other? We must work on all fronts at the same time. And although we should be on guard against "bourgeois thinking", I think clearing out one's own most private taboos can be defended.

I originally called this book a manual, by which I meant various things.

I think it would be fine if some readers used it for its P-ratings. Pornography and similar things can help you to become aware of your own sexual reactions.

But naturally it should also be used for other purposes: as a survey of what different people in art, science and elsewhere have found out over the years about masochism; as a detailed (unfinished) *case history* – my own – with the object of show- ing how masochism functions on an individual level; as a sketch of how masochism functions on the collective level and in society; as an attempt to free masochism from its taboo- label, which makes us treat it like a bad egg and prevents us from dealing with it and eventually disposing of it.

The aim must be to allocate our problems – our female masochism – their right place and no more. No less, either, or we will get no further, for although authoritarian masochism is the most dangerous and destructive part of female masochism and therefore demands most of our attention, we also have to deal with sexual masochism and if possible dispose of it – not because it is shameful, but because in itself it is muck we can well do without. But in future, no one will be able to come and say to *me* that I am a slave, who would rather bundle all ideas of freedom and equality together and sweep them under the carpet just because I imagine all kinds of grotesque torments while I masturbate. I will try to be cured of my sexual masochism, or else to live with it without feeling compromised when faced with the women's movement or the rest of the world.

I would never have dared write this book if it had not been for the women's movement. That was what freed me of my authoritarian masochism. That is what showed me – in theory and especially in practice – that there are other places to live than down in a mousehole or inside a pocket buttoned from the outside. The movement showed me that women are strong, that I myself am strong, and that is quite a new and amazing feeling.

It has also taught me that masochism is no less dangerous than sadism, although the books say the opposite. The sadist can beat his victim both physically and psychically, but the masochist, especially the female masochist, can cripple other women and prevent them from wanting strength and freedom. In that way, female masochism is not simply our cross, but also our worst enemy – female masochism in other women, and the masochism within ourselves.

This is why we must set about discussing masochism in all its nuances. You started, young woman at the meeting with Germaine Greer, and so it was actually you who gave me the decisive shove to get started.

You were also the one who made me realise that if there were to be any point in it, I had to try to write about things so that they could be understood. It is good that people do research, but it is not good when academics are the only people initiated into the language, so that you have to be an academic in order to know yourself better.

You were also the one who made me understand that I had to lay bare my own experiences, and that it would be cowardly if I did not put my own name to this book. Too cowardly – and a confirmation that masochism is mortal sin and our darkest patch and our most burning shame, besides being in our nature.

There is also the advantage that all you other readers can take up your own stance in relation to the book. Naturally it may well be used against us, but our silence can also be used.

Naturally I hope that you will come down in favour of the book. Purely personally, I can foresee all the abuse I am risking. Can't you see the headlines – Women's Libber Admits She's a Masochist – TV Executive Discloses her Intimate Sexual Fantasies – and so on? For although by writing this book I have dispersed a great deal of the anxiety linked with a sexual taboo, there is still a little of it left. So I cannot help appealing to you, friends of all sexes, please do not be too upset by my admissions. I have tried to isolate one side of myself, but I am neither especially exhibitionistic nor especially perverse, nor anything else especially bad. I am no different now from what I have always been. So please don't give me a wide berth. I simply thought it was time we started dusting off the cobwebs. We can only be freer, safer and stronger from that.

We have to face our anxiety dreams. Then there is a chance that the monster will transform itself into a puff of smoke and disappear up into the blue sky.

Should things not go so easily – well, then we have anyhow faced it and not been swallowed up, so at last we can use our strength to fight it seriously, because we are no longer silenced and crippled by fear. Who knows – perhaps one day it will all end in victory (if not before, then for our children) so people will no longer be divided into those who love freedom and those who hunger for oppression.

So next time *you* get up in an assembly and speak, I think you should express yourself in a slightly different way:

"For Heaven's sake, Sisters, I bet a whole lot of us sitting here in this hall are unhappy and afraid because we feel we are masochists. So, what about setting about making the women's movement hum!"

Notes and References

CHAPTER 2

p. 20   FABRICIUS-MØLLER, J., *Kønslivet (Sexual Life)* not translated

p. 26   KRAFFT-EBING, RICHARD VON, *Psychopathia Sexualis. With Especial Reference to the Antipathetic Sexual Instinct*, translated from the twelfth German edition and with an introduction by Franklin S. Klaf, Staples Press, London, 1965

CHAPTER 4

p. 43   KINSEY, ALFRED C., and others, *Sexual Behavior in the Human Male*, W. B. Saunders & Co, Philadelphia and London, 1948; *Sexual Behavior in the Human Female*, Institute for Sex Research, Indiana University, Indiana, 1953

p. 43   AUKEN, KIRSTEN, *Undersøgelser over unge Kvinders Sexuelle adfaerd*, Rosenkilde og Bagger, Copenhagen, 1953

p. 44   see also DE MARTINO, MANFRED F., *The New Female Sexuality*, Julian Press, New York, 1969; and

HOLLENDER, M. H., 'Women's Fantasies During Sexual Intercourse', *Arch Gen Psychiat*, 8:86–90, 1963

p. 44   HUNT, MORTON, *Sexual Behavior in the 1970's*, Playboy Press, New York, 1973

p. 48   CLAESSON, B. H., *Boy Girl Man Woman, A Guide to Sex for Young People*, Revised Penguin edition, Harmondsworth, 1980

p. 50   HEGELER, INGE and STEN, *An ABZ of Love*, translated from the Danish by David Hohnen, revised for English readers by Alex Comfort, Neville Spearman Ltd, Sudbury, 1963

p. 53   ULLERSTAM, LARS, *The Erotic Minorities. A Swedish View*, translated from the Swedish by Anselm Hollo, Calder & Boyars, London, 1967

CHAPTER 6

p. 68   SACHER-MASOCH, LEOPOLD VON, *Venus in Furs*, Sphere Books, London, 1967

p. 73   DE SADE, DONATIEN ALPHONSE FRANCOIS (MARQUIS), *The Complete Justine, Philosophy in the Bedroom, and Other Writings*, compiled and translated by Richard Seaver and Austryn Wainhouse, with introductions by Jean Paulhan and Maurice Blanchot, Grove Press, New York, 1965

p. 87   In another version of the *Taming of the Shrew* story, the American musical *Annie Get Your Gun*, Annie does not get the man she loves until she becomes the 'little one'.

p. 88   KAFKA, FRANZ, *The Trial*, translated by Willa and Edwin Muir, Secker & Warburg, London, 1945

CHAPTER 7

The quotations from Freud are to be found in *The Standard Edition of the Complete Psychological Works of Sigmund Freud*, translated and edited by James Strachey, 24 vols, The Hogarth Press and the Institute of Psycho-Analysis, London, 1953-74

The most important essays are the following:
'Instincts and their Vicissitudes', S.E. *14* (117–40)
'A Child is Being Beaten' S.E. *17* (177–204)
'From the History of an Infantile Neurosis', S.E. *17* (7–122)
'The Dissolution of the Oedipus Complex' S.E. *19* (173–182)

'The Ego and the Id' S.E. *19* (12–66)
'Civilisation and Its Discontents', S.E. *21* (64–145)
'Female Sexuality', S.E. *21* (225–243)
'Beyond the Pleasure Principle', S.E. *18* (3–64)

p. 99   For an experience of LSD treatment, described by a patient, see NEWLAND, C. A., *My Self and I*, New York, 1962

CHAPTER 9

p. 125   FROMM, ERICH, *The Fear of Freedom*, International Library of Sociology & Social Reconstruction edited by Karl Mannheim, Kegan Paul, Trench, Trubner & Co Ltd, London, 1942

p. 129   HORNEY, KAREN, *New Ways in Psychoanalysis*, Kegan Paul & Co., London, 1939
Feminine Psychology, edited by Harold Kelman, Routledge & Kegan Paul, London, 1967

p. 135   DEUTSCH, HELENE, *The Psychology of Women*, 2 vols, Grune & Stratton, New York, 1944
'Psychologie des Weibes in den Funktionen der Fortpflanzung', *Int'l Zschr. für Ps. und Imago/International Journal of Psychoanalysis 11 (Eleven)*, 1930 (48–60)

p. 144   BONAPARTE, MARIE, *Female Sexuality*, translated by John Rodker, Imago Publishing Co Ltd, London, 1953

CHAPTER 11

The most important of the writings of Wilhelm Reich dealt with in this chapter are: *The Function of the Orgasm*, translated by Theodore P. Wolfe, Orgone Institute Press, New York, 1942; Panther Books, London, 1970
Character Analysis, translated by Theodore P. Wolfe, Vision Press, London, 1976
Selected Writings, translated by Theodore P. Wolfe, Farrar Straus & Giroux, New York, 1970

CHAPTER 12

p. 178 'The Unfinished Story of Alexandra and Wilhelm' was published in the Danish periodical *Vindrosen* in 1972

p. 181 GREER, GERMAINE, *The Female Eunuch*, MacGibbon and Kee, London, 1970
see also FIRESTONE, SHULAMITH, *The Dialectic of Sex*, Morrow, New York, 1970; Cape, London, 1971 and MITCHELL, JULIET, *Psychoanalysis and Feminism*, Allen Lane, London, 1973
MILLETT, KATE, *Sexual Politics*, Rupert Hart-Davis, London, 1971

p. 183 DE BEAUVOIR, SIMONE, *The Second Sex*, translated by H. M. Parshley, Jonathan Cape, London, 1953

p. 186 HORNEY, KAREN, *Feminine Psychology*, op cit

p. 190 For other examples of comparisons of women's roles in different cultural backgrounds, see the works of Ruth Benedict and Margaret Mead

CHAPTER 13

p. 191 RÉAGE, PAULINE (pseud), *The Story of O*, with an essay by Jean Paulhan, Olympia Press, London, 1970; Corgi Books, London, 1972

CHAPTER 14

Much of the material for this chapter is drawn from the analysis of relations between the coloniser and the colonised in *The Wretched of the Earth* by FRANZ FANON, translated by Constance Farrington, Grove Press, New York, 1965; MacGibbon and Kee, London, 1965, and from descriptions by Karl Marx and his successors of the phenomenon of 'false consciousness'

p. 222 The concept of neuroses 'falling in line' comes from the book *Deliver Us from Love* by SUZANNE BRØGGER, Dell, New York, 1976; Quartet, London,

1977. S. Brøgger's book deals too with sexual fantasies

CHAPTER 15

p. 234 LEAH C. SHAEFER gives a number of examples of the means mothers have used to frighten their children when they masturbated, in *Women and Sex*, Pantheon, New York

CHAPTER 16

p. 243 The advertisements quoted could be seen on a number of Sundays in 1974 in the Copenhagen newspapers *Politiken* and *Ekstra Bladet*

p. 254 FORD, C. S. and BEACH, F. A., *Patterns of Sexual Behaviour*, Harper and Bros, Paul B. Hoeber, New York, 1951; Eyre and Spottiswoode, London 1952, offers several examples of role patterns in animals and 'primitive' peoples